A Hermeneutics of Contemplative Silence

Studies in the Thought of Paul Ricoeur

Series Editors

Greg S. Johnson, Pacific Lutheran University/Oxford University (ELAC), and Dan R. Stiver, Hardin-Simmons University

Studies in the Thought of Paul Ricoeur, a series in conjunction with the Society for Ricoeur Studies, aims to generate research on Ricoeur, about whom interest is rapidly growing both nationally (United States and Canada) and internationally. Broadly construed, the series has three interrelated themes. First, we develop the historical connections to and in Ricoeur's thought. Second, we extend Ricoeur's dialogue with contemporary thinkers representing a variety of disciplines. Third, we utilize Ricoeur to address future prospects in philosophy and other fields that respond to emerging issues of importance. The series approaches these themes from the belief that Ricoeur's thought is not just suited to theoretical exchanges, but can and does matter for how we actually engage in the many dimensions that constitute lived existence.

Recent Titles in the Series

A Hermeneutics of Contemplative Silence: Paul Ricoeur, Edith Stein, and the Heart of Meaning, by Michele Kueter Petersen
The Phenomenology of Revelation in Heidegger, Marion, and Ricoeur, by Adam J. Graves
Reading Religious Ritual with Ricoeur: Between Fragility and Hope, by Christina M. Gschwandtner
Reading Scripture with Paul Ricoeur, edited by Joseph A. Edelheit and James F. Moore
Paul Ricoeur and the Hope of Higher Education: The Just University, edited by Daniel Boscaljon and Jeffrey F. Keuss
Paul Ricoeur and the Lived Body, by Roger W. H. Savage
A Companion to Ricoeur's The Symbolism of Evil, by Scott Davidson

A Hermeneutics of Contemplative Silence

Paul Ricoeur, Edith Stein, and the Heart of Meaning

Michele Kueter Petersen

LEXINGTON BOOKS
Lanham • Boulder • New York • London

Published by Lexington Books,
an imprint of The Rowman & Littlefield Publishing Group, Inc.
4501 Forbes Boulevard, Suite 200, Lanham, Maryland 20706, www.rowman.com

Copyright © 2021 by The Rowman & Littlefield Publishing Group, Inc.

Unless otherwise noted, Scripture quotations are from New Revised Standard Version Bible, Copyright © 1989, Division of Christian Education of the National Council of the Churches of Christ in the United States of America. Used by permission. All rights reserved worldwide.

The Prelude, Chapter 3, Chapter 6, and Chapter 8 contain a (in some cases revised) version of material that was previously published: Chapter 6: "A Ricoeurian Hymn to Humanity: You Are Better Than Your Actions," in *Moral Powers, Fragile Beliefs: Essays in Moral and Religious Philosophy*, edited by Joseph Carlisle, James C. Carter, and Daniel Whistler (London: The Continuum International Publishing Group, 2011). Used by permission of Bloomsbury Publishing Plc.

The Prelude, Chapter 3, Chapter 6, and Chapter 8 contain a (in some cases revised) version of material that was previously published: "A Heart Full of Meaning: Stein and Hermeneutics," in *Edith Steins Herausforderung heutiger Anthropologie*, edited by Hanna-Barbara Gerl-Falkovitz and Mette Lebech (Heiligenkreuz im Wienerwald: Be&Be-Verlag, 2017). Used by permission of Be&Be-Verlag.

All rights reserved. No part of this book may be reproduced in any form or by any electronic or mechanical means, including information storage and retrieval systems, without written permission from the publisher, except by a reviewer who may quote passages in a review.

British Library Cataloguing in Publication Information Available

Library of Congress Cataloging-in-Publication Data

Names: Petersen, Michele Kueter, author.
Title: A hermeneutics of contemplative silence : Paul Ricoeur, Edith Stein, and the heart of meaning / by Michele Kueter Petersen.
Description: Lanham : Lexington Books, [2021] | Series: Studies in the thought of Paul Ricoeur | Includes bibliographical references and index.
Identifiers: LCCN 2021020548 (print) | LCCN 2021020549 (ebook) | ISBN 9781793640000 (cloth) | ISBN 9781793640017 (ebook)
ISBN 9781793640024 (pbk)
Subjects: LCSH: Ricœur, Paul. | Silence. | Contemplation. | Hermeneutics. | Stein, Edith, Saint, 1891-1942.
Classification: LCC B2430.R554 P68 2021 (print) | LCC B2430.R554 (ebook) | DDC 128/.4--dc23
LC record available at https://lccn.loc.gov/2021020548
LC ebook record available at https://lccn.loc.gov/2021020549

∞™ The paper used in this publication meets the minimum requirements of American National Standard for Information Sciences—Permanence of Paper for Printed Library Materials, ANSI/NISO Z39.48-1992.

To Daniel, Elizabeth, and Nicholas with love and gratitude
To Mom and Dad with love and respect

In loving memory of dear Rosy
January 13, 2010 (March 24, 2010) – June 14, 2020
Who has graced life with her spirited presence and
adorned the silence with her beauty and love

Set me as a seal upon your heart, . . . for love is strong as death, ...
Song of Solomon 8:6 (NRSV)

Contents

Preface	ix
Acknowledgments	xv
Prelude: A Poetic Presence	xvii
Chapter 1: Fallible Human	1
Chapter 2: Fallibility Gives Rise to Hermeneutics	23
Chapter 3: Capable Human and the Role of Silence in the Creation of Meaning	35
Chapter 4: The Practice of Contemplative Silence as a Historical Phenomenon	69
Chapter 5: Edith Stein and the Carmelite Tradition: Blazing a Prophetic Path in the Light of Love	97
Chapter 6: The Practice of Contemplative Silence as a Transformative Spiritual and Ethical Activity	113
Chapter 7: The Meaning of Capable Human	149
Chapter 8: A Song of Hermeneutical Existence	167
Postlude: Toward a Third Naiveté	185
Bibliography	191
Index	201
About the Author	211

Preface

How one questions and names the reality of what it is to be a human being and the meaning of being is of ethical import and a concern of the philosophical community and of communities of discourse across the various disciplines of the humanities, as well as an exercise of spiritual and religious import, a concern of faith communities, and more generally, of people of good will everywhere. Self-reflexive, critical, and self-critical thinking is always already a part of everyday life in confronting the harsh realities of pain and suffering on this planet, even as it is possible to affirm the joy of being alive and the wonder of human existence. In a shrinking and, in some ways, more "connected" world, there is ample reason to make the case that it is disconnection and fragmentation along with isolation and alienation that prevail. Moreover, discourse about the other human being and emphasis on alterity and difference can sometimes serve to betray an understanding of the fundamental humanity that is shared by all and the unity and solidarity of the human family. At its worst, it can help to incite a culture of fear and violence, and inculcate and perpetuate injustice—especially insidious, systemic injustice.

And so, how can I be discriminative in my discernment to honor what is precious and unique about individual human life and, at the same time, do justice to the fact that I share my humanity with every other human being on the face of the earth? Moreover, how can I do justice in my relationship with other forms of life? Is it possible to be generous and hold competing claims in loving attention and honor my relational realities without falling prey to some form of relativism, all the while looking beyond myself for greater coherence to a larger field of shared meaning and value? Can I suspend judgment by giving someone the benefit of the doubt, and at the same time, not assume that just because I did not judge I will not, in turn, be held accountable? Can

I challenge myself to a higher standard of accountability for the sake of all of life on this planet?

These times call for human cooperation and human community of a magnitude heretofore unimagined, for communities of discourse to be forged in conversation with those with whom I share my most cherished goals and desires, and most especially, with those with whom I disagree. There is profound wisdom in learning to accept mutual vulnerability. Likewise, there is humble intelligence in coming to understand that while I cannot resolve or reconcile the issues that divide or separate myself from another, it is possible to find ways to learn to relate to one another, and to grow in mutual respect and reverence for one another. The field of hermeneutics and hermeneutical philosophy can provide insight on the relationship between the unique individual human and a shared humanity—and the relationship between language and experience at the most crucial and value-laden moments of human life. So often those meaning-saturated moments are characterized by multitudinous forms of human suffering. How can I meaningfully embrace and share in the suffering of my sisters and brothers, and do so with integrity such that if I cannot alleviate the suffering altogether, I can at least help to bear the burden? Can I give priority to the other? Dare I hope to lift the other up in loving acts of human compassion and understanding?

Paul Ricoeur (1913–2005) and Edith Stein (1891–1942) both are seminal figures in twentieth-century philosophy and theology and Catholic-Jewish relations who have overriding concerns with the meaning of being and what it is to be a human being and regard the embodied human as someone who both acts and suffers. Both Ricoeur and Stein also have firsthand experience of the ravages of war: For Stein, she interrupts her studies to train as a Red Cross aide and nurses the wounded during World War I. During World War II, in 1942, she is abruptly taken by SS troops from the Carmel in Echt, Holland, along with her sister. They are deported to Westerbork Concentration Camp, and then transferred to Auschwitz where they tragically die. Meanwhile, Ricoeur is called up to military service during World War II, is captured shortly thereafter, and spends most of the war in a POW camp.

They both also share philosophical roots in phenomenology. Stein studies under its founder, Edmund Husserl, along with several other early phenomenologists and writes her doctoral dissertation, *On the Problem of Empathy*.[1] Upon completion of her dissertation, she serves as Husserl's private assistant for the next eighteen months, and when she decides it is time to move on, Martin Heidegger succeeds her in working with Husserl. Ricoeur, very early in his career, writes a paper concerned with phenomenology entitled "Attention: A phenomenological study of attention and its philosophical connections."[2]

Further, Stein anticipates the field of hermeneutics that passes down through Heidegger, Hans-Georg Gadamer, and to Ricoeur and attempts to carry out hermeneutical inquiry beginning with her dissertation. In its final section, which is entitled "Empathy as the Understanding of Spiritual Persons," she poses the question of whether or not purported religious experience is genuine or not among spiritual persons given that delusion is possible.[3] Moreover, one can have motives that can become "idols of self knowledge."[4] In the end, she recommends to the reader that further inquiry warrants the study of religious consciousness. Ricoeur, for his part, in an interview with his biographer, concedes that with hermeneutics, any intuitionist philosophy, whether it involves Platonism, Neo-Platonism, or some other equivalent, must be forfeited, as it (as well as any form of philosophy) cannot reestablish immediacy.[5] He refers to hermeneutics as a task that involves interpretation. He says that one must come to terms with the fact that the relationship to reality is indirect when one engages in hermeneutics; that is, one remains relationally distant to oneself as interpretation is carried out. Given this position, self-knowledge can be tenuous, indeed, and is easily subject to distortion.

Ricoeur was raised along with his sister in Rennes, France. He lost both of his parents when he was young, his mother having died shortly after his birth and his father having been killed in battle in World War I. He had an inquisitive and restless mind in his youth and in later years attributed that unsettledness to the conflict within him between his Protestant upbringing and his intellectual formation, influenced as he was by his high school philosophy teacher, Roland Dalbiez, who had a neo-Thomist background. He was also deeply influenced by Henri Bergson's *Two Sources of Morality and Religion* and Karl Barth's *God's Word and Man's Word* as well as his first commentary on the *Epistle to the Romans*. While Ricoeur held a strong conviction that the "Word of God" preceded the "word of man," he also admitted to being ridden with intellectual doubt as a result of his philosophical studies.[6]

The early conflict that he experienced between faith and philosophy would exercise a profound influence on his subsequent prolific career. He held prestigious faculty appointments throughout his tenure as a university professor in France and America and lectured extensively. He also abided by the pact that he made with himself early in his career to maintain a distinction between the nonphilosophical sources of his conviction and the arguments that would comprise his philosophical discourse. He sought to delineate between conviction and critique, between biblical faith and philosophy. His vast corpus of philosophical works span the areas of the religious and theological, the poetic and literary criticism, analytic language theory, semiotics, aesthetics and metaphysics, the ethical and the moral and the important distinction between the two, the humanistic sciences, psychoanalysis, and the historical.

Stein was born into a large German-Jewish family in Breslau, now Wroclaw, Poland. She lost her father when she was young. Stein was precocious in her youth and was considered smart in her studies. Later in life, she referred to her teen years as a period when she "Deliberately and consciously ... gave up praying...."[7] She eventually pursued the study of philosophy and her admittedly rationalistic prejudices and leanings gave way to the world of faith once more, influenced as she was, in part, by some of her peers in the phenomenological circle at Göttingen.

While always acknowledging the Jewish tradition, her Jewish origin and roots, and the Jewish faith of her family and her people, Stein also moved outside Judaism, and eventually entered the Roman Catholic Church. She was deeply influenced by Carmelite spirituality and the work of Teresa of Avila and John of the Cross. She taught at an educational institute and traveled throughout Europe, giving lectures to Catholic audiences over the course of several years. Initially because she was a woman, and later because she was of Jewish roots and heritage, under National Socialism in Germany, she was unable to pursue an academic university teaching career. She finally entered the Carmelite monastery at Cologne—her long-desired wish. Her philosophical training was influential in the texts she wrote as a Carmelite nun. Throughout her lifetime, she wrote on a vast array of topics that reflected the wide-ranging scope of her interests as both a philosopher and a person of faith.

One of the topics that Stein discusses and which Ricoeur does not explicitly address is that of contemplative silence—initially from a philosophical perspective, and later, from a religious perspective—about which more will be said later. Here I want to note that while Ricoeur addresses linguality (*Sprachlichkeit*), he has much more to say about textuality (*Schriftlichkeit*). I also want to note that while human beings have the capability for expression in various forms of discourse, he does not take up the role of silence in relation to discourse. Stein, for her part, in her early philosophical treatise on sentient causality, describes a state of resting in the divine, "of complete relaxation of all activity, in which you make no plans at all, reach no decision, much less take action, but rather leave everything that's future to the divine will, 'consigning yourself entirely to fate.'"[8] The editor notes here that Stein's reference to both the deity and fate signals that this is not necessarily a religious, i.e., a Jewish or Christian stance in the passage, but rather a sign that she is referring to a kind of stoicism commended by the philosopher, Epictetus, who regarded fate as divine as well as impersonal.[9] Later, in her personal letters, Stein expressly offers religious advice about the practice of contemplative silence.[10]

The interdisciplinary, multidisciplinary, and transdisciplinary work of Ricoeur and Stein lends itself to rich engagement in the humanities and the humanistic sciences. Their work is also relevant to sociocultural issues having to do with religious diversity and religious pluralism. While there is a robust body of secondary literature on Ricoeur, Stein's work is not as well known in the Anglophone world. Stein held a variety of positions and had many academic interests prior to her entry into formal contemplative life. It is my hope that this study can, in some modest way, help lend coherence to the wide-ranging scope of her interests and her works. And, the notion of coherence of meaning over a lifetime is an issue that remains close to her heart—one which she addresses in her later dense text, *Finite and Eternal Being: An Attempt at an Ascent to the Meaning of Being.*[11] That text is, in part, I believe, an exercise in hermeneutics in which she engages in philosophical discourse in order to more coherently embrace both critical thinking and her faith life. In the end, in bringing together the work of Ricoeur and Stein, this study will set forth the role of silence in the creation of meaning and show the ways in which the understanding and living out of mystical consciousness—and of contemplative awareness—is part of ordinary, everyday human reality.

NOTES

1. See Edith Stein, *On the Problem of Empathy*, 3rd rev. ed., vol. 3, The Collected Works of Edith Stein, trans. Waltraut Stein (Washington, D.C.: ICS Publications, 1989) (hereafter Empathy).

2. See Charles E. Reagan, *Paul Ricoeur: His Life and His Work* (Chicago and London: The University of Chicago Press, 1996), 7; 7n2.

3. See Stein, Empathy, 91–118.

4. Ibid., 118.

5. Reagan, *Paul Ricoeur, His Life and His Work*, 100.

6. See Paul Ricoeur, "Intellectual Autobiography," *The Philosophy of Paul Ricoeur*, vol. 22, The Library of Living Philosophers, ed. Lewis Edwin Hahn, trans. Kathleen Blamey (Peru, IL: Open Court Trade and Academic Books, 1995), 5.

7. See Edith Stein, *Life in a Jewish Family: An Autobiography, 1891–1916*, vol. 1, The Collected Works of Edith Stein, trans. Josephine Koeppel, eds. L. Gelber and Romaeus Leuven (Washington, D.C.: ICS Publications, 1986, 2016), 148 (hereafter Life).

8. See Edith Stein, *Philosophy of Psychology and the Humanities*, vol. 7, The Collected Works of Edith Stein, trans. Mary Catharine Baseheart and Marianne Sawacki, ed. Marianne Sawacki (Washington, D.C.: ICS Publications, 2000), 84 (hereafter PPH).

9. Ibid., 84n115.

10. See, for example, Edith Stein, *Essays on Woman*, 2nd rev. ed., vol. 2, The Collected Works of Edith Stein, trans. Freda Mary Oben (Washington, D.C.: ICS Publications, 1996), 143 (hereafter Woman). See also Edith Stein, *Self-Portrait in Letters: 1916–1942*, vol. 5, The Collected Works of Edith Stein, trans. Josephine Koeppel, eds. L. Gelber and Romaeus Leuven (Washington, D.C.: ICS Publications, 1993), (hereafter SPL). Stein to Sr. Callista Kopf, OP, February 12, 1928, Letter 45, in SPL, 54–55.

11. See Edith Stein, *Finite and Eternal Being: An Attempt at an Ascent to the Meaning of Being*, vol. 9, The Collected Works of Edith Stein, trans. Kurt F. Reinhardt (Washington, D.C.: ICS Publications, 2002) (hereafter FEB).

Acknowledgments

I wish to express my deep and profound gratitude to David E. Klemm, Keith J. Egan, Lawrence S. Cunningham, Gerald O'Collins, SJ, David Jasper, Raymond A. Mentzer, Christopher Merrill, John Durham Peters, Diana Fritz Cates, Ralph Keen, Morten Schlütter, and the Members of the International Association for the Study of the Philosophy of Edith Stein—IASPES—the collegial community that is The Stein Circle. I am also deeply grateful for Rabbi Michael A. Signer, may his name be for a blessing.

I wish to offer special thanks to friends, family, and colleagues—fellow travelers in this life—for all of their love, support, and encouragement, especially Kimberly Baker, Paul Bobay, Jane Davis, Norm Freund, Irene Friend, Kerry Murphy Giangobbe, Fr. Walter Helms, Helene Hembreiker, Fr. Andrew Kelly, Kimberley Kintzle, Binita Vinod Mehta, Joseph Molleur, Gael Mooney, Carolyn Nicholson, Josephine Petersen, Eileen Pollack, Rabbi Jeff Portman, Carol Potter, Betty Signer, Tom Wetzel, Lorraine Whittington, and Mary Ann Zollmann, BVM.

I also owe a special debt of gratitude to the editors at Lexington Books as well as the series editors and the anonymous readers who so generously shared of their time and wisdom, and to Gael Mooney whose work of art graces the cover of the book.

I wish to thank my family for joyously sharing the way, and for the great gift of their love, presence, patience, and wisdom—for my spouse, Daniel Petersen, my daughter, Elizabeth Petersen May, my son, Nicholas Petersen, and for Dustin May, Ericka Meanor Petersen, Aurelia Marjory Petersen, Jude William Petersen, Leo Danny May, Carl B. Kueter, Diane S. Kueter,

Lisa Kueter Adolphs, Renee Kueter Gray, and importantly, Rosy, Teddy, and Finnegan, ever faithful companions.

Michele Kueter Petersen
Iowa City, Iowa
August 9, 2019
Memorial of Edith Stein
Remembrance of Nagasaki

Prelude

A Poetic Presence

The primary task of this study is to develop a hermeneutics of the religious phenomenon of contemplative silence that is in conversation with the philosophical hermeneutical theory of Ricoeur. As part of that endeavor, I want to locate the role of silence in the creation of meaning. I also engage the work of Stein with the objective to illuminate the significance of her texts for contemporary philosophical and theological inquiry, especially given her lifelong philosophical interest in the relation between individual uniqueness and a shared humanity, and between person and community.[1] Further, in addition to her concern with meaning, Stein is a practitioner of contemplative silence. The practice of contemplative silence is not merely a theoretical phenomenon. Contemplative silence does not exist except as it is embodied in the activity of contemplating silence—an activity that is also the mode of being it intends to achieve. I therefore will approach the phenomenon of contemplative silence as a practice that produces the end that it seeks. It has also the nature of an ethical activity since it is a practical mode of being. The practice of contemplative silence, in its manifestation as a mode of capable being, is a self-consciously spiritual and ethical activity that aims at a transformation of reflexive consciousness.

My goal is to engage in a constructive analysis and a creative interpretation of contemplative silence in which I assert that contemplative silence manifests a mode of capable being in which I have an awareness of the awareness of the awareness of being with being whereby I can constitute and create a shared world of meaning(s) through poetically[2] presencing my being as being with others. The doubling and tripling of the term "awareness" refers to five contextual levels of contemplative awareness, which include (1) immediate self-awareness, (2) immediate objective awareness, (3) reflective awareness, (4) reflexive awareness, and (5) contemplative awareness. I will analyze all five levels and make the case that contemplative silence manifests a mode of capable being, one which creates the condition of the possibility for contemplative awareness. Contemplative awareness includes both an experience and an understanding of the virtuous ordering of my relational realities. My claim is that contemplative awareness can and should accompany the practice of contemplative silence in order to appropriate the meaning of a silence embodied in the here and now, through the hermeneutical endeavor. Contemplative awareness elicits movement in thinking and involves the ongoing exercise of rethinking those relational realities in and for the world. The continuous movement of rethinking my relational realities—including the relation to God (theology) and the idea of God (philosophy)—is itself integral to ethical action, insofar as I am thereby open to new motivations and intentions for acting in relation to other human beings. In appropriating contemplative silence, there is the actualizable possibility to live as a transformed human being.

In considering the purpose of this study, on the one hand, a theoretical description of a phenomenological/hermeneutical mode of being bears upon how the practice of contemplative silence is possible. On the other hand, there is the history of texts that give witness to that practice. They can be considered primordial texts in giving a description of the practice. They are an image around which I can constellate the practice. They also give principles of the practice itself through the itinerary of the threefold path, or the three ways—the purgative, illuminative, and unitive. The three ways denotes the fundamental structure that religious writers through the ages have used to articulate the experience of contemplative silence in marking the passage of spiritual growth. The texts have a descriptive and an expressive quality to them that invites participation in their multi-leveled meanings. Ricoeur's philosophy enables reflection on the condition of the possibility of the practice. At times, his work is a reflexive consciousness in a theoretical mode. Thus, I will deal with both sides—how to talk about a tradition with a practice, and textual instruction, together with Ricoeur, whose work allows me to explain both the role of silence in the creation of meaning and the practice itself.

There are a few provocative questions that animate this study: First, how best can one live with, in, and even through the conflict of interpretations? Second, in the light of intersectionality, what are some ways in which one can work for transformative change at personal, communal, and sociocultural levels, simultaneously and therefore at times paradoxically, both within and outside of institutions that perpetuate systemic injustice? Third, is it possible to expansively, generously account for faith tradition belonging and acknowledge the fluidity of relational reality without being reductive (reducing the question solely to identity or a litmus test for orthodoxy), or closed-minded (refusing to consider the question a legitimate one), while avoiding religious syncretism? That is, how best to account for the figure of Edith Stein in terms of the study of philosophy of religion?

One final note before proceeding: For the seasoned scholar of Ricoeur, the initial chapters provide the reader with an opportunity to ponder the profundity of his thought as I rehearse his philosophical anthropology and his hermeneutical philosophy, albeit with a subtle difference in that eventually I insert the notion of silence where appropriate as I begin to build my argument. For the new reader of Ricoeur, my aim is to capture the different frames of his seminal texts and the moving, shifting horizons of his rich explorations as he writes a portrait of the acting and suffering human in the world. Any finality to this expressive portrait is continually elusive in his concern with the mystery and meaning of human being.

A BRIEF OVERVIEW OF THE STUDY

I present a conceptual framework that opens to hermeneutics, and a way to think about ongoing appropriation of a mode of capable being as continual growth in the human capacity to make, unfold, discover, and carry meaning.[3] I want to note that capacity is Ricoeur's central concept. Also, there is reflexivity to the structure, because a study of the practice is an exemplification of the practice, which produces the very practice that it is talking about.

In Chapters 1–3, I address the question, How is the practice possible? In order to respond to this question, I turn to the work of Ricoeur. Everything contained in those chapters, or Steps 1-6 of my argument, lays the groundwork for providing a context within which to situate the practice of contemplative silence. The context is theoretically determined in terms of fallibility and capability within the basic capacity of fallible existence.

The context is religiously determined in terms of the purgative, the illuminative, and the unitive ways, or the path to transformative spiritual and ethical maturity according to the Christian tradition. The purpose of Chapter 4 is to introduce a succinct historical discussion of the threefold path. A historical context is therefore established in addition to a hermeneutical and phenomenological context for the practice of contemplative silence. A description of the practice is presented in this chapter by focusing on material about the practice dating from Origen and extending into the twentieth century with Edith Stein and Thomas Merton. This highly selective exposition also includes a short discussion of negative theology and self-reflective critique. And whereas in Chapter 4, both John of the Cross and Stein are contextualized and assume their place within the Christian contemplative tradition, Chapter 5 is dedicated to the life and work of Stein in order to show her in continuity with the Carmelite tradition. John of the Cross is privileged in that it is his work that Stein interprets and interpolates—and which enables her to build on the tradition. She does so in language that resonates with contemporary existence. I then proceed to an analysis of the practice of contemplative silence—that includes Step 7 of the argument—and the philosophical thinking that grounds the five levels of awareness in Chapter 6, engaging the texts of Ricoeur and Stein for the most part, but of other thinkers as necessary.

In Chapter 7, I ask and address the following questions: (1) What does the practice mean? The meaning is the intended transformation. And, are those transformations real? This is where texts are brought in that exemplify those transformations. How so? First, given Ricoeur's notion of the semantic autonomy of the text, it transcends the author's finite horizon; and, the meaning of the text now is considered more important than what the author meant in the event of writing it.[4] Second, discourse carries dual meaning: Meaning is objective in that in the textual sentence a noun-verb conjunction yields an utterance meaning; meaning can be considered subjective insofar as it has to do with what it is the speaker intends to utter, or an utterer's meaning.[5] In contrast to spoken discourse, textual discourse is different, however, in that insofar as a reader responds to a text, the text can be regarded as a subjectivity that takes the place of the speaker's subjectivity.[6] These texts are capable of uttering then, and are capable of the transformed consciousness that I refer to in previous chapters. (2) Does it, i.e., the transformed consciousness exist? So far I have only said that it is possible. Work is carried out that articulates the transformation that is being discussed. Textual evidence for transformations are brought to bear. A case is made for the possibility of transformation, and the interpretive part shows how the transformations have been actualized using the language of the Carmelite tradition. The creative imagination is brought to bear, but it is unitive through and through. The transformation of reflexive consciousness, as well as what happens to the summoned subject, are interpreted in each of the final three steps of the argument, Steps 8 and 9, which span Chapter 7, and then, Step 10, in Chapter 8, points the way forward.

AN OUTLINE OF THE STUDY

The opening chapter lays out the philosophical anthropology of Ricoeur, taken primarily from the work, *Fallible Man*. His thought and anthropological model provide the best conceptual framework and structure, as well as the origin point for a hermeneutics of contemplative silence, despite the fact that Ricoeur rarely, if ever, discusses silence. Human being is a mediating being between the finite and the infinite, but these mediations are partial, and so, a fallible human being. Language is the medium of the fragile mediations between receiving and acting in the world. This is the articulation of the possibility of human being.

Chapter 2 explains the move from reflective philosophy to hermeneutics, Ricoeur's change in method. The concept of fallibility, the relationship between freedom and evil, and Ricoeur's work on a hermeneutics of symbol serve as focal points. To consider human being fallible is to say that the non-coincidence of human being to itself is a primordial weakness that can give rise to evil. The evil arising in its being posited leads to a symbolics of evil: "The symbol gives rise to thought."[7] Through the giving of the symbol, the circumstances arise to be able to engage in thought. Thought is confined, and yet free, as the immediacy of the symbol and thought are held together with hermeneutics. The mixture of original affirmation and existential difference increasingly appears as a "fault." The fault affirms as well as negates in "the Joy of Yes in the sadness of the finite."[8] The activity of mediating outside reality results in a fragile mediation.

Through the exercise of human freedom, evil is made manifest only if it is recognized as such.[9] That I am fallible and capable of failing is due to my weakness—the limitation from which my capacity for evil derives; this is so only in positing it.[10] Evil is the source of actualized self-awareness in language and confession of responsibility, as well as the occasion for the human search for redemption. With Ricoeur's move to hermeneutics as a transition point, there is a shift in emphasis away from the fallible human in order to focus on the capable human.

I identify four elements in Chapter 3 that contribute to what it is to be capable human for purposes of this study. Further, the basic capacity of fallible existence "needs the 'how much more' of superabundance" in the ever present struggle with dysfunction and error, and fault and evil, so that constitutive goodness can be liberated."[11] This mediating work involves the reform of attitudes, motivations, intentions, and patterns of acting with regard to human being's life and world. Ricoeur's second naiveté is a critical and interpreted immediacy, which includes his "hope for a re-creation of language."[12] His interest in hermeneutics is a qualitative one of depth that aims at transforming reflexive consciousness. He explains that the disclosure of a new mode of being gives the interpreter a new way of understanding herself.[13] Acknowledging his debt to Kant's work, especially *Religion within the Boundaries of Mere Reason*, Ricoeur unequivocally affirms goodness as originary, a constitutive part of the ontological structure of the human person.[14] I want to emphasize this point about his work, a point that cannot be overstated. He also says that "there is a hermeneutics of daily life that gives introspection the dimension of an interpersonal practice."[15] While admitting of interpersonal dimensions to this inner space, there is still the dialogue of the soul with itself articulated using the phrase "*for intérieur*, one's heart of hearts—literally a 'forum' in which one speaks to oneself"—a deep interiority with its own particular standing that eludes scientific knowledge.[16]

An explanation of Ricoeur's hermeneutical theory is foundational here: Expression as the thought and experience of human being is at the center of this discussion of the nature of discourse as it appears in the mediating function of language. However, a discussion of discourse is incomplete without an explanation of the relation of silence to discourse. Here, I turn to the phenomenological analysis of Bernard P. Dauenhauer to elucidate this relation. Ultimately, I build upon his work with the insertion of contemplative silence into it, and I bring that to the fore. Ricoeur's move to hermeneutics, discussion of expression and discourse as developed in his text, *Interpretation Theory*, and the relation of silence to discourse, which builds on the work of Dauenhauer, provide three of the four key elements that contribute to an explanation of what it is to be capable human.

The fourth key element is the hermeneutical self, derived primarily from Ricoeur's text, *Oneself as Another*. There are two aspects that comprise personal identity in that work, "*idem*-identity" and "*ipse*-identity."[17] It is possible both to create a moving, meditative image of reflexivity, in which one thinks about thinking, and to portray it as a moral space.[18] He presents a dynamic of thinking that is always already open to the ongoing reality of human becoming and that constitutively forms the self through the movement of reflexivity. The human person is thought through "composition," rather than directly, as Ricoeur employs "the dialectic of original affirmation and existential difference."[19] In the dialectical reflexivity between self and self as other on the one hand, and between self and other on the other hand, interiority is cultivated as reflexivity creates depth. The hermeneutical self has a narrative identity that is expressed in the question, "Who am I?"[20] The hermeneutical self has the capacity to speak, to act, to tell a story, and to be imputed.[21] These capacities are moral powers. The hermeneutical self has, too, a moral identity that is expressed in the statement, "Here I am!"[22] Finally, the hermeneutical self has, I assert, an aesthetic identity insofar as the self understands the relation between silence and discourse. With these aspects of selfhood in place, the chapter closes with a discussion of the notion of recognition. Recognition is critical to an understanding of the event of transformation.

Chapter 4 deals with the practice of contemplative silence as a historical phenomenon and culls out of texts an image of contemplative silence and its fundamental principles and specifies this tradition as one of practice—that there is textual testimony or avowal to the practice which tells what the practice of contemplative silence is. Chapter 5 contextualizes the work of Stein within the long and rich tradition of Carmelite spirituality in order to bring out what Stein has in common with the other Carmelites. In Chapter 6, an examination of the five levels of consciousness that comprise the phenomenon of the practice of contemplative silence round out and complete discussion of the capable human. This discussion will position me so that I can eventually interpret the meaning of capable human.

It is essential to note at the outset of the study that silence is less an act of fleeing the world and more a focus for life and action (while also acknowledging that harmful action, for example, in the form of crimes against humanity have been perpetrated throughout human history, sometimes under the guise of, and in, complicit silence). Hermeneutical activity assumes the quality of an ethical action, emerging beyond the confines of formal thinking. Moreover, there must be knowledge of the five levels of awareness ingredient in the phenomenon itself as potentialities in order to understand the transformation involved. The first contextual level of a hermeneutics of contemplative silence is immediate self-awareness, the direct experience of the self. It is the awareness that I am here—the I to whom I ascribe actions. Immediate awareness of my own being refers both to "what is," to the manifest and present, and rather oddly to "what is" as unmanifest and absent as well.

The second contextual level of awareness is immediate objective awareness, the direct experience of the world. It is the awareness of a perceptual flow and is a conversion of sense impressions into percepts or perceptions. This is the awareness of what is not I—although it can include awareness of the self's productions. Perceptual awareness includes the imagination as well as perceptions. The flow of sense impressions is stabilized by an image *en route* to perception. It is awareness of the world. Ricoeur says that it is to the world that I am first directed.[23] The body is read as an openness unto the world, so that through the body things or persons that are perceived appear. The world is a correlate to existence and immediate self-awareness.

The third contextual level of awareness is reflective awareness. With reflection, I can say what that immediate awareness is—it is awareness of objects in the world. It has to do with the formulation of proper concepts that define percepts. The concept, when joined with a percept, and expressed in the linguistic form of subject-copula-object, produces a judgment. The meaning of a judgment can be ascertained or denied. Hence the possibility of reflection on truth appears at the reflective level. The important point is that being appears in the form of a judgment in language as well as in the world as reality, in the connectedness of the universal and the particular.

The fourth contextual level is reflexive awareness. This level of awareness has to do with the truth about truth, or reflection on the temporal event of being in truth. The truth about truth brings out the temporality of being—that being is not just the awareness of being but has a temporal structure in appearing. There is consciousness of the identity and difference linking thinking and being-with, being with tended being, when I think about my acts of thinking. There is a distinction here between "being-with" (*mitsein*) as a mode of being, and "being with" as a gerund plus a preposition, which is awareness of time. There are strong interpretive possibilities concerning the meaning of this primary relation, in terms of both the givenness of the object and of the receptivity of the subject. The study involves an inquiry into what kind of being in the world there is at this level, and the shape and the givenness of being. I can inquire into what is manifest in the being of the temporal object; it is not just a placeholder but a "being-with" that has to be brought out. The temporal object has a meaning—namely a meaning of being. Its meaning reciprocally determines the meaning of my being, and so it discloses a mode of being. Hermeneutics enters into discussion at this point. The activity of methodically grasping and responding to symbols is interpretation. Discussion is extended to objects not only grasped intellectually, but also to symbols, language (such as the word-event), and anything that appears with power and meaning.

The fifth contextual level of a hermeneutics of contemplative silence is contemplative awareness, a transformation of reflexive consciousness, which culminates in the idea of the summoned subject with contemplative awareness. Contemplative awareness includes negation, absence, and presence, in addition to discourse and silence. With the consideration of the practice of contemplative silence and the five contextual levels of awareness, I have all of the essential elements in place in order to understand the meaning of capable human.

Transformation is interpreted in the final two chapters of the study. In Chapter 7, the transformation entailed includes metaphor and overturning in Ricoeur. First, I reinterpret Ricoeur's four "I can's" in terms of the practice of contemplative silence as a transformative spiritual and ethical activity. Second, I interpret texts of the Carmelite tradition—specifically those of John of the Cross—to elucidate transformation as contemplative action. The activities of contemplative awareness have to do with carrying out ordinary daily life with a heightened degree of awareness. Authentic life is seeing the unity of opposites which through the very seeing is to transcend them; this is the unitive way. In the ongoing practice of contemplative silence, there is further deepening and understanding of the meaning of capable human.

The manifestation of this mode of capable being is considered a creative way of being on the way, that is, a way of poetically presencing our humanness in conscious solidarity with all of humanity. The summoned self is the unitive way. The theory of discourse couples with the capable self who is capable of being summoned and responding. There is an opening onto a mode of capable being that is summoned to ongoing response to the Word in silence. The awareness of absolute poverty and dependence along with ardent desire together correspond to the awareness of the greatness of the Word and the inability of adequate response. In humble acceptance of finitude, there is joy and gratitude for the grace of the silence of the Word.

The story moves between an understanding of finite freedom and human fallibility, and infinite capacity and human capability, which ultimately gives way to a new mode of capable being. The summoned self continues to respond to the symbolic mode of capable being through ongoing mediation of fallibility (the acceptance thereof) and capability (openness to new meaning). Through the practice of contemplative silence, human being recognizes in understanding the relation between silence and language within the Word, that it has an infinite capacity to transcend itself through ongoing transformation of reflexive consciousness. Truth claims are referred back to lived existence in the moral striving to live life with integrity and in greater depth.

In Chapter 8, the emphasis is on transformation as movement and the continuity of movement—a concern that Ricoeur has. Stein, too, attempts to show how from a hermeneutical perspective, one can experience and express an awareness of a shared humanity. Ultimately, the practice of contemplative silence manifests as an operative force for good in the world. I conclude the study by briefly proposing the contours of a third naiveté.

NOTES

1. See Sarah Borden Sharkey, *Thine Own Self: Individuality in Edith Stein's Later Writings* (Washington, D.C.: The Catholic University of America Press, 2010), xxvin18. It is noted here that "Stein well recognized that we must distinguish philosophical and theological investigations, but she also has an account of the appropriate way philosophers may include theological truths."

2. See Mark S. Burrows, "'Raiding the Inarticulate': Mysticism, Poetics, and the Unlanguageable," *Minding the Spirit: The Study of Christian Spirituality*, eds. Elizabeth A. Dreyer and Mark S. Burrows (Baltimore and London: The Johns Hopkins University Press, 2005), 342–43. Burrows explains that "Poetics points through language toward the *in*articulate, toward a transcendence not *beyond* but *within* speech. The play of words and meanings and feelings—this 'making' that is the meaning of *poiesis*—is the gift brought by the poetic imagination. Our speaking and our very being are shaped at these margins. Theological thinking oblivious to these edges, which lure us like an ocean's horizon where the immensities of sea and sky mingle and play, becomes little more than a thinking strategy without depth or draw."

3. "Carry" is a transitive verb, but it is also a teleology that I am bringing forward. "Carry" in the hermeneutical tradition of Gadamer and Ricoeur is to transmit and carry meanings from one context to another, and is associated with a tradition. See Paul Ricoeur, "Religious Belief: The Difficult Path of the Religious," *A Passion for the Possible: Thinking with Paul Ricoeur*, eds. Brian Treanor and Henry Isaac Venema (New York: Fordham University Press, 2010), 27–28. Ricoeur explains that "it is in my desire to be, in my capacity to exist, that the arrow of the religious comes to hit me. I have adopted in my works on philosophical anthropology a condensed

expression that serves as a heading for detailed analyses, the expression *capable man*. Under this expression I gather all the figures of power and impotence, as indicated by linguistic constructions using the auxiliary verb *can*. Power is the whole of what I can do; impotence, the sum of what I cannot. In the broad sense of the word, it is about an approach to the human phenomenon in terms of acting and suffering, of *praxis* and *pathos*." See also Richard Kearney, "Capable Man, Capable God," *A Passion for the Possible: Thinking with Paul Ricoeur*, 49. Kearney remarks that Ricoeur, in what was to be one of his final communications with him, indicated his intent to write a work entitled *Capable Man* as a counterpart to *Fallible Man*.

4. See Paul Ricoeur, *Interpretation Theory: Discourse and the Surplus of Meaning* (Fort Worth: Texas Christian University Press, 1976), 29–30 (hereafter IT).

5. See Ricoeur, IT, 12–13. See also David E. Klemm, "Philosophy and Kerygma: Ricoeur as Reader of the Bible," *Reading Ricoeur*, ed. David M. Kaplan (Albany: SUNY Press, 2008), 50.

6. Ibid.

7. Paul Ricoeur, *The Symbolism of Evil*, trans. Emerson Buchanan (Boston: Beacon Press, 1967), 348 (hereafter SE).

8. Paul Ricoeur, *Fallible Man*, rev. trans. Charles A. Kelbley, intro. Walter J. Lowe (New York: Fordham University Press, 1986), 140 (hereafter FM).

9. Ibid., xvi.

10. Ibid., 146.

11. See Brian Treanor and Henry Isaac Venema, "Introduction: How Much More Than the Possible?" *A Passion for the Possible: Thinking with Paul Ricoeur*, 5.

12. Ricoeur, SE, 349.

13. Ricoeur, IT, 94.

14. Paul Ricoeur, "Ethics and Human Capability: A Response," *Paul Ricoeur and Contemporary Moral Thought*, eds. John Wall et al. (New York and London: Routledge, 2002), 284.

15. Jean-Pierre Changeux and Paul Ricoeur, *What Makes Us Think?: A Neuroscientist and a Philosopher Argue About Ethics, Human Nature, and the Brain*, trans. M. B. DeBevoise (Princeton, NJ, and Oxford: Princeton University Press, 2000), 68.

16. Ibid., 69.

17. Paul Ricoeur, *Oneself as Another*, trans. Kathleen Blamey (Chicago and London: The University of Chicago Press, 1992), 2–3 (hereafter OA).

18. See David E. Klemm, *The Hermeneutical Theory of Paul Ricoeur: A Constructive Analysis* (Lewisburg, PA: Bucknell University Press, 1983), 103 (hereafter HTPR). In connection with Ricoeur's hermeneutical theory, Klemm explains that "Reflexivity is a subjectivity that understands its own understanding and could just as easily be called the hermeneutical subject."

19. See Ricoeur, FM, 140.

20. Ricoeur, OA, 167.

21. See Ricoeur, OA.

22. Ibid., 167.

23. Ricoeur, FM, 19.

Chapter 1

Fallible Human

Precisely what is the reality of human being (here I place emphasis on the act) and being human (here I place emphasis on the state of existing)?[1] The starting point, and the first step of the argument is that human being is originally endowed with finite freedom and life. Ricoeur refers to human reality as "willed existence and existence undergone," which constitutes a totality in that I exist as the one that I am.[2] Here, act and state are joined in this one that I am. This structure is two-in-one, in that I can conceive of the act and the state of existing as two, but they are lived, in human reality, as one. Embodied human being constitutes freedom that is in reciprocal relatedness with nature; freedom and nature are in a dialogue. I understand myself initially as a person who says "I will."[3] Embodied freedom is equivalent to the structure of the will and governs my motivations, intentions, and powers. Necessity is at the core of human freedom. Human being, as embodied freedom, assumes responsibility for the decisions, actions, as well as the consent that issue forth and that constitute living experience.

Embodied freedom is both mystery and paradox. The mystery has to do with a concealed unifying consciousness that is willed, and yet endured. The acts that I perform are joined to the state of living in the one that I am. The necessity that I feel is the brute fact that I discover I exist. Because consciousness cannot bestow being nor persevere, I often suffer, although I sometimes experience joyous complicity in a reality beyond myself.[4] Freedom is dependent not only upon the finite and limited nature of the body, but on consciousness and the elusive "I" as well.

In order to complete the determination of human freedom in his work, Ricoeur mediates, and in so doing, contextualizes human freedom through the use of a limit concept, which he also regards as a presence—that of genuine transcendence.[5] It is through the introduction of presence that he presents and brings into view a poetic dimension of reality. He considers this new dimension as being an innovation in the theory of subjectivity. Yet, to be sure, human freedom is not divine freedom in that it is not an absolute positing; to will is not the same thing as to create.

His meditation on a mythics of bad will prompts him to think about the point at which evil is inserted into human reality. How is evil possible? and How could it enter the world? The movement from innocence to fault, and from original goodness to human evil in experience, cannot be approached by description. Myths of the fall and exile, for example, cannot be directly introduced into philosophical discourse. Rather, they must be placed into their own proper world of discourse—that of pre-philosophical expression—where they are understood as being secondary elaborations of a quite basic language of avowel.[6] A symbolic language can speak indirectly to what human fault and human evil are.

Ricoeur therefore must broaden his anthropological perspective from a study of the structure of the will to a study of the conditions of its possibility in the constitutional structure of human being. Through reflection on pre-philosophical expressions, and the reduction of discourse to the ontological structure that provides for their possibility, his presupposition is that he can make intelligible where it is that the possibility of evil becomes visible in the inherent structure of human being. He engages in transcendental reflection that begins with an object (i.e., the expression) and proceeds back to the conditions of its possibility in order to ascertain the fundamental elements that comprise the theory and structure of fallibility.[7] He explains how the inherent structure of human being as fallible is a weakness that gives way to evil. Fallibility as an ontological characteristic is inscribed in human being. His goal is to give conceptual clarity to the pre-philosophical discourse by way of an explanation. The goal is not fully realizable, however, in that no amount of conceptual analysis and explanation can articulate in full what it is that primary expressions are capable of saying. With this dual beginning in the pre-philosophical and the philosophical, the pathetic (*pathétique*)—constituted and characterized by avowals of misery—and the transcendental—Ricoeur establishes the elements for the conceptual elucidation of his philosophical anthropology.[8]

Humans are subject to imperfections, and so, are prone to err. The possibility of moral failing resides in a disproportion, which is the non-coincidence of human being with itself. Human being lives a paradox as it is situated in the middle of two poles—the infinite and the finite: Human being is infinitude insofar as it can conceive concepts, engage in rational thinking, and participate in ideas, and thus make things intelligible in universal terms. Human being is finitude insofar as it can perceive percepts and intuit the sensible in a limited and particular way given its restricted perspective on reality. Human being is infinitude, while finitude, as a sign, indicates the limited nature of infinitude.[9] The opposite holds as well: infinitude, as a sign, indicates a transcending of that finitude. Understanding this finite/infinite polarity is crucial. The instability of the ontological condition consists in the human being who is both greater than and lesser than itself. Below, I will examine more closely the constitutive structure of human being.

THE PHILOSOPHICAL ANTHROPOLOGY OF PAUL RICOEUR

Given the relation between theology and philosophy for Ricoeur, his philosophical anthropology can be said to be bracketed and he accepts that it is.[10] There is a Word as source or origin that falls outside his philosophy and there is a last word that remains outside his philosophy as well.[11] His philosophical anthropology becomes a detour in this respect. Human capability is at the center of his philosophical anthropology. Humans have a capacity for fallible existence. He analyzes three levels at which human reality fails to coincide with itself—at the levels of knowing (or thinking), doing (acting or willing), and feeling. Each of the three levels is explained below in terms of theoretical, practical, and affective mediation. The three levels that are considered as a single structure and articulated in triadic terms in the opening of *Fallible Man* as the infinite, the finite, and mediation, are expressed as originating affirmation, existential difference, and human mediation in the closing of the study.[12] He thereby acknowledges the task of transposing and incorporating the Kantian categories of quality—reality, negation, limitation—into his philosophical anthropology. Through employing the dialectic of knowing, acting, and feeling, his goal is to make a more concrete determination of feeling as that which truly represents our humanness and humanity. By beginning the analysis with knowing, and moving downward through acting and feeling, originating affirmation grows increasingly richer and more inward in the progression. Through the pole of the infinite, I am assured that my existence can be continued in an openness that includes thinking and acting; "the originating affirmation is felt here as the Joy of 'existing in' the very thing that allows me to think and to act; then reason is no longer an other: I am it, you are it, because we are what it is," he explains.[13]

While the power of originating affirmation (the "effort to exist" or the "power to *posit*"), constitutes human being, I am intelligible only by participating in a particular negative notion of nothingness, which is in true relation with that affirmation.[14] This existential negation serves to negate my perspective, my character, and my felt love for life through denial; it limits my originating affirmation and appears as a difference. For example, suppose that I can play the French horn, and was once accomplished at it. I have been motivated to audition for the local symphony orchestra. I will audition out of love and the desire to play, as well as to hear great music. I am drawn to the beautiful music and hear in it the call of what is desirable and loveable. Further, when I desire to play in the orchestra, I also experience a feeling of myself as desiring to participate; this is a form of self-love. This is the affective perspective.

I visit with my friend, who is an amateur musician herself, about this desire. She tells me that more than likely I will not succeed in the audition, as there are other musicians much more accomplished than I who have professionally trained for their positions. I begin to doubt myself and my abilities, to the point that I am tormented by the thought of the possibility of the audition. Then too, I know that I would be overextending myself with the commitment if I were to be chosen. My body has been both an opening in willing something, and a closing in resisting the desire. I have persevered. This is the practical perspective.

My self-doubt turns to interiorized anguish. I know I am correct in having come to the realization of the constraints on my time because of the other professional and personal goals that I have set. I now become accustomed to the reality that indeed, I chose not to audition for the orchestra. A feeling of my finitude closes in and envelops me, pressing in on me; I feel sadness about this lost opportunity to expand my horizons, and feel and know that I am human and finite. My character as a combination of both the affective and the practical perspectives, is the finite openness I have demonstrated above. Thus, existential difference manifests "as a difference between me and the other, then as a differing of myself from myself, and finally interiorizes itself in the sadness of the finite."[15] Initially, I felt the difference, but it was outside of myself; however, I then interiorized it as a result of my feeling of contingency. The recognition of my contingency insofar as it is not necessary that I exist as I am, nor that I even exist, that there was both a possibility that I could have been some other, or not existed at all, entails this ground that is sadness: "I am the living non-necessity of existing."[16]

In the dialectic between originating affirmation and existential negation or difference, the Kantian term, limitation, synonymous with my human fragility is, in Ricoeurian terms, human mediation. Indeed, the limitation is the human itself as a mediating being. Finite freedom and mediating being come together. The human being is thought through composition rather than directly in this mixture of originating affirmation and existential negation. The human "is the Joy of Yes in the sadness of the finite."[17] This sadness is regarded as a primitive affection or sufferance that focuses on the negative through a constricting of consciousness. This joy is the exhilarating, felt knowledge and exuberance of simply being aware that I am alive, of being in love with life, which results in an expansiveness of consciousness. Feeling discloses the fissure, the split that I am as primordial conflict, which appears as a fault resulting in human fragility. I appear, then, as a synthesis—a fragile mediator of reality, or existential self-contradiction. Discontinuity and conflict are inscribed into the structural constitution of human being.

The human being is a thinking being who brings about mediations.[18] There is a vertical and a horizontal pole which establish the limits of critical thinking. The arché, or ground, of the vertical pole out of which thinking emerges is the lower threshold, and the mode of discourse it signals is "original affirmation." The unity of opposites of the polarities remain altogether undifferentiated at this point. The opposite end of the pole, the telos, the goal or end toward which thinking strives is the upper threshold, and the mode of discourse it signals is "eschatological hope." Now, the unity of opposites is differentiated through human mediation. Ricoeur employs the terms "original affirmation" and "eschatological hope" to signify that thinking at either limit is nonconceptual; at the limit, thinking is negated and gives way to immediacy.

The horizontal pole is associated with the notion of critique on the infinite pole, and conviction on the finite pole, and of "Being" on the infinite pole in opposition to "God" on the finite pole. In Kantian terms, the idea of pure reason, which is the concept with no intuition (percept) on the infinite pole can be opposed to the aesthetic idea, which is intuition (percept) with no concept on the finite pole. Ricoeur affixes limits to thinking on the horizontal plane as well. If I abstract one side of the mediating activity from the other when regarding them in reciprocal terms, a limit is reached in thinking. Both elements in the oppositional pair must appear, according to the rule of active synthesis. For example, in the theoretical synthesis, the "I" synthesizes percepts with the appropriate conceptual determination in language by following the system or relations and rules governing words, and the lexicon of word-meanings. With the practical synthesis, what is projected is the intention to follow a plan of action so that happiness is achieved. It is at the level of the affective synthesis that the deepest conflict, the inner conflict of the heart takes place where intention and affection come together. Essential feelings such as having, power, and worth, come into conflict with the characteristically spiritual feelings of joy and sadness, anxiety and courage, hope and fear.

Theoretical Mediation

Ricoeur begins with a transcendental reflection that examines the power of knowing. The other two levels of human being—action and feeling—will have to undergo transcendental reflection as well in order to be considered categories of anthropological investigation. First, it is through an investigation into the power of knowing that the initial disproportion is presented. The myths and avowals of misery are transposed into fallibility. Second, the reflection (as distinct from introspection) begins with knowing from the thing or object known, through the process of discerning the power of knowing, that is at work, in order to uncover the disproportion between receiving and determining an object. It is transcendental reflection because it makes appear on the object precisely what it is in the subject that enables the synthesis to be possible. This power of synthesis is called "consciousness," i.e., consciousness of the object that is not yet self-consciousness.

At each stage—the theoretical, practical, and affective levels—the mediation unites an element that is universal with one that is particular. The middle (final) term must combine something universal with something particular. The mediating figure that defines me as a finite and fallible human is composed of a transcending element that opens to infinity and a self-constricting that closes me in.

Seeing

Seeing is the particular element and the finite pole in the first mediation. What first appears to me is other living persons or things in this world, toward which I am directed. My body serves to open me out to the world, and, at the same time, to isolate me in my suffering. The openness of my body is self-constricting, however, and is, therefore, finite in terms of my receptivity and my limited perspective, or single point of view, as I can only perceive one side of an object, for example, at any given point in time. When I determine, however, I must think, which involves exerting mastery over that presence; this is the opposite side, the infinite pole, of the theoretical mediation. Upon the thing, there is a scission between a receiving, i.e., seeing, and a determining, i.e., saying. Reflection involves combining and sundering. This reflection distinguishes between receiving the presence of objects and determining what their meaning is.

Saying

Saying is the universal element and the infinite pole in the mediation. To speak of my finitude is to transcend that finitude, so that there must be a moment of surpassing being finite that is the condition for the possibility of expressing that finitude. A depiction of finitude is deficient if it fails to account for what it is that enables a discourse on finitude to be possible. It follows that in order for there to be a complete discourse on finitude, there has to be a discourse on finitude and infinitude. It is in this way that I can, as a human, account for the transgression that occurs through discourse. For example, I could not recognize a perception as just that, perspectival, if I did not somehow go beyond my own perspective. The being who speaks is a human who, through intending and expressing, transcends perspectival perception in the capacity to determine the entirety of some thing, including the non-perceived sides of the thing. Any discussion of Ricoeur's philosophical anthropology is incomplete without attending to the infinite as well as the finite.

Imagination

The imagination as the middle term must combine something universal with something particular. The finding of a disproportion between seeing and saying, which is a rupture between finite perceiving and infinite signifying, or between the look and the expression, gives rise to a problem with the third term, the pure imagination. The pure imagination resists direct observation and is simply impossible to understand, although it does appear in the thing, or the unity that is already realized between point of view and speech, or between the percept and the concept. Ricoeur names this unity "objectivity," which indicates the "ontological dimension of things."[19] The ontological dimension of things combines appearance (presence), or the finite pole, and meaning, or the infinite pole, and is, therefore a synthesis; this is the mode of being of the thing.

The being of things is not in consciousness; however, consciousness takes an active role in determining what is the being of things by projecting itself into the mode of being of the thing.[20] This is a transcendental reflection and not a psychological reflection. A psychological reflection is description at an empirical level. The transcendental and the empirical are two different standpoints that I can occupy. The empirical standpoint is the everyday: I dodge and catch a bus, for example. The transcendental standpoint is the philosophical standpoint that I occupy when I stand back from the empirical standpoint to reflect on how what happens at the empirical standpoint is possible. A transcendental reflection is what is used to justify the necessary use of concepts that have no empirical correlates—concepts like substance and causality. A good example is time, which is a condition of the possibility of empirical experience. I can come close to intuiting time in the everyday empirical standpoint, but not quite, according to Kant. Time and space are pure intuitions which make other intuitions possible.

I am a synthesis of speech and perspective in being capable of connecting meaning and appearance in the thing.[21] I cannot, however, conceive the "I" of synthesizing activity, because "I" is not a concept. Concepts are universal, and the "I" is singular. Neither can I perceive the "I," because "I" is not a percept. Percepts are empirical, and the "I" is the origin-point of percepts that can never appear empirically to myself. The "I" is transcendental, as a necessary condition of experience. I think the "I" transcendentally (as the necessary condition of experience), therefore, and not directly, in the intellectual intuition which takes the place of thinking.[22] In terms of reflexivity, I could say that intellectual intuition is the self-awareness of myself acting, the immediate consciousness of acting, and what I do when I act. And, further, the self-awareness could be *ad infinitum*.

Ricoeur uses two images so that I may be guided in thinking the pure activity of synthesizing: First, the image of openness suggests a combination of perspective and the transgression of it, in that each perspective does not enclose me because I hold access to a space of expressibility by virtue of the thing's very appearance under its successive aspects.[23] Second, is the image of light or clarity, in that light is a space of appearance and intelligibility. If I consider light to be an openness, then it becomes the medium of both appearance as well as expressibility.[24] The transcendental "I" schematizes and forms an image in the mind in order to synthesize the universal concept with the particular appearance. The (transcendental) image is capable of mediating between concept and percept because it meets Kant's "homogeneity" requirement: the image is particular like the percept, yet it is also universal, like the concept. Kant's example is that of a dog. I see something and call it a dog. The transcendental imagination mediates by forming an image of a dog in general. As the being of the thing (e.g., the "immediacy") is the actual connection between the concept and the intuition (percept), then critical consciousness questions what is the truth of being, insofar as it is self-evidently given in appearance. Knowledge is the result of the correspondence between the concept as intellectually derived, and intuition as sensibly derived.

A schematized category is a category plus time. When I schematize a category so that it has a time-determination, then it is intuitively available and accessible to me, whereas a category is not. I must think a category. The pure image is a transcendental time-determination, so that in apprehending a percept, time is generated. The important thing behind the doctrine of schematism is the Kantian claim that time itself is a particular, and I therefore intuit time. Time is not, therefore, a universal that I can think as a concept; I intuit something in time (and space), and, again, I can imagine empty time and space—but I cannot imagine the absence of time and space.[25] In the attempt to do so, however, I seem to intuit time and space intellectually as *a priori* or pure forms of intuition. This is the result of the Transcendental Aesthetic of Kant's *Critique of Pure Reason*.[26] Moreover, time is diversity and allows itself to be understood; it scatters and orders. Time is particular and universal; time is the finite pole of the particular and sensible, and the infinite pole of the universal and intelligible. Through time-determinations, it also unites the finite pole of appearance, in the percept, with the infinite pole of meaning, in the concept.

Time is determinable by my understanding because the categories are embedded in my understanding in the structure of a schemata, which is to say that I can temporalize these categories. Time can come in different determinations such as permanence (substance), necessary succession as in "first this, then that" (causality), and fullness of time, as opposed to emptiness of time; it is the filling of time (quality). Because I cannot think time, I cannot construct a philosophical order on its basis. Ricoeur explains that to know being (to have an ontology) is not only to allow it to appear, but "to determine it intellectually," to order and express it, as well.[27] But if being is time, in some way I cannot do it; I do not have it. I can let it appear, but I cannot say what it is that I am pointing out. Time is inscrutable.

Practical Mediation

As I descend into Ricoeur's philosophical anthropology, I move from "I think" to "I will." Transcendental reflection alone is not enough to account for the human person. I must include a world of persons who express themselves in human works. Hence, my reflection progresses from the "thing" that is known to the "person" in the practical world of finitude. Concerning the finite pole, what is "perspective" at the first level, can be summarized in the concept of "character" at the second level.[28] The infinite pole can be comprehended and summarized in the concept of "happiness" at the second level. "Respect" is the third term and mediates these notions of character and happiness. The practical mediation enlarges the first level of mediation by the transcendental imagination. At this second level, the disproportion is between character and happiness.

Character

Character is the particular element and the finite pole in the second mediation. There are three steps in composing a concept of character—affective perspective, practical perspective, and character.[29] Whereas perspective is disinterested at the first level of knowing in the theoretical mediation, here Ricoeur restores the affectivity of perspective. The will is fed with motives, which in turn, project its desires outside of consciousness onto the world. I go outside of myself in giving myself over entirely to a project. Human freedom advances in terms of motivated projects for which I have reasons in constituting my actions. Sensory receptivity is analogous to motivation. That is, I see exactly why it is that I act in a given way.

The feeling of myself is a form of self-love. When I desire something, I also experience a feeling of myself as desiring that thing. In addition to being mediatory, there is immediacy to the body as well.[30] There is an element of opening of the body to the world insofar as the will is thrust outward to the world.[31] The body also possesses an element of closing insofar as it resists desire, which is inertia; practical finitude is such a kind of perseverance.

Character combines affective and practical perspective. Character has to do with the finite openness of my existence to humanity as well as with the totality of my field of motivation, which is considered in its entirety. This totality is given in adumbrations of expression in the way, for example, that I love, which reflects on my entire personality. Character is expressed in the quiet gesture or the thoughtful and telling comment, which gives me occasion to recognize who the person is through these inimitable expressions.

Happiness

Happiness is the universal element and the infinite pole in the second mediation. The disproportion between happiness as universal, and character as particular, in practical reason, is what denotes finitude in the practical mediation. Ricoeur is attempting to express at this second level of his anthropology the global nature of disproportion. He says that Aristotle thinks of happiness in terms of "the Good [which] has rightly been said to be that at which all things aim"; happiness has to do with discriminating the goal of desire in the human.[32] A naïve sense of happiness has to do with acting in a way that produces pleasure and, at the same time, avoids pain, with the emphasis placed on result in consciousness. What is achieved is temporary peace or repose. The naïve sense makes of happiness a finite term. The proper sense of happiness is one that reflects a totality of projects in discerning a decision and considering personal factors that contribute to realizing a greater meaning to life.

The important point that Ricoeur makes here is that Aristotle's idea of happiness as "merely sum of pleasure" is insufficient in that he lacks a transcendental level of reflection. Ricoeur proceeds from a sum to a whole in connecting the will to Kantian reason. Adding the demand of the totality of reason to the totality of contentment brings to view a deeper meaning in the task Aristotle engaged in: practical reason demands a totality of meaning. The supreme destination, the supreme Good, now becomes the worthiness to be happy. Here happiness and virtue are joined, which is demanded by reason, so that the good is complete as well as perfect.

The idea of totality resides in the will and is the source of an extreme disproportion between character, which is of finite origin, insofar as it is the point from which I can open to something, and happiness as the opposite, insofar as it is an infinite end. At times, I may receive a sign or premonition of the happiness that is my destiny in moments of feeling the immensity of reality when I am assured of being on the correct path. There are indications, however, of a perceptual narrowness, as the field of my attention is limited. I ascertain that narrowness and feeling of constriction when I experience being at odds with others. While it is reason that demands totality, the sense of direction that is experienced in my feeling of happiness is assurance that reason, indeed, is interior to my destiny.

Respect

Respect as the third mediating term must combine the universal term of happiness with the particular term of character in the practical mediation. The synthesis of happiness and character is discovered in a person, the self of the Kantian "I think." In this personal process of moral striving, self-consciousness arises out of consciousness. The humanness of human beings is the individual person that strives to be. In the self that I represent to myself, there is a synthesis between the human as end and of absolute worth, and an existence as a presence so as to be able to enter into relations of mutual understanding.

Respect can mediate between character and happiness because it is the rational feeling—it is both felt in the body and is the embodiment of rationality. It inscribes genuine happiness, based on the Good, onto the individuality of character. Respect is felt in terms of myself as well as others and constitutes right human relationship in Kant's imperative to act in such a way that I am treating humanity as an end, and not solely as a means. Respect is proper to the faculty of desire, as it operates to provide incentive for the will to act. Respect is duty as a felt obligation in striving for the highest good. Respect is proper to practical reason inasmuch as it is a feeling that is elicited by reason. Self-esteem becomes a kind of attestation of the genuineness with which the moral law has been appropriated into the mind.[33]

There is a reflexive structure of the will in which "I" am a commanding sovereign, and "this one here" as obeying subject. Respect for others and self-respect must work together. Respect, insofar as it mediates between character and happiness, is the center of the disproportion, and the possibility of discord, or "the existential 'fault'" (meant in a geological sense), that is the cause of human fragility.[34] There is a fault line in the structure of the will. Ricoeur follows Kant's *Religion within the Boundaries of Mere Reason* in that while humans have an original predisposition to the good, human nature contains an original propensity to evil.[35] Propensity is understood by Kant as a subjective ground of a possibility of an inclination, or a habitual desire, and arises when an experience of what is desired has occurred, and a concrete inclination, or habitual desire, arises as a result. The human being has choice: The will, in its freedom is the locus of a moral wrestling as it makes either an evil choice, in which duty is subordinated to happiness, or it makes the good choice, in which happiness is subordinated to duty. For example, either I can freely determine to subordinate the claims of the moral law to the claims of my sensible nature or, I can freely determine to subordinate the claims of my sensible nature to the claims of the moral law. I must choose the appropriate relationship between the two goods so that there is an ordering involved.

As for the origin of evil in human nature, (in that an effect descends from a first cause), origin can be considered with regard to reason (i.e., noumenally), or with regard to time (i.e., phenomenally). Cause and effect pertain to freedom, and moral evil is the effect of this freedom; thus, the origin of moral evil is in reason rather than time. Human nature can be regarded as reason. Kant says that there is no cause in the world which results in free agency being taken away from humans in each passing moment. The origin of evil can be located in the power to exercise choice with regard to maxims governing my actions. To speak of no comprehensible ground from which moral evil in human nature originally derives, is to ascribe evil to human beings. Evil originates in the improper use of freedom and is ever present as a possibility for freedom.

There is not a presupposition of downfall in the practical mediation. The mediating term of respect, Ricoeur says, is based in my desire for rationality that involves both free will and emotion deep within my body.[36] He refers to an anthropology that is symbolized in the term, *Gemüt*, a region whereby reason, as a force takes preference.[37] The important property of feeling (*Gemüt*) is receptivity (*Empfändlichkeit*), which is the capacity to experience and endure the force of a moral incentive.[38] This is a region of mindful interiority characterized by admiration and awe. Admiration and awe are not merely sought but are seen and are accordingly connected with consciousness of my existence. Admiration and awe testify to the affinity that sensibility has for rationality. This positive relation is the human destination, which in turn raises human worth, and infinitely so. The locus of respect is in the faculty or disposition of desire to be rational; the activity of the free will and passion come together. Feeling is precisely the area in which reason has force and can take preference.[39]

To conclude, the aspects of finitude can be reorganized under the notion of finite perspective. The aspects of infinitude can be reorganized under the notion of meaning. Respect, the third mediating term, is a fragile synthesis whereby a person's form is constituted. It is respect as an affective moment that gives itself to making known this "texture"[40] of feeling.

Affective Mediation

Ricoeur sets out to fill in what is missing in his reflective analysis of the structure of human being with the third mediation that involves the heart of human reality—the dimension of feeling. If it is possible to construct such a philosophy, then it must be capable of expressing the fragility that characterizes human reality as intermedial being. In other words, what he is questioning is the gap between a transcendental exegesis concerning disproportion, and a lived experience that can be characterized as misery.

Feeling and knowing arise together. It is through the powers of knowing that degrees of feeling can be ascertained. Feeling gives rise to the intentionality associated with knowing; I have a feeling about "something"—whether I characterize it as the loveable or the hateful, for example. Feeling can be considered an intentional act in that I feel qualities of love and hate. And yet, feeling discloses the way in which I am inwardly affected by such acts. Ricoeur refers to this situation as a perplexing paradox in that "an intention and an affection coincide in the same experience, a transcending aim and the revelation of an inwardness."[41] Feeling cannot posit being. The paradox of feeling is that it indicates a "thing-quality" and expresses an inwardness of the "I."[42]

Whereas knowing establishes a fissure between subject and object and divides, feeling precedes duality and manifests my relation to, and restores my involvement in and belonging to the world, and is, therefore, unitive—this is profound. Feeling can be considered a paradoxical unity of intention (directed toward the world) and affection (of the self). This paradox is a sign of the mystery that is associated with feeling—"the undivided connection of my existence with beings and being through desire and love."[43]

Feeling adds another dimension to a transcendental understanding of my human reality. Feeling interiorizes a division at the heart of human reality. When abstractly and indeterminately considering, for example, a relation between love and what is loveable, up to now, there has been no necessity to specify whether I am referring to a thing, a person, an idea, a community, or the idea of God. Now, my relation to the object entails ranking tendencies and differentiating the inwardness of feeling. In moving to a vertical discussion of degrees associated with feeling that are in accord with degree of the objects, the disproportion emerges. The disproportion of knowing reaches a completion in feeling, in the inner conflict, which remains unresolved. The humanness of my humanity is "that divergence of affective tension between the extremities of which is placed the 'heart.'"[44]

There are two types of terminations that feeling takes the form of: 1) pleasure as self-love, which is characterized by a constricted view of reality, and 2) happiness or beatitude, which is characterized as an openness to the whole of reality.[45] It is between the two, living and thinking, that the self is constituted. The first type of termination above, pleasure, is the affective movement that completes and perfects finite acts. The second termination, a fullness of happiness or beatitude, is the affective movement of perfection that is the work of the human in its totality, or its destiny. Hence there exists a duality of ends in feeling. Pleasure and beatitude, respectively, constitute the finite and infinite poles of this mediation.

Pleasure

Pleasure is the particular element in the third mediation. Sensuous desire or *epithumia* is a felt intention which brings together separate finite acts. It is in this way that pleasure is a finite perfection of life. Pleasure shows how living is the condition on which all other activities are based. Pleasure has a totality about it that mirrors happiness in that it is representative of happiness in the moment. I should, however, consider the long view of reality, in terms of what would be a just activity that could be engaged in over time that contributes to, and is a rejoicing in life lived with a view to the fullness of spiritual joy that is beatitude. Ricoeur follows Aristotle in noting that pleasure in taking the form of one activity can limit me or hinder me from engaging in other activities. When pleasure is engaged in for its own sake, it is deficient in terms of a higher aim.

Beatitude

Beatitude is the universal element in the mediation. Beatitude is rational desire, the desire for and love of the good, or the *eros* of *logos* in the fullness of happiness. This kind of desire is desire for the sake of desire, or spiritual happiness. I can characterize it, too, as the desire for God—love of God. Once again, Ricoeur follows Aristotle here.[46] Any final purposefulness that happiness may hold has to do with the activity itself, and not with any pleasure derived from that activity. The Good surpasses what is pleasurable. Happiness can be considered the highest form that pleasure assumes.

Eros is regarded as the fundamental feeling, and "is particularized in a diversity of feelings of belonging that are, as it were, the schematization of it."[47] These are termed spiritual feelings and constitute the pole of infinitude of the affective life. The spiritual feelings split, developing in two different directions: (1) in the "We" (or the individual who transcends itself together with other individuals who transcend themselves) through interhuman participation in all of its variety, and (2) in "Ideas" through participation in the tasks that transcend the individual work.[48] Ricoeur explains that "loving participation in ideas is the noetic or spiritual feeling *par excellence*."[49] It is in and through this feeling that I gain the certainty that reason, rather than being something alien, is who I am.

Conflict

The heart—*thumos* or spirit, serves as the mediating principle between pleasure and beatitude. Ricoeur considers the heart to be the schema of ontological feeling: "*Being-with*," is considered an interpersonal schema, "*being-for*" is a supra-personal schema, and "*being-in*" is the fundamental intention.[50] Heart is a fundamental openness to and availability of being.

It is no small task for the heart to synthesize two desires, and herein lies conflict: the desire for pleasure and the desire for beatitude or spiritual love. The disproportion between the principle of pleasure and the principle of happiness arises in this affective tension. He follows Kant's discussion of the human passions of possession (*Habsucht*) or having, domination (*Herrschsucht*) or power, and honor (*Ehrsucht*) or worth.[51] He relates this trilogy of affective human passions to the appropriate dimensions of objective life in order to show how distortions as well as realization of ideals are possible within life. First, having has to do with desires in connection with the economic dimension of life, or human relations as "an *available* good."[52] Availability creates a cycle of feelings such as acquisition and possession, for example. There is an interiorization of the human relation with the economic thing whatever it may be. The temptation is to equate having with happiness, but it cannot substitute for genuine happiness. There can be an innocent relation of the human self with having in that I can imagine a form of having in which goods are justly distributed and persons possess only what they cultivate and create themselves.

Second, power has to do with desires in connection with political and social situations in life, which is how humans are connected to communities comprised of communicative networks of relationships. Those who exercise control hold power over other people, and that creates dominance which carries over into the political sphere. Again, the error is in thinking that possession of power can ward off the losses of finitude. There is also an ideal in which that power is exercised in an altruistic way, without personal gain or reward in order to improve other human lives, as well as all forms of life.

Before I take up discussion of the third passion of possession, honor, it should be noted that Ricoeur presupposes a threefold structure of recognition. I present these three steps as a mini-phenomenology that is derived from Hegel. These three moments, as they appear in Hegel, and are inherited from Fichte, are the following: (1) immediate self-consciousness, (2) intersubjective self-consciousness, and (3) universal self-consciousness. In the process of recognition whereby "oneself" recognizes "another," the other negates me, and yet, at the same time negates the negation so that I am seen by the other, just as the other is seen by me. There exists the desiring to be seen by the other, and vice versa; this process sets up the Kantian notion of worth, that is, it is a value to be recognized by the other.

The first moment is an immediate self-consciousness that is appetitive self-consciousness, in that desire is a part of this. It is recognition of the other that redounds on the self, but just as conscious agents, or beings, or persons in general. It is immediate, particular self-consciousness, or simple self-identity. Each self-consciousness is itself by a refusal of what is the other self-consciousness.[53] Private certainty, and not truth, is expressed. The truth is going to demand the inclusion of the other who is suppressed.

The second moment, intersubjective self-consciousness, is the relation of one self-consciousness to another self-consciousness, with the process of recognizing occurring between the two. A "we" breaks into self-consciousness in that "I" am part of this intersubjective "we." There is the emergence of "my" freedom as limited and mirrored by "yours"; and, freedom is mutually self-limiting. A struggle ensues that must be undergone in order that the private certainty of each one, respectively, might be raised to the level of truth. Each one sees the other as an elusive presence who must be eliminated, because the other has called that one into question. In this case, each risks their own life, which is critical so that freedom can be demonstrated. The point of the second moment is not to rid one of the other, however. The point is to secure the recognition, and legitimate in intersubjectivity the certainty of one's own self-consciousness.[54] Ethical life and spiritual life emerge when there is reciprocal self-recognition, and the other is recognized as constituting a freedom characterized by respect. It is fair to say that an enduring ethical relationship of reciprocal recognition is one of love. Love has to do with a mutual releasement in which there is a "letting the other be."[55] When the freedom of the other is acknowledged, and the other is freely recognized, then intersubjective mediation does not collapse into self-mediation, and the other is not reduced to the same.

The third moment is the universal self-consciousness in the movement from the intersubjective "we" consciousness to universal self-consciousness, where now the "we" is sublated. The sublation occurs by seeing the difference between "I" and "you," but also, and most importantly, the identity of "I" and "you," which points toward some universal structure. Reason, my process of recognition, stands within the universal structure of recognizing me. Universal recognition, or *Geist*, is recognition itself through my recognizing it. Recognition is essential to reason so that it can acquire a genuine universality.[56] The passage to reason, that is, rational self-consciousness, is representative of the achievement of universal self-consciousness. Reason is already there in the world before, as well as independent of, any human subjectivity. The movement that has been traced through these three moments of recognition proceeds from an exclusive particularity to an inclusive universality, or the "We," through the process of reciprocal recognition. Intersubjective mediation is crucial to reason, otherwise reason is just subjective assurance. Having established the groundwork for recognition, I shall now return to discussion of the third possession of passion, or honor.

Honor has to do with desires in connection with the quest for worth and esteem in the view of the other. Here it is difficult to ascertain erroneous intentions from the constituting intentions of esteem. Subjects become constituted in and through the process of self-recognition by another subject. The "moment" of self-esteem involves a search for my own self-esteem by way of the esteem of the other, and has the identical nature of the esteem that I experience for the other. Ricoeur explains that "If humanity is what I esteem in another and in myself, I esteem myself as a thou for another," which is to say "I esteem myself in the second person."[57] I can say, then, that I love myself as if I were loving an other.

This kind of otherness is connected to a feeling of value. Self-esteem is the indirect relation of mediating oneself to oneself while passing through "the valorizing regard" of the other.[58] This relation to oneself is the interiorized relation to the other. Worth is believed. Ricoeur says that the feeling of our worth is constituted by this belief.[59] In the case that the other is considered as myself, an extreme case to be sure, the feeling of worth is an appreciative affection or affective appreciation, and is the summit of self-consciousness.

The disproportion in knowing, acting, and feeling can be considered in feeling as fragility. Here there is human duality. The first sign of the duality can be discovered between the finite goals of pleasure, and the infinite goal of happiness, or beatitude. The heart is restless so that no amount of having, power, or worth is enough. The fragility of feeling is taken up into the indefiniteness of the spirit or *thumos*. The heart is restless in asking, When will I be satisfied in having enough? When will I receive in sufficient measure appreciation and recognition? Between pleasure as finitude, and happiness as infinitude, there must be a transcending intention that dwells in the great ventures of human existence.

Passion receives from *eros* a power of abandon and devotion. Through the interiorization of relation of the self to the world, feeling displays a new rift in which the self is alienated from itself, which is a disproportion of feeling.[60] Out of the disproportion of feeling, emerges a mediation that is parallel to the silent mediation in the transcendental imagination in knowledge. That is, the devoted and passional life lived is one of passivity that is of a more primordial nature than "passional captivity and sufferance"; other modalities of this passion are grafted onto that first passion.[61] Yet, the human places the entire capacity for happiness onto the objects that constitute the Self. This is a shifting of totality onto objects that characterize the cycle of having, power, and worth; this is the schematization of happiness. This schematization is an extension of the schematization of the transcendental imagination into the third mediation of feeling. Thus, the person who wants to have it all, so to speak, forgets that what is existing between happiness and the desired object is of a symbolic character; the symbol is made an idol. Ricoeur comments that "the impassioned life becomes a passional existence."[62] The locus of fallibility resides in a relation between the impassioned and the passional.

Conflict serves to function as part of the primordial constitution of human being. The self is conflict given the disproportion of living (*bios*) and thinking (*logos*), as my heart suffers this primordial discord.[63] The very humanness of humanity emerges out of this moral and aesthetic striving. There will be both distorted and undistorted forms of having, power, and worth. Concepts such as justice (distribution of power), and truth (in recognition whereby people are seen for who they are), come into play here. This is the weak point where evil enters the world; I displace genuine mediation for one-sided mediation. At this third level, the disproportion is between a feeling of pleasure and a feeling of beatitude. This is how the possibility of evil comes in.

THE POSSIBILITY OF HUMAN BEING

For Ricoeur fallibility is the ontological structural weakness of human being. Human being is that non-coincidence of self within itself and between its selves that feeling reveals—the disproportion of being intermediate in bringing about mediations between an element of the finite and an element of the infinite. In the presentation of his reflective model, human being has the capacity to think, to act, and to feel. The second step of the argument is that the finite creature is suspended between opposite poles of perceiving and conceiving. These capacities of finite existence are brought about through language. Language is the medium of the fragile mediations between these poles of receiving and acting in the world. This is the articulation of the possibility of human being. In the more extensive initial presentation of Ricoeur's model above, the role of language appeared briefly. For my purposes here, it is the function of language as a medium that warrants attention. The nature of my short presentation below is to meet the purpose of providing a formal introduction to the role of language in this study.

Language means a system of relations and rules governing words, in addition to a lexicon of word-meanings. To think in language requires joining and separating words in sentences with meaning. The sentence is the primary unit of meaning. Because of this joining and separating of word-meanings in sentences, I will show eventually how language is always punctuated by silence. Language is the medium of being, because the activity of being is the joining/separating, and the being of a thing is what is joined and separated in the thing by language. Furthermore, I speak the being of things by connecting the particular subject-term with the universal predicate-term in a sentence. Being is the connection and separation of universal and particular. In speaking the being of things, I also bespeak my own being as the connecting process. I am the connecting of meaning—the disclosure of meaning—within a historical language with a particular worldview. The being of a person is connection and separation of the "I" and "this one here." In speaking the being of things, I also combine and differentiate the "I" and "this body," because "I" appears as "here" in "this one" in speaking, yet the "I" announces itself as always in principle more than and transcendent to "this one here."

In *Fallible Man*, the dialectic of signifying (saying) and perceiving (seeing), is primordial.[64] Ricoeur references the first of Husserl's *Logical Investigations* and explains how expression can serve as a sign insofar as I proclaim what I mean to someone else.[65] Expression as a sign indicates a sense that is the represented content, which accordingly signifies the referent. Hence, through signification, language conveys the sense that transgresses my own unique and finite perspective. Everyone else to whom the same sense has been conveyed fulfills it in reference and relation to their own perception, or imagination, or it may not be fulfilled at all. Meaning is arrived at rather than directly bestowed. Meaning also has the property of being capable of excess in that by virtue of signifying, I am always saying more than what I actually am seeing. This dialectic is therefore one of infinitude and finitude.

Because of the transcendence of speech (saying) over perspective (seeing), further attention is accorded the concept of expression and the delineation between a noun and a verb, the unity of which comprises the essential element of human discourse. Ricoeur follows Aristotle's thinking in *On Interpretation* and says that the verb has a noun-meaning as an action that has additional meanings: First, verbs specify a tense as that of past, present, or future, which posits the activity of existence in temporal terms. Second, verbs attribute the activity to a subject. Third, verbs contain the power to either affirm or negate something in someone.[66] In this way, the noun-verb combination expresses not only truth, but being as well. The volitional moment of affirmation includes the seeking of assent as well as improvement, or the remedy of error. Finally, in terms of the transcendence of speaking as accomplished by the verb, what is disclosed is that the heart of the verb lies in affirmation, which entails freedom of judgment in relation to truth insofar as the verb points to the truth. What I have hoped to show is how meaning is made in the noun-verb combination, and that it is shot through with being; being enters language.

To conclude, the purpose of presenting Ricoeur's philosophical anthropology is to show how the practice of contemplative silence is possible. For that reason the ontological structure that is the condition of the possibility of the practice is explained. The human being is the activity of mediating at three levels and as a whole, and a hermeneutics of the practice of contemplative silence is grounded in this ontological structure. The practice is a highly refined, self-conscious instance of mediating activity that both establishes and transcends both the being of the self and the being of language in silence. The fragile mediations that are performed occur through language. In language, the saying in coordinating with seeing expresses more than it knows in such a way that metaphorical and philosophical language arises. In pursuing the notion of fallibility, one context for the practice is determined that centers on human lived reality. Fallible human is in relation to a world. Accordingly, Ricoeur changes his method from reflection to hermeneutics, which is the focus of the next chapter.

NOTES

1. See Paul Ricoeur, *Freedom and Nature: The Voluntary and the Involuntary*, trans. and intro. Erazim V. Kohák (Evanston: Northwestern University Press, 1966), 484 (hereafter FN). The act should not be understood as "pure act" since freedom, according to Ricoeur, has moments of activity as well as receptivity in that "It constitutes itself in receiving what it does not produce: values, capacities, and sheer nature." See also Kearney, "Capable Man, Capable God," 49; 51n9. Kearney comments that Ricoeur does, however, see continuity between potency and act, (or between "possibilizing and actualizing" in the "I can"), in that this phenomenology—the aim of which is a concrete event—is a mix of the two.

2. Ricoeur, FN, 412.
3. Ibid., 5.
4. Ibid., 413.
5. Ibid., 486.
6. Ricoeur, FM, xlii.
7. Ibid., 5.
8. Ibid.
9. Ibid., 3.
10. Boyd Blundell, *Paul Ricoeur between Theology and Philosophy: Detour and Return* (Bloomington and Indianapolis: Indiana University Press, 2010), 158.
11. Ibid., 147.
12. Ricoeur, FM, xliv; 135.
13. Ibid., 137.
14. Ibid. Ricoeur follows Spinoza here.
15. Ibid., 138.
16. Ibid., 139.
17. Ibid., 140.
18. See Klemm, "Philosophy and Kerygma: Ricoeur as Reader of the Bible," 53–56. This is an excellent presentation of Ricoeur's abstract model of human being, and from which this discussion is drawn.
19. Ricoeur, FM, 38.
20. Ibid. Ricoeur says that the consciousness as synthesis is not "self-consciousness," and therefore, not yet human.

21. Ibid., 40.

22. See Frederick C. Beiser, *German Idealism: The Struggle Against Subjectivism, 1781–1801* (Cambridge, MA, and London: Harvard University Press, 2002), 297–98. Beiser says that for Fichte "the first principle of the *Wissenschaftslehre* is a postulate that demands that the subject intuit itself, that it think of itself and in doing so construct itself in intuition." Beiser explains, too, that "The transcendental ego, [or the "I"] is not a thing-in-itself, Fichte contends, but a transcendental idea because it can be 'realized in intellectual intuition' . . . . By appealing to intellectual intuition, then, Fichte could keep transcendental philosophy within its own self-imposed limits of possible experience." Beiser comments that this context illustrates how Fichte did not develop the theory by an abstract reflection on self-consciousness, or from a general examination of "the conditions of consciousness. Rather, he formed it in reflecting on the conditions of transcendental self-knowledge, and in attempting to build a strictly immanent transcendental philosophy."

23. Ricoeur, FM, 40.

24. Ibid.

25. See Immanuel Kant, *Critique of Pure Reason*, trans. and ed. Paul Guyer and Allen W. Wood (Cambridge and New York: Cambridge University Press, 1998), 175 or A 24/B 39 and 178–79 or A 31/B 47 respectively. With regard to the absence of space, Kant explains that "One can never represent that there is no space, though one can very well think that there are no objects to be encountered in it." With regard to the absence of time, Kant explains that "Time is a necessary representation that grounds all intuitions. In regard to appearances in general one cannot remove time, though one can very well take the appearances away from time. Time is given *a priori*. In it alone is all actuality of appearances possible. The latter could all disappear, but time itself (as the universal condition of their possibility) cannot be removed."

26. Ibid., 172–92 or A 19/B 33-A 49/B73.

27. Ricoeur, FM, 43.

28. Ibid., 49–50.

29. Ibid., 51.

30. Ibid., 55.

31. Ibid., 58.

32. Ibid., 64n10.

33. Ibid., 74. See also 74n28.

34. See Ibid., 75n32.

35. See Immanuel Kant, *Religion within the Boundaries of Mere Reason*, trans. and ed. Allen Wood and George di Giovanni, intro. Robert Merrihew Adams (Cambridge and New York: Cambridge University Press, 1998).

36. Ricoeur, FM, 77.

37. Ibid.

38. Ibid.

39. Ibid.

40. Texture denotes both appearance and feel.

41. Ricoeur, FM, 84.

42. Ibid., 85.

43. Ibid., 89.
44. Ibid., 92.
45. Ibid., 95; 97; 107.
46. Ibid., 96n9. Ricoeur quotes Aristotle in stating that "Happiness is the 'desirable in itself' and not 'for the sake of something else.'"
47. Ibid., 103.
48. Ibid.
49. Ibid., 103–4.
50. Ibid., 104.
51. Ibid., 111.
52. Ibid., 114.
53. Robert R. Williams, *Recognition: Fichte and Hegel on the Other* (Albany: SUNY Press, 1992), 173. For this discussion, see also, Georg W. F. Hegel, *The Phenomenology of Spirit (The Phenomenology of Mind)*, trans. J. B. Baillie (LaVergne, TN: Digireads.com, 2009).
54. Williams, 174.
55. Ibid., 184.
56. Ibid., 197.
57. Ricoeur, FM, 124.
58. Ibid.
59. Ibid.
60. Ibid., 131.
61. Ibid.
62. Ibid.
63. Ibid., 132.
64. Ibid., 27.
65. Ibid.
66. Ibid., 33. Ricoeur says that what was not considered by Aristotle was the power to judge that the verb reveals.

Chapter 2

Fallibility Gives Rise to Hermeneutics

As an opening exercise, I will rehearse Ricoeur's thought once more so as to ascertain the linguality and textuality associated with human reality. It was shown how in pure reflection he expresses the mediating activity that is intermedial being, and that reflective philosophy becomes the reflexive activity of thinking about thinking, which entails a philosophical anthropology. An iteration of that structure is to characterize it as a continuous theoretical striving of critical thinking to mediate among disproportionate and opposite powers and capabilities, as intermedial being relates to self, other and world.[1] Theoretical striving is a desire to know—the desire for knowledge and its fulfillment. Fallibility characterizes this movement of rigorous thinking that is on a par with the richness of a pathetic understanding of misery.[2] The mediations that are performed in thinking become more fragile, however, the more interior they become, in moving from the theoretical, to the practical synthesis, and finally, to affective fragility. I can think about the meaning of thinking insofar as performing fragile mediations are mediations of my very being as thinking. Through the dialectic of originating affirmation and existential negation, the effort to exist and the desire to be that are manifest in perspective, character, and felt love for life, are negated through denial, as seen in the example presented in Chapter 1. This existential "difference" of intermedial being in the becoming of an opposition is the felt conflict of human reality, which is interiorized by the self in the depths of the human heart. The primacy of willing means that human being is striving toward something; the human is act before representation. However, human being cannot confer being upon itself and persist in it; the human suffers an untold original woundedness. Human being is received.

That human being is received leads to the next step of the study. I want to introduce and briefly develop the idea of human reality as including both silence and language, which is the third step of the argument. Human life, according to Ricoeur, is a combination of animal life (instinct and appetite), which is *bios* or living being, and rationality, or the capacity for rational thinking, which is *logos*, or thinking. The disproportion between *bios* and *logos* is the primordial discord suffered in the human heart. The term, *logos*, is not purely abstract and ideal. "*Logos*" refers to the capacity for, and possibilizing and actualizing of, abstract thought; it is the capacity for reasoning, and it is the resultant rationality as well. Here, "thought" means an abstract, invisible, spiritual or ideal meaning held in the mind. To think a thought is soundless and occurs in silence. *Logos* as abstract meaning in thought is dependent upon language that is suffused with silence.

It is with the practical synthesis that there is an ideal to attain through the intention that the self represents to itself in striving, as freedom in thinking, to become someone. An iteration of that structure is to characterize it as moral striving in the desire for the Good, and in terms of how I behave; I ought to comply with the Good. Thinking is appropriated as this freedom by explaining and thereby making clear its expressions in the characteristically linguistic world in which it is immersed.[3] Hence "thinking qua thinking for Ricoeur has the identity of a moral striving."[4] A self of such representation is a combination of a specific and concrete living existence, and an idea of humanity. The experience wherein is constituted a synthesis between existence and reason, of presence and end, or between living being and thinking, is the moral feeling of respect. Here, there is a synthesis of *bios* and *logos*, of living being and thinking. This moral feeling can be considered a moral schema, as it belongs both to sensibility and to reason, through the power of desiring and the power of obligation that issue forth from practical reason. Respect is both a sensible form of reason in the incentive to yield to the moral law in human actions, as well as an actual empirical, felt appearance of reason. With respect as a mediating term, respect for others and self-respect are deeply intertwined. I become who I desire and ought to be inasmuch as I act and conduct myself in accordance with others who have inherent worth, and who, as such, are deserving of my highest esteem. This is precisely the locus of tension and strife, as well as the condition of the possibility of existential fault with the resultant human fragility. It is at this point that Ricoeur looks to a theory of feeling in addition to reason. The characteristic power and capability of feeling is receptivity. Recall that he defines receptivity as the capacity to experience and endure the influence that the moral impulse exerts. I sometimes experience and endure the feeling of misery in living up to this demanding imperative. *Bios* as concrete living meaning contained in avowals of misery is dependent upon symbolic language and the silence within which it is held, as will be shown.

With affective fragility, I reach the heart of human reality, or the heart of hearts—an interiority that localizes a duality of feeling "here" in this one who

"I" am. An iteration of that structure is to characterize it as the experience of aesthetic striving, which is a personal felt aesthetic and a striving for the beautiful; it is a shared experience and a felt sense perception. Here, there is the tension between the intimation of beatitude and the lure of pleasures, but the aim, in the form of a goal, is to subordinate pleasure to beatitude. As beatitude suggests at this affective level, it is directing me to the beautiful. The movement that occurs is from self-consciousness, to the free part of the "we," to the person embodied in universal reason; and, it is the relation of goodness and truth to beauty. These are regulative ideals that direct our thinking and acting rather than constituting metaphysical entities.

Feeling and knowing arise together. Feeling, insofar as it is a paradoxical unity of intention directed toward the world, and yet, of being inwardly affected, at the same time, is a paradoxical sign of mystery, too: it points to the undivided nature of my existence in relationship both to other beings and to being, in and through desire as well as love. Given the duality of feeling in the desire for pleasure and the desire for spiritual love, heart as the fundamental openness to, and availability of being, must hold both desires in conflict. The summit of spiritual feeling is to lovingly participate in thought that transcends individual work. *Bios* and *logos* are principles of meaning for a finite creature because they function at the limit; I cannot approach either one without the other. The disproportion of *bios* and *logos* as ultimate meaning in the struggle that is living being and thinking, of which my heart suffers a primordial and resounding dissonance, is dependent upon language and silence. That is, the experience of language that is integral to human being as intermedial between finitude and infinitude includes silence.

FROM REFLECTIVE PHILOSOPHY TO HERMENEUTICS

I have shown how fallibility for Ricoeur is a constitutional weakness that makes moral evil possible insofar as there is a disproportion, a noncoincidence (which is a limitation) of the self to itself. Included in the notion of fallibility is the capacity to fail, which is a "*power* to fail" insofar as it makes the human "*capable* of failing."[5] That is, a fragile mediation makes an appearance as the condition of the possibility of the appearance of evil. The human who is a center of reality must reconcile extreme poles and is a weak link in respect to the real. The human by virtue of existence must connect opposites theoretically in consciousness as well as practically in intention, while engulfed in deep conflict. The gap between the possibility of evil, and the reality and actuality of evil is the leap, or the enigma of fault. The actuality of human being comes with the capacity for fallible existence. Evil becomes the source of actualized self-awareness in language and confession, as well as the occasion for the search for redemption. Thus, fallibility gives rise to hermeneutics. This is the fourth step of the argument. Pure reflection cannot explain so as to remediate the fault and the movement from innocence to guilt. The reality of actual evil cannot be elicited from its mere possibility. I cannot deduce the actuality of evil from the structure of fallibility. It is impossible to describe evil in empirical terms. So Ricoeur therefore turns to the interpretation of linguistic expressions such as utterances in the form of avowals and confessions of sin, fault, and guilt to reveal the humanness of this existential experience.[6]

He explains how language serves as "the light of the emotions" in that initially a blind experience, such as dread, fear, or anguish—an experience that most often occurs in silence, I would add—becomes objectified in discourse through the emotional note that is struck.[7] A confession expresses and pushes to the exterior this emotion; without it, this emotion would remain an interior impression. Thus, through this confession the human remains speech, but again, the human is also silence insofar as the experience of absurdity and suffering are felt and embodied, to be sure. This feeling is not only blind but equivocal in its multiplicity of meanings, which require the elucidation of language. Finally, this experience of alienation, of being myself, and yet, alienated from who I am, is immediately transcribed in language as interrogative thought, e.g., What have I done? How long must I live like this? I am, in the silence of soundless thought, incomprehensible to myself in this experience, lost to myself, which communicates with a need and desire to understand; self-alienation is a scandal and astonishing to the self!

Ricoeur makes the change from pure reflection to hermeneutics because he hopes to gain deeper insight into the problem of personal identity. As such, the hermeneutical turn is a significant change in the goals of his project. The human is an acting and suffering being. Given the conditions of existence, the self is alienated from itself in silence and language as well as in the middle of a world in which the self has become objectified. In the philosophical tradition the first truth is "*I am, I think*," which is a positing of both being and act, a positing of both existence and the functioning of thought.[8] "I" exist insofar as "I" think. This truth is not verifiable. It can only be posited by reflection. "Self-positing is reflection" (he refers to Fichte here), which is the starting point of philosophical reflection.[9] This first truth, however, is abstract, empty, and invincible. Reflection therefore must be more sufficiently characterized. Reflection is an effort to recapture the "I" precisely where it has been objectified—in its works, acts, institutions, monuments, ideas, and images. The first truth is mediated by what objectifies it.[10] The "I" must lose itself in the objects and discover the meaning of itself anew in the act of existing by "deciphering" or interpreting the meaning of the "I" in the "signs scattered in the cultures in which our language is rooted."[11] He also makes hermeneutic detours through symbol, metaphor, and narrative that give perspective on my own identity. By taking a detour through texts, I gain the critical distance on myself to realize new possibilities for my life—something he further develops in *Oneself as Another*.[12]

Hermeneutics as reflection appropriates and reappropriates the effort to exist and the desire to be. In so doing, "I" discover something that was lost, but that had been originally a part of me in language, and which through time and space and distance had become separated from me. Reflection is a task in that I must make my concrete living experience on a par with the "I am" as posited. Now, I can say that positing is a task. I experience being myself, yet I am alienated from myself, which gets transcribed in silence and language.[13] Hermeneutics can reunite what is an astonishing alienation with what is lost through the experience of silence and language. Further on, I will discuss the way in which silence, together with mythological language and symbolical language, function in this respect. Hermeneutics, as an expansion of philosophical reflection, takes on ethical and spiritual import insofar as there is movement from alienation to freedom and beatitude.[14] Through appropriation and reappropriation, the alienated self is transformed through arriving at knowledge of the whole.

FALLIBILITY

For Ricoeur, to refer to the human as fallible means that in the constitutive structure of human being there is an inherent possibility of moral evil.[15] Fallibility has explanatory power in terms of how moral evil is possible, while the occurrence of evil, that is, the actuality of evil, is inexplicable. He considers two sorts of clarifications of this explanation. The first one has to do with "limitation" and fallibility. The second one has to do with fallibility and the possibility of "fault." First, it is not the notion of limitation (or finitude in general), that brings me to what is "the threshold of moral evil."[16] Rather, it is a specific limitation that has explanatory power in that the possibility of failing resides in human reality, in the self that does not coincide with itself. Finite and infinite aspects of the self constitute the human disproportion. This disproportionate relation constitutes an ontological locus that lies between the "quantity of being" that is human—"being and nothingness."[17] He says that *"It is this relation that makes human limitation synonymous with fallibility."*[18]

Given the movement of his study, what is playing out is an increasingly more real determination of the term, mediation, as representing the humanity of human being. The guiding concept in the anthropology is most definitely not finitude; finitude is what results rather than being the origin.[19] In order to be able to identify human thinking with human being, all three levels of human reality must be analyzed. It is at the third level of feeling that I really am this humanity that is thinking.[20] Eros and love illustrate this goal that is immanent to my human functioning in the anticipatory happiness that comes with a consciousness filled with direction as well as belonging. It is the infinite pole of feeling, or beatitude that provides this assurance. With originating affirmation comes a Joy about existing in what it is that enables me to be able to think as well as act.

However, original affirmation must become concretely human by proceeding through the existential negation of perspective, character, and vital feeling. Existential negation, the negation of the affirmation, is the most inward of negations.[21] Feeling as conflict is revelatory of the human as this primordial conflict. It illustrates that the mediation is merely intentional, and merely aimed at in the task that is performed. The possibility for evil comes in at the third level, the level of feeling, in the conflict between the feeling of pleasure (self-love without beatitude), and beatitude (without self-love).

The second clarification concerns fallibility and the possibility of fault. This fragility to fail is meant in three increasingly complex terms—it is an occasion to fail, the origin of failure, as well as the capacity to fail. In terms of the occasion, fallibility indicates the mere point or space through which there is the possibility of evil for the human. The gap is between the possibility of evil, and evil as a reality. Ricoeur says that his philosophical anthropological reflection remains behind in the leap, while ethics appears too late. I have the enigma of the "leap" from fallibility to what is already fallen. The only way to capture that leap is to make a new start and engage in a hermeneutical reflection that focuses on avowals of evil and symbols of evil. It is solely through the present evil condition of the human heart that I can ascertain a condition that is more primordial than any evil: "it is through hate and strife that one can perceive . . . respect . . . ; it is through misunderstanding and lying that the primordial structure of speech reveals the identity and otherness of minds . . . it is always '*through*' the fallen that the primordial shines through."[22] This movement reveals fallibility as a capacity. It is important to reiterate the primacy of "capacity" in his work, and for purposes of this study, the emphasis will be kept on the actualizable possibility of human capacity. It is in the mode of the imagination—mythological-poetic language—that I can both express the primordial and investigate the possible. Fallibility becomes the origin of evil whenever evil is actually posited in the world in and through human action. It is then that fallibility is a capacity that is realized. I shall briefly turn to a discussion of the relation of freedom to evil before discussing his hermeneutics of symbol. It is in the avowal of evil that the circumstance of freedom becomes apparent.

THE RELATIONSHIP BETWEEN FREEDOM AND EVIL

Feeling discloses the fissure, the split that I am as primordial conflict.[23] I traverse the enigma of evil in the leap from fallibility to fault, from the possibility of evil to its actuality. Imaginatively, I can understand evil insofar as I understand good; goodness is even more primordial than what is bad. That I am fallible and "capable" of failing is due to my weakness—the limitation from which my "capacity" for evil derives; this is so only in positing it.[24] In discussing the good life in *Oneself as Another*, Ricoeur explains that I should act in conformity "with the maxim by which [I] . . . can wish at the same time that what *ought not to be*, namely evil, will indeed *not exist*."[25] He refers to the experience of suffering as "evil," "a problem," and "irreducible."[26] Further, he is "haunted" by suffering in his thought, which explains his concern with duration in human action.[27]

I can engage in an ongoing effort to understand freedom and evil, each in terms of the other.[28] Evil manifests in and through the exertion of my freedom. This space of the manifestation of evil becomes apparent to me solely in the case that I can recognize it. To recognize it is to purposefully decide to attempt to understand evil in light of freedom—it is my conscious decision to contend with evil. The decision is this announcement of a freedom, an avowal of evil that acknowledges responsibility by exercising agency to see that it is not perpetrated. Awareness of freedom and the ethical view of the world come into being concomitantly. The "grandeur" of the ethical vision consists in my continually striving to comprehend evil and freedom by each other. Freedom arrives at self-understanding laden with meaning. The avowal of evil is the condition of conscious awareness of my finite, limited freedom.

A HERMENEUTICS OF SYMBOL

The concept of fallibility is given profundity in the movement from innocence to fault that is disclosed in and through the positing of evil. Ricoeur's "meditative" reflection on symbols begins within the fullness of the language and the meaning that is already present; in a sense everything has already been said, but it wants to be thought again—including any presuppositions—in the endeavor to "recollect" itself.[29] This meditation includes both a moment of forgetting and a moment of restoring, in which a dim recognition of forgetting (of Sacred signs and human belonging to what is Sacred) rouses me to bring integrity back to language. An infinite discourse commences through this symbolic manifestation of a thing.[30] "The symbol gives rise to thought," in two respects: I am given something and I am given the opportunity to think about something.[31] The symbol also introduces a radical cultural contingency to discourse, as the philosopher speaks from a particular standpoint, which will influence the way in which the investigation is oriented.[32]

All language that has to do with evil is symbolic language. Symbol supplies the language for confession and avowal. The symbolism of evil begins with primary symbols, which come from human experience in nature, whereby I am oriented in space. I become aware of myself in the world in different modalities by means of primary symbols. My consciousness is posited in an expressive cosmos that communicates through them. Primary symbols carry a literal meaning.[33] Mythical symbols include narratives that have to do with the origins and end of an experience for which primary symbols serve as the avowal.

A symbol is like a sign in that it points to and intends some other thing, and stands for that other thing. A symbol can be distinguished from a sign, in that a sign is a single-meaning expression, whereas a symbol is a second-meaning expression signifying a mode of my being in the world.[34] Not all signs are symbols, however. Hidden in the symbol is a double-intentionality—a double-meaning expression. The first literal and apparent meaning intends through analogy the second meaning, which otherwise would not be given except by way of that first meaning. The second meaning points to the circumstance of human being (e.g., a material stain in terms of a deviation in space, which points to a predicament of humanity with regard to the Sacred), an expression of what it is to be human; and it signifies a mode of being in the world (e.g., fallenness as an existential mode of being in the world). Hence the situation of stained and guilty being, as the literal meaning, points beyond to that "which is *like* a stain, *like* a deviation. . . ."[35] The symbol, in this way, "gives" a second meaning.

I will consider first of all, the interior movement of the primary symbols of "stain," "sin," and "guilt," and think of them as constellations. For example, a "stain" is more than just a "spot" as the "whole" person as penitent is affected; physical washing is insufficient to remove whatever it is that is affecting the penitent. Ricoeur explains that in the performing of interchangeable acts (he mentions, for example, spitting and the covering of the body with earth), these rituals of purification so intend an integrity that can only be spoken by using symbolic language.[36] Second, a schema of exteriority lies at the heart of the symbolism, insofar as I am infected by evil: Evil can only be evil if it is posited by human freedom, and yet, evil is already there, which is affirmed in the symbol of the ancient stain.[37] Symbols destroy prior symbols; symbols are overturned. For example, when a new category of religious experience is introduced in the phrase, "before God," in terms of the covenantal relationship of Judaism, evil becomes a broken relationship, and so, nothing—no thing is expressed in images such as "emptiness" and "God's absence."[38] "A new positivity of evil arises" again, however, in the form of "a real enslaving power," as captivity serves as a symbol, and transforms historical events—Ricoeur mentions the Egyptian and Babylonian captivities, for example—into "a schema of existence, [that] represents the highest expression achieved by the penitential experience of Israel."[39] The first symbol of stain is once again taken up as "the schema of exteriority is recovered," but at the ethical rather than at the magical level.[40]

The linguistic expression of the experience of evil is, in turn, an interpretation of symbolic expressions. Primary symbols derive from the literal meaning of words. Both Greek mythology and the biblical rendition of fallenness disclose new countenances of the undergoing and suffering of evil, and recount the beginning and end, or how experience is directed "from memory toward hope"—which reflects the temporality of living reality.[41] Any admission or acknowledgment of fallenness, finitude, and guilt is connected to the assertion of the innocence of created being. Thus, in addition to their expressivity, there is exploratory value to these symbols of evil as they bestow universality, temporality, and an ontological significance on those expressions. With Ricoeur, hermeneutics becomes a global theory of understanding.[42]

Three dynamic stages of this original symbolic consciousness emerge in the form of reflective thinking from the Judaeo-Christian tradition: The first stage manifests as surprise at the stain that is corrupting me, and which I can feel, although I refuse to impute this evil deed to myself and externally project it onto something Other. The second stage of deviation demonstrates cognizance of falling short relationally with God. Evil is the consequence. The third stage of bondage of the will admits of personally being responsible for the evil in symbolic terms. Reflective thinking arises out of the primary symbols, the myth that schematizes the primary symbols, and symbolic avowals of fault that respond to mythical meanings, which serve as preparation for not only theological notions but metaphysical concepts as well.[43]

Symbolism is always subject to its being surpassed through an oppositional dynamic between myths that relate the origin of evil to primordial conflict, which predates the human, such as Greek tragedy does, and myths that attribute evil to human being who makes an evil choice, such as in the Book of Genesis where the person is immersed in evil through her own fault; this is an ongoing participatory activity. This temporalizing process results in two different forms of symbolic consciousness, which hinge on the issue of timing with regard to evil. There is, too, the juxtaposition of a schema of exteriority in the notion of evil considered as stain, versus a schema of interiority, which is captured in the pain-ridden experience of guilt and scrupulosity of conscience.

Yet the conflict does not only pertain to two different kinds of myths, but within the single Adamic myth, there is the moment of the Fall attributed to

32   *Chapter 2*

one human, while the narrative concerning the temptation plays out over the duration of time and is spread out among several characters and episodes. This is the conflict of myths contained in the single myth. The serpent symbolizes the preexisting evil that attracts the human; the human discovers evil rather than beginning it. For the human, to begin means to continue. The serpent represents what is Other in terms of human evil.[44] While theology in tragedy is unavowable and cannot be thought, the unavowable is shown, however, through the tragic hero who is at once innocent and guilty.

Critical thought is crucial for Ricoeur's hermeneutics and ensures the authenticity and perfection of the process of appropriation.[45] The function of hermeneutics is to transcend criticism by means of a restorative criticism. Symbol and thought are held together in hermeneutics; the meaning of a symbol and the task of understanding bond in the hermeneutical circle: "We must understand in order to believe, but we must believe in order to understand," explains Ricoeur.[46] The interpreter and the expressions of life form a kinship of thought with the intended aim of that life—the thought and the thing in question. Philosophical hermeneutics entails a philosophy that begins with the symbols and strives to form the meaning through a creative interpretation. The symbol is a way of deciphering my human reality in such a way that the space of avowal or confession is illuminated. The symbol, in the power to make itself known, augments my self-awareness, while at the same time, a philosophy that is taught by these symbols has the task of "a qualitative transformation of reflexive consciousness."[47] It is in this regard, with Ricoeur's shift to hermeneutics, that I change the focus from fallible human to capable human.

NOTES

1. See David E. Klemm, "Searching for a Heart of Gold: A Ricoeurian Meditation on Moral Striving and the Power of Religious Discourse," *Paul Ricoeur and Contemporary Moral Thought*, eds. John Wall, William Schweiker, and W. David Hall (New York: Routledge, 2002), 100 (hereafter "Searching for a Heart of Gold"). He comments that "I think that it would be entirely fair to Ricoeur to add that dialectical thinking about thinking therefore means to question the meaning and truth of these mediations—and to put into question one's own being as thinking."

2. Ricoeur, FM, 6.
3. Klemm, "Searching for a Heart of Gold," 102.
4. Ibid.
5. Ricoeur, FM, 141; 145.
6. Ricoeur, SE, 4–10.
7. Ibid., 7.

8. Paul Ricoeur, *Freud and Philosophy: An Essay on Interpretation*, trans. Denis Savage (New Haven and London: Yale University Press, 1970), 43 (hereafter FP).
9. Ibid.
10. Ibid.
11. Ibid., 47.
12. See Blundell, 40.
13. Ricoeur, SE, 8.
14. Ricoeur, FP, 45.
15. Ricoeur, FM, 133.
16. Ibid.
17. Ibid., 134.
18. Ibid.
19. Ibid., 136.
20. Ibid., 137.
21. Ibid.
22. Ibid., 144.
23. Ibid., 141.
24. Ibid., 146.
25. Ricoeur, OA, 218.
26. See Reagan, 135. See also Paul Ricoeur, *Evil: A Challenge to Philosophy and Theology*, trans. John Bowden, intro. Graham Ward (London and New York: Continuum, 2007), 18.
27. See Reagan, 135.
28. Ricoeur, FM, xvi-xlix.
29. Paul Ricoeur, "The Hermeneutics of Symbols and Philosophical Reflection: I," *The Conflict of Interpretations: Essays in Hermeneutics, I*, ed. Don Ihde, trans. Denis Savage (Evanston, IL: Northwestern University Press, 1974), 287-88 (hereafter "The Hermeneutics of Symbols: I").
30. Ricoeur, SE, 11.
31. Ibid., 348. See also "The Hermeneutics of Symbols: I," 288.
32. Ricoeur, FP, 48.
33. Klemm, HTPR, 70.
34. See Ricoeur, SE, 14-18.
35. Ricoeur, "The Hermeneutics of Symbols: I," 290.
36. Ibid., 291.
37. Ibid.
38. Ibid., 291-92.
39. Ibid., 292.
40. Ibid.
41. Paul Ricoeur, "The Hermeneutics of Symbols and Philosophical Reflection: II," *The Conflict of Interpretations: Essays in Hermeneutics, I*, trans. Charles Freilich, 316 (hereafter "The Hermeneutics of Symbols: II"). See also Ricoeur, SE, 6.
42. See Ricoeur, SE, 9.
43. Klemm, HTPR, 70-71.
44. Ricoeur, "The Hermeneutics of Symbols: I," 295.

45. Ricoeur, SE, 350.
46. Ibid., 351.
47. Ibid., 356.

Chapter 3

Capable Human and the Role of Silence in the Creation of Meaning

This chapter signals a shift of emphasis to center on capable human and therefore reflect the move to hermeneutics. Given the conditions of human existence—the alienation from self that occurs in language, and the objectification of self in the world—these linguistic expressions require interpretation. It is through the hermeneutical process of appropriation that language is experienced, and the self comes to better situate itself in being.[1] The avowal of evil, as the source of actualized self-awareness in language is the impetus behind the human search for redemption. The symbol of evil, in its revealing power, does not merely augment my self-awareness; that would be tantamount to my severing it from the ontological function that it is meant to serve.[2] After all, to "know thyself" is not purely reflexive. Rather, each human receives the entreaty to locate herself in a more excellent way in being, which is to say, that I should be wise.[3] The symbol also expresses what is the situation at the core of my being, that is, the circumstances and condition of my heart, wherein I exist, move, feel, and will.

The being who posits itself has yet to discover in the act of abstracting itself away from what is the whole, that it does not stop sharing in the challenge that being presents through the symbol. Both the symbols of guilt and the myths convey the situation that I am in—the being of human in the middle of the world.[4] The task, therefore, is to elaborate upon worldly existential concepts in beginning with symbols. Now, structures of existence, and not merely structures of reflection, demand explanation, as existence is what comprises being human. However, why these particular symbols rather than other ones? Ricoeur thinks that by virtue of a culture hitting upon them, then it becomes the task of philosophy, through the exercise of reflection as well as speculation, to make known the rationality that is their foundation.

While the situation of being human is one in which I am ridden with fallibility, fault, evil, dysfunction, and error, given my basic capacity and my capabilities, that is, my powers, there is a constitutive goodness, an original predisposition to goodness that has only to be freed. The fifth step of the argument holds that progress toward spiritual and ethical maturity is both positive and negative. Human being requires an overflow, a superabundance so that it may be liberated. I hope to show how as growth in maturity occurs, there is increasing awareness of both fallibility and capability. The mediating work is accomplished, in part, through language in the reform of attitudes, behavior, motivations, intentions, and patterns of acting, as the will is conformed, and ultimately, the mind—consciousness—is transformed.

While the human being is language, it is also capable of and has the capacity for so much more. Ricoeur offers a "critical supplementation" to Gadamer's hermeneutics of tradition, as he makes the move from linguality to textuality so as to emphasize the significant role that distanciation plays.[5] And while he considers the various forms of discourse that human beings use to express themselves, I want to reiterate an important point I previously made—that nowhere in his work does he directly take up the role of silence. Further, I want to refine the notion that human reality consists of both silence and language. My assertion here is that silence is integral to language and expression. Moreover, I want to show in this chapter how in order to express myself in discourse, I have to include a discussion of silence in relation to discourse. The work of Dauenhauer on a phenomenology of silence can serve as an important supplement to Ricoeur, in this regard.

What I aim to accomplish in this chapter is to set out a creative arrangement of the essential elements that comprise capable human. I explain each of the elements in the sections that follow (with the exception of Ricoeur's move to hermeneutics, which has already been discussed), which are (1) the move to hermeneutics and the hermeneutical philosophy of Ricoeur, (2) expression and discourse in the interpretation theory of Ricoeur, (3) the relation of silence to discourse as set out in the phenomenology of Dauenhauer, and the grafting of contemplative silence onto that structure, and (4) an explanation of the hermeneutical self as derived from Ricoeur. The fifth step of the argument encompasses the first three elements, while the sixth step of the argument encompasses the fourth element. Finally, the chapter closes with a discussion of the concept of recognition. This discussion is an extension of the mini-phenomenology of recognition that is presented in Chapter 1.

RICOEUR'S HERMENEUTICAL PHILOSOPHY

It is through the act of interpreting that I am able to hear the call of being once again. With his change in methodology from reflective philosophy to hermeneutical philosophy, Ricoeur distinguishes between first naiveté, critique, and second naiveté. It is the task of the second naiveté to reunite thinking and being, and the split that defines the subject and consciousness. I noted the experience of self-alienation of human being. He places hope in the re-creation of language that extends beyond a "desert of criticism."[6] In his hermeneutical theory, the critical juncture of his endeavor lies between the thought that is articulated and given in the symbol, as well as the actual thought that posits and thinks. This circumstance brings together all that has already been said, albeit enigmatically, along with the necessity to start over, and begin again in the space of thinking; it is a hermeneutics of ordinary daily living that he is aiming for. I proceed now to what is a brief exposition of his hermeneutical philosophy.

First Naiveté

The literal or precritical level of original understanding is subjectivity that corresponds to the expression of mythic-symbolic language. The primary symbol (the avowal or confession), and the myth (the narrative that tells a story about origins and end), coalesce in the emergence of language. The primary symbol carries the literal meaning; however, as discussed in Chapter 2, the second-meaning expression is carried in human subjectivity and becomes, through response, an expression of what it is to be human under the conditions and influence of the symbol's literal meaning. Myth reestablishes in intention the self in its unity with the world by narrating the primordial story of the fall from essence to existence, from fallibility to fault.[7] It is not only that I discover myself in the midst of evil, but that I am at present implicated in yielding to the evil by way of actions issuing forth out of the present moment.[8] Symbols "are like a voice of Being."[9] It is not so much that language is spoken by the human, than that language is spoken to the human.[10] The self can be characterized as naïve immediacy in its relation of openness and response before the sacred cosmos which expresses itself through the primary symbol. There is minimal difference between the self and the sacred cosmos with which it identifies in regard to responsivity and receptivity. There is some questioning at this level; however, what transpires is not critical questioning and the distanciation that that implies.

In order to round out discussion of the first naiveté, I want to make a few remarks about the reader of a text within this context. An example of the relation between the reader/interpreter and the text would be that of a person who reads a sacred text without yet having analyzed and separated it into constituent parts. Everything is understood to be in reality as it appears in the language of the text without submitting it to critical questioning and reflection. It can be likened to the wide-eyed sight of an innocent child. Ricoeur explains that "consciousness is originally false consciousness, 'the pretension to self-knowledge.'"[11] There is no calling into question the symbol. The naïve appropriation is characterized by passive receptivity in relation to the content in that the self tracks the moving image, but remains unaware of the dynamics that are occurring—that this is an event, and that it is in and of time.

Critique

The questioning of how knowing is possible forces away the first immediacy. Critical reflection results, then, in the negation of immediacy. I question the "how" of the knowledge of what appears in reality by asking if what appears is really as it appears, which can be traced back to Kant and his "Second Copernican Revolution." Objects are only representative of appearances and realities unto themselves from the perspective of the viewer. The question bans the immediacy of the consciousness of the first naiveté by severing the relation between the expression and what appears as reality. The dynamism that is at work in symbolism entails the surpassing of symbolic meaning, which involves a destruction of the immediacy associated with the symbolic meaning. This is the "desert" of criticism.

I want to note that the desert of criticism refers to the reflexive endpoint of critique: (1) it cancels the givenness of objects; (2) it cancels the givenness of the totality of objects; (3) it cancels the subject; and (4) it cancels the connection between subject and totality of objects (being). I can say that critique leads literally to nothing—in fact, beyond nothing to what is not nothing, and so on *ad infinitum*. Critique cancels all values and absolutes—even the value of critique, and it is incapable on its own of restoring any positive value or absolute. Or, so it seemed . . . (to Romantics). Critique, taken to its absolute power, signals the advent of nihilism! That is the "desert" of criticism.

Critique is considered a second level of subjectivity in ontological terms, while the structure of a text corresponds on the object side. Critique can be defined as the infinite capacity I have as a human being to dislodge the meaning or being of whatever appears to me as self-evident. With critique, the myth as self-evident disintegrates: the gods are driven out of naïve consciousness. The referential activity of language is suspended so that distinctions can be drawn and separations be made to determine the relations fixed in the text under analysis. As a result, in terms of subjectivity, there is maximum difference and minimal identity with critique. It is the work of critique to delineate the textual structural features that direct the text world. If I consider critique within the context of the movement of detour/return in Ricoeur's work, critique lies at the midpoint between an original simplicity and an intellectually refined conviction.[12]

Second Naiveté

With the second naiveté, or the third level of subjectivity, the "I" embraces the naïve state and identifies with its symbolic expressions, so as to show consideration for the original understanding of the symbol. The "I" also methodically examines the expressions that emerge out of symbolic consciousness using the implements of critical thinking. What is restored by means of empathetic imagining, together with the consequences of the engagement of critique, are set in productive tension so that I can continue to think the symbol's meaning. The "I" is not the existential self in immediate and unbroken relationship with the symbol, but rather, is the transformed "I" that purposefully engages relations of self-world. Objective consciousness is transformed, enhanced, and can be mediated successfully with other forms of consciousness, as movement between immediacy and critique is facilitated. This movement is accomplished by connecting/combining immediacy of belief with the results of critical consciousness. This level of subjectivity is rooted in the manifestation of reflexivity as it occurs at the point at which the naïve sense is mediated by way of the critical consciousness.

The text is read both naïvely, as in the first innocence and simplicity of original understanding, and critically, insofar as I rigorously examine the parts of the text to therefore become at once adult critic and naïve child; then I can reposition my life and understanding now within the range of the reality of the text.[13] This is another step or logical distinction. In so doing, a second immediacy is restored, but it is an interpreted immediacy at the level of the possible. I am aware that I am engaged in reading a text, but the possibility of being becomes for the reader the subject of the interpretation. The reader is drawn into the possible as possible. Thus, immediacy and the mediation of thought are held together.

The power inherent in new possibilities precedes the power of decision and choice. The imagination of subjectivity can respond to the poetic text. A poetics of existence responds to the poetics of discourse.[14] Self-critique is central to the process of understanding the text, because my understanding is always ingredient as I permit the text to speak.[15] Critical reflection has to be forever grafted into reflection that is not mere representation, but truly critical examination into motives, intentions, decisions, leading up to action; the fateful step is action.[16] The action is the mediating work that is carried out with the resultant transformation coming about through and appearing in language, and the way in which I relate to language. I would note that it is through transforming my relationship to language that I transform my relationship to myself. And, in transforming my relationship to myself, I transform my relationship to language, and integrally so. Next, I will turn to an examination of expression and an explanation of the nature of discourse in the mediating function of language—the second essential element in the discussion of capable human.

THE ROLE OF EXPRESSION AND DISCOURSE

Expression includes the thought and experience of human being who is situated in the middle of the world. Ricoeur is interested in approaching language in terms of discourse that is used, and not merely objectified, or considered in terms of its structure and system. He looks to linguistic development and the distinction that is made between semiotics and the system of sign as a basic unit, on the one hand, and semantics and the production of the sentence, which is made up of noun-verb combinations as a basic unit, on the other hand. There is a stark contrast between these two units of language in that the sign is an abstraction that lacks any reference to actual living conditions, while the sentence is an actualization of the virtual, as "the very event of speaking," by a living being who is situated in the being of the world.[17] Semiotics involves the separation of language into its structural constitutive parts, or "the science of signs," while semantics involves an integrative procedure that has to do with meaning, or "the science of the sentence."[18] He wants to return (ontological) priority to the semantic level of discourse by performing a mediation between these two opposing elements of discourse.

Ricoeur makes a basic distinction in language between *langue* and *parole*. He explains that "*Langue* is the code—or the set of codes—on the basis of which a particular speaker produces *parole* as a particular message."[19] Whereas the message is individual, the code is considered collective. The message comes about as the result of an intentional, free act, and is, therefore, unnecessary and contingent; it is an individual speech event in time that participates in a successive series of events, sequentially, in diachronic time.[20] The code, in its collectivity, exists as part of synchronic time insofar as it is "a set of contemporaneous elements" that is anonymous and unintended; it emerges from a structuring process that is unconscious at the level of culture, and is not only systematic, but compulsory for the given speakers of the community.[21] Semiotics, as a model, brackets the message, the event, the intention, and the contingent, free act in order to prioritize the code, the system, the structure, and systematic combinations of the synchronic systems. This bracketing results in an objectification of language. He proposes to counter this objectification by distinguishing between language as discourse and language as merely a system. He achieves this task by establishing a basic subject-object structure of discourse, which mirrors the basic subject-object structure of the self.[22] He establishes two dialectics that are set in tensive motion—the dialectic of event and meaning, and the dialectic of sense and reference, which I shall, in turn, consider below.

The Dialectic of Event and Meaning

The first dialectic in discourse is the concrete polarity between event as the subjective pole, or subjective side of discourse (the actualization of codes), and meaning as the objective pole, or objective side of discourse (the propositional content in a sentence). This dialectic of event and meaning is an inner dialectic which involves the meaning of discourse. While Ricoeur considers discourse as an event of language, there is an epistemological weakness with *parole*, or the message, because of the fleeting character of the event that soon vanishes in time; whereas the system is stable and remains.[23] The message needs to be related to an ontological priority about discourse, which is the consequence of the actuality associated with the event, in contradistinction to the virtuality associated with the system; a message bestows actuality on language and has a temporal existence, while a system has a mere virtual existence.

On the objective pole, an act associated with discourse is not just transitory in its vanishing aspect; an act of discourse can continually be identified or reidentified as the same in that it may be repeated, or it may be said using other words. In addition, the act can be said in another language or translated into another language. This build-up of identity through all of these acts of discourse is the propositional content of a sentence. In any given sentence, the subject identifies only a single item, such as a proper name, a pronoun, a demonstrative such as "this and that" or "now and then," and a definite description.[24] The predicate, however, delineates some universal quality, class, or type, whether it be relation or action of the subject. An objective meaning is formed in the sentence by joining together a singular identification with a universal predication by means of the verb, which ascribes what is, in relative terms, the universal, to what is the particular, followed by the addition of a reference to existing in actual time.[25] The idea of speech as an event is a reminder to me that discourse occurs and is temporally realized in the present moment, whereas if language is considered strictly in terms of a system, then it is merely virtual to me, and remains outside of real time. If there is an actualization of all discourse as an event, then all discourse can be understood as meaning.[26] While an event is transient, the meaning that is understood endures through the joining together of noun and verb. Discourse affirms a purposefulness about language itself, and the subject-object structure. If I consider language to be an intending, then through the actualizing and canceling of the event, discourse is transient and vanishing; however, discourse understood as meaning endures and lives on in the propositional content.[27]

Performative discourse, such as the speech-act of actual promises, is a locutionary act. The speaker does what she says in the saying of something in the first-person singular. The doing of the deed in the saying is the illocutionary act in the event of discourse, and differentiates the promise from the order, or a wish, for example. The perlocutionary effect is what is yielded in the doing of a saying.[28] The interlocutionary act in discourse is addressed to someone and includes a speaker and a hearer, which means that discourse is communication.[29] Ricoeur explains that communication is an enigma, however, for any existential investigation:

> My experience cannot directly become your experience. An event belonging to one stream of consciousness cannot be transferred as such into another stream of consciousness. Yet, nevertheless, something passes from me to you. Something is transferred from one sphere of life to another. This something is not the experience as experienced, but its meaning. Here is the miracle. The experience as experienced, as lived, remains private, but its sense, its meaning, becomes public. Communication in this way is the overcoming of the radical noncommunicability of the lived experience as lived.[30]

Discourse as event is assumed into what is the propositional content so that private experience through discourse becomes public. The sense which becomes public is considered to be an event, while the actual experience as lived is, and remains private.[31] It remains private, I would add, due to the silence that suffuses discourse and to an existence that is imbued with silence. The sense of the sentence is communicated in the event of dialogue. The exteriority of discourse is what opens discourse to someone else. The ground of the communicability of the message is in the meaning's structure.

The locutionary and illocutionary acts are events to the degree that they are recognized in terms of what they are—the singular identification, the universal predication, a statement, or an order, a wish, or a promise, etc.[32] Because of the role of recognition, intention itself becomes communicable to a particular degree. There is, of course, a psychological aspect that can only be experienced by the speaker, insofar as in a promise is the commitment, and in the assertion is a belief; however, they are not radically incommunicable. The intention of identification, acknowledgment, and recognition by an other comprises the intention.[33] This is how the noetic, or what is intellectual, is part of the psychic. The criterion for the noetic is the intention of communicability, and the expectation for recognition in the intentional act. The illocutionary includes the presence of an intention to bring forth in a listener a particular mental act through which that listener will recognize what is the intention. This reciprocity constitutes dialogue as an event. In conclusion, language is considered the process by which what is private experience becomes public. With language as exteriorization, an impression by way of being transcended becomes what is an "expression," which results in a transformation of what is psychic into what is the noetic.

The Dialectic of Sense and Reference

In addition to the dialectic between event and meaning, the relation between sense and reference constitutes the other dialectic that Ricoeur devises in his theory of discourse. On the objective side of discourse, meaning is divided into a second dialectic of "sense" (*Sinn*) and "reference" (*Bedeutung*).[34] The sense is the "what" with regard to discourse, and the reference is the "about what" of discourse.[35] The distinction applies to language that is used, and is not applicable to signs because signs refer merely to the other signs that are in a particular system. The sense of the sentence directs itself to its outside referent.[36] The reference has to be given independently of comprehending the sense.[37] Sense correlates both the identification and predication function in the sentence, whereas the reference is what relates that language to a world, and establishes the truth claim of discourse. In my experience and ontological condition of being in the world, I work toward expressing my experience in language; however, language is not merely directed toward some ideal meaning, but refers also to what actually is. Again, I would draw attention to the role of silence in the creation of meaning as my experience and ontological condition involve expressing that experience in language, but it also happens bodily in silence through what is commonly referred to as body language.

The dialectic of sense and reference is related to the dialectic of event and meaning: Reference is tied up in the event of discourse inasmuch as "to refer" is what the speaker accomplishes in a given situation. However, the sense meaning structures the actual event. The sense is traversed by the speaker's referring intention.[38] Semantics relates the inner sense to the transcendent intention of reference.[39] The practice of actual discourse refers backward to the speaker and forward to the world.[40] I now have in place two of the four essential elements that constitute capable human. I want to creatively extend Ricoeur's notion of discourse and consider the role of silence as it relates to discourse in the next section of the study. Before I do so, however, I will complete discussion of his theory of discourse. I must address the move from speaking to writing and the written text.

There are two points that Ricoeur makes evident concerning textual language. First, meaning is exteriorized, but separated from the event of discourse. I no longer have access to the original event. This is precisely where hermeneutics comes into play insofar as the alienated meaning must be freshly appropriated through the event of understanding. Ricoeur explains that "Inscription [of meaning] becomes synonymous with the semantic autonomy of the text, which results from the disconnection of the mental intention of the author from the verbal meaning of the text, of what the author meant and what the text means."[41] It is in this way that the text can transcend the finite horizon of the author. Although there is no longer the coinciding of authorial intention and textual meaning, it can become newly inscribed through the hermeneutical process. Furthermore, he places a premium on what the text means "now" as opposed to what was meant when the author originally wrote it.[42] Moreover, as a result of the positive role that distance plays as part of the text in extending the "said" and prioritizing it over whatever the original author meant to "say," that is, decontextualization—from the author, reader for whom it was intended, and life situation—recontextualization can now be carried out by its subsequent readers.[43] As Boyd Blundell explains, "distanciation now belongs to the textual mediation itself, and . . . constitutes the textuality of the text [which] is the very thing that has allowed human discourse to span historical distances."[44]

Second, discourse carries dual meaning. Ricoeur makes a distinction (in terms of utterer's meaning and utterance meaning), concerning the concept of meaning, which can be interpreted in two different ways because of the subject-object structure of discourse; it is a mirroring, too, of the dialectic of event and meaning. Meaning is subjective insofar as it has to do with what the speaker means and has the intention of saying—the utterer's meaning; and, meaning is objective insofar as it has to do with what a sentence means in that in the textual sentence, a noun-verb conjunction yields an utterance meaning.[45] Within the objective sense of meaning, i.e., the utterance meaning, which is within the inner structure of the sentence itself, a reference is made back to a speaker's intention, i.e., the utterer's meaning, by means of grammatical procedures, or "shifters."[46] There is no objective meaning in personal pronouns such as "I"—the only function of this shifter is "to refer the whole sentence [back] to the subject of the speech event," that is, to a speaker who is the "I."[47] There are other shifters, i.e., grammatical bearers that refer the discourse back to the speaker, as well, such as verbs in the present tense, and accordingly refer to what is "now" a speech event and a speaker. Adverbs are also included here that have to do with time and space, and demonstratives. These are all ways for discourse to refer back to the speaker. There is, then, a dialectical relation between the meaning of discourse and the event of discourse. Also, there is a nonpsychological interpretation, that is, a semantic definition of the speaker's intention, or utterer's meaning. As he explains, "No mental entity need be hypothesized or hypostasized. The utterance meaning points back towards the utterer's meaning thanks to the self-reference of discourse to itself as an event."[48]

Furthermore, there are differing elements that constitute the structure of discourse in the text as opposed to the situation of conversation in living speech. While in the case of living speech there is a shared horizon, a common world that exists between two subjects, with the text there comes into play a new dimension to the dialectic between event and meaning. Moreover, the semantic autonomy of the text entails that there is no longer a dialogical conversation occurring between two interlocuters who are conversing face-to-face. Because there is no subject—an actual person—who through gesture, body language, or phonic clues can give indications while speaking as to how the conversation partner should interpret the event of meaning, the text must take up the position of subject in relation to the reader. That is, with textual discourse as distinct from spoken discourse, the text takes on subjectivity, whereas before subjectivity resided with the live speaker. Since with the text there is no shared horizon of speakers, the world now must be worked out by the interpreter. So the interpreter/respondent has to figure out how to understand the event of the disclosure of meaning.[49] This is where the objective structure of the text (wherein the code has to be figured out), becomes important to discern as one goes about the process of actualizing meaning. In the end, it is through this process that the text assumes the role of subject in relation to the reader/interpreter. The gap or distance that exists between the inscription of meaning from the written text, and the existing isolation and separation from the original event, sets the stage for the disclosure of language—for the depth and power of language to renew and refresh through its creative capabilities. Ricoeur explains that "The inscription of discourse is the transcription of the world," which is not a reduplication, he says, but its metamorphosis.[50] I have the capability to participate in the re-writing of reality, to participate in "the revelation of a real more real than ordinary reality" or, the augmentation of reality.[51] Finally, it should be noted that the characteristic quality of the text is the appearance of structure, which makes of discourse a work.[52]

The text can grasp (1) understanding as a mode of knowing, but it will not grasp (2) understanding as a mode of being. Thus, he wants to (1) interpret the text, and (2) understand the text in terms of sense (what it says) and reference (what it is about). He is, in his philosophical hermeneutics, engaging in a fundamental enterprise of commenting upon a text. The hermeneutical arc unfolds in five steps: (1) initial understanding (as one transfers the meanings of signs, one translates them into a first reading characterized by openness, which is a naïve understanding, and the conviction of accepting the text); (2)

structural explanation (this could be semiotics, and is a critical objectification); (3) sense and reference (this has to do with what the text says and what the text is about); (4) ideological critique (one bends back on the interpretation to take into account a distortion so as to account for being unaware of ideology); and (5) assessing and evaluating (one asks what is significant and important about the text, so that the text may be critically appropriated). In following this process, I move from conviction through critique to critical appropriation. With critical appropriation, self-understanding occurs. A text can transform the reader insofar as subjectivity is transformed. What Ricoeur is doing is calling attention to the need to think about thinking insofar as I can gain an understanding of the principles underlying what I am doing. Worlds appear in the text, so I must understand a philosophy of language and the different kinds of texts. I also must think about the aesthetic and ethical use of language. In addition, while he presupposes that I must think about what it means to be human within language, in laying out a systematic dynamic of thinking, he is saying that there are many different theoretical starting points, and there is, therefore, a conflict of interpretations.

Ricoeur's interpretation theory is born out of the conviction that in a definite suggestive sense, the human person "*is* language," and because writing is considered the fulfillment of language, in laying out the principles that pertain to textual meaning, there is something that may be disclosed that points not only to human being, but to being as well.[53] For Ricoeur, capable human being has to do with linguality, textuality, and my capacity to express myself, my being, in discourse. If I follow him here, then I must acknowledge the important role that silence plays in relation to discourse, something Ricoeur never did. To his textuality and interpretation theory—his hermeneutical theory, and his philosophical anthropology, therefore, let me add silence. That is, the human person *is* silence as well as language. This statement represents a flowering of the third step of the argument. Further, any discussion of discourse remains incomplete without a discussion of silence. I am positioned now to take up the role of silence.

THE RELATION OF SILENCE TO DISCOURSE

My aim is to discuss silence and its relation to discourse, and to being human, and therefore show how integral silence is to discourse and to human life itself. Indeed, it is the third element of what constitutes capable human in this study. I want to note that Heidegger considers the relation of silence to discourse in *Being and Time*.[54] Heidegger characterizes silence as providing the possibility for discourse.[55] He uses the example of how conscience, insofar as it never comes to utterance, entails silent discourse. This silent interior call emerges out of soundlessness and once summoned returns to stillness. While it remains beyond the task of this study to take up Heidegger's silence about his political failings during the years of National Socialism in Germany, it is important to note the controversy surrounding him in this regard. Given that he clearly associates silence with conscience, this omission is all the more poignant and complex and is a subject deserving of comprehensive treatment in and of itself.

I turn now to the work of Dauenhauer who illuminates silence as a phenomenon.[56] In his phenomenological analysis of silence, he constructs the phenomenon of silence as essential to discourse, and accomplishes this task by engaging in a transcendental argument. He begins with a description of the ontic (or existential) phenomenon, i.e., in this case, silence, and then gives a formal analysis with respect to a noetic-noematic structure. His study thereby becomes a phenomenological analysis of the intentionality of consciousness. Intentionality itself divides into the aforementioned noetic-noematic or subject-object structure. The "noetic" refers to an act of consciousness, or an act of knowing. The "noematic" refers to an object of consciousness. This structure is a reduction to some "eidos," or in transcendental terms, to the condition of the possibility of the ontic phenomenon. The eidos is silence as a positive phenomenon.[57] Silence is a turning point in discourse, and is, therefore, integral and preeminent in the dialectic between silence and discourse. Silence can be considered as an interruption of modes of discourse in everyday language. I will take a closer look at his argument.

Silence as a Phenomenon

Silence is positive and equiprimordial with the utterance. This thesis involves the two claims that (1) silence is both the necessary condition of utterance, and is also coordinate with the utterance, and (2) there is a describable temporality about silence that is its own, so that its temporality does not come from the temporality deriving from the utterance to which it is joined.[58] Silence is linked to the human performances of activity that he calls "utterances." Utterance is "any performance employing systematically related signs, sounds, gestures, or marks having recognizable meanings to express thoughts, feelings, states of affairs, etc."[59] Utterances can include not only word phrases and musical notes, and the aforementioned gestures, for example, but painted and sculpted shapes, as well. Each specific utterance is considered a moment of actual discourse, with discourse being comprised of utterance in its totality. Without utterance as such, there is no silence.

There are three kinds of silence which precede his phenomenological analysis and that are bound up with utterances. They are as follows: (1) "intervening silence," (2) "fore-and-after silence," and (3) "deep silence."[60]

First, intervening silence can be considered as a kind of punctuating silence in that it serves the function of punctuating words as well as phrases. Intervening silence also has a rhythmic function similar to sound phrases in music. Finally, it has a temporal structure of its own in addition to the temporal structure that it has as being constituent to what is the actual utterance.[61]

Second, fore-and-after silence is constituted in the silence that precedes the first and last sound phrase of an utterance. They each have a time structure, too. Fore-and-after silence assists in distinguishing a particular utterance from all other utterances, while intervening silence has to do with distinguishing an individual sound phrase from all sound phrases in general. This sameness of function points to their unity in that these aspects comprise a background silence, positive in character, against which there is an unfolding of a determinate utterance that starts, runs a course, and reaches completion.[62]

The third kind of silence is deep silence. Deep silence is involved in all utterances, and is not subordinate to an utterance. Deep silence is distinct from the previous two kinds of silence in that it is not possible to identify numerically distinct instances of this kind of silence for every occurrence of an utterance. Dauenhauer explains three different modes of deep silence, which are (1) "the silence of intimates," (2) "liturgical silence," and (3) "the silence of the 'To-be-said,'" which is characterized as a silence that transcends all saying.[63] It is also a philosophical or a mystical silence. Deep silence runs through not only utterance, but the other two kinds of silence as well. It has its own time structure just as any type of silence does.

Discourse and Silence

Dauenhauer distinguishes between two types of discourse, topic-centered discourse and interlocutor-centered discourse, and builds on Ricoeur's work on discourse, which makes his work compatible with and integral to this study. Topic-centered discourse refers to a world and not merely a situation, and is non-ostensive; whereas interlocutor-centered discourse is ostensive, and refers to the spatio-temporal situation of the participants, as well as intending a dialogical situation. Examples of interlocutor-centered discourse are discourse with family, friends, or acquaintances. Examples of topic-centered discourse are scientific, technological, political, moral, religious, and artistic discourse.[64] Each different facet of discourse manifests as joined together with a different aspect of silence.[65] And, just as the facets of discourse are positive, so, too, are the aspects of silence positive.

In the case of religious discourse, to cite one specific example, there is a reference to the world wherein both the moment of creation and the end moment of time are privileged and singled out. The silence that accompanies religious utterances binds and joins them to the originary utterance. An originary utterance can be considered a response to a manifest appearance of the divine. Religious utterances can be considered to be repetitious insofar as they repeat an eternal word that has always been uttered and will continue to be. A paradoxical recognition occurs because the utterer realizes that she has to utter what has always and everywhere already been uttered, and yet that her word matters greatly. Finitude is recognized in the fact that the only sufficient response is one that her predecessors have already made, and that those who follow after her will make.

A second example is with artistic discourse, which at least in the modern world, has to overcome referential values having to do with routine discourse so that new expressions can be articulated. The new utterance is, in its moment of origin, filled with a silence that reveals the finitude associated with the artistic discourse that preceded its own, in addition to being filled with its sense of finitude. Hence silence reveals "its own finitude" against the background of historical consciousness.[66] In the end, silence can be thought of in terms of "cuts" or "breaks" between discourse, or as "moments" of discourse, or even at the deepest cut, it is silence that creates the condition for the possibility of discourse and therefore makes discourse possible at all.[67]

"Three Irreducible Moments" of Silence

Dauenhauer's intentional analysis of silence illustrates how the temporal structure associated with silence appears in combination with the various kinds of discourse, such as soliloquy (where the uttering is merely a reuttering), bipolar discourse (between the author and the audience) which includes monologue as well as dialogue, and codiscourse (where there is a sublation of the author and the audience as the "I-you" becomes a "we").[68] The cuts between them are interpersonalizing silence and deindividualizing silence.[69] Living within the domain of discourse entails all three levels and a "shuttling" between the levels, although a specific utterance occurs within a particular level.[70] The cut at the level of codiscourse has a distinguishing feature in that it serves to direct movement toward interpersonal coalescence. The capacity to engage in discourse deepens as a result.

There is a final cut that is known as terminal silence that closes off the region of discourse, and interrupts what is the "and so forth" of the domain of discourse in its entirety.[71] Terminal silence and deep silence have the same structure, but terminal silence is also connected to after-silence which involves savoring the discourse such that a series of utterances can achieve their full existential weight.[72] So after-silence, with its digesting in which nothing more that is determinate is added to discourse, is connected to terminal silence, as the digesting is essential in acknowledging the pointlessness of expanding upon the utterances.[73] The opening cut, or originary silence is what establishes the gap that exists between the domains of intentional performances—perceptual and pictorial as well as signitive performances.

Based on his depictions, in the final analysis, there are three kinds of silence, which I shall refer to as (1) originating silence, (2) pervasive silence, and (3) terminal silence. That is, there are "three irreducible moments" of silence, according to Dauenhauer, that constitute a temporal structure in regard to silence.[74] First, silence originates, that is, opens a way and provides a departure point for the domain of discourse in its entirety. Second, in terms of pervasive silence, silence spreads or disperses the domain inasmuch as it enables the shifts to be made from one shape to another, and from one level to another within discourse. Further, it preserves movement that takes place within the discourse that commenced with the first moment of silence. Third, in terms of terminal silence, silence closes off and turns discourse back to its departure point, its origination, which results in establishing a unity about the entirety of the region of discourse. This also entails silence being turned back to its originating moment, but Dauenhauer does not explain how this is so. I want to develop the idea that it has to do with my capacity to remember, and my memory as retrieval; it is an interpretive retrieval that involves the process of recognition, about which more is discussed below. Through the process of the third moment, discourse is situated within a context that includes the entire scope of human experience. Discourse arises by means of silence, and reaches completion as a unitary domain by means of silence. Terminal silence can be given specificity by virtue of being interpreted.

Dauenhauer's analysis affirms that silence is an active performance. Further, it discloses silence as being established on prepredicative experience—the world of perception, which includes sensory and feeling—as silence arises from looking at the world around me.[75] The prepredicative world is a necessary condition for silence. My being in the world precedes even the active world of silence. Silence, in turn, is a necessary condition for predicative and postpredicative experience.

Now I can further delineate and develop these three moments in terms of (1) prepredicative, (2) predicative, and (3) postpredicative. First, the prepredicative moment corresponds with originating silence; and there is an original identity of silence and discourse. This is the level of perceptual and affective consciousness. Second, the predicative moment corresponds with pervasive silence; and the original identity becomes divided. This is the level of discursive experience or consciousness as a moment of reflection. Acts of reflexivity are still within the predicative world, as I can talk about reflexivity. Third, the postpredicative moment corresponds with terminal silence, and this is the cut that opens and that follows discourse. There is a different form of reflexivity here that is in silence and not talk. I stop talking and the mind turns back and starts thinking, as in the German word, *nachdenken*. This thinking may not be formal thinking; it could be remembering, recalling, and recognizing. By bringing discourse to a close, a unity is brought about. Discourse continues on, and nevertheless within the finitude of silence, discourse is bound, and yet silence muses. With reflexive silence, I can muse back on originating silence, pervasive silence, and muse about discourse itself. I can muse about its (silence) own state of terminal silence—this silence is a recollective silence.

There is a 1–2–3 structure above, and this is a moment within a larger analysis. But nonetheless, this 1–2–3 structure is valuable. "1" can be considered in terms of "paradise" with the original unity of subject-object. "1" corresponds to the first naiveté. "2" can be considered in terms of "fallibility" and everything that that entails in terms of fault, guilt, evil, dysfunction, and error, with the moment of reflection and the division of subject-object. "2" corresponds to critique. "3" can be considered in terms of "redemption" and "capability" with the recovery of paradise. "3" corresponds to the second naiveté with reference to silence. Terminal silence is a musing upon my own musing, and is word-filled, as I muse on my own words. It is a recapturing of what was lost, but not a perfect recapturing. I cannot ascend to absolute knowledge in the Hegelian sense here. Ricoeur would say, instead of absolute knowledge, that my primordial finitude is shining through. This leads to a conflict of interpretations in Ricoeurian terms. Dauenhauer, too, says that silence yields with the recognition of finitude, and there is a multiplicity of discourse.[76]

Situating the Practice of Contemplative Silence

It is in this third moment of postpredicative silence that I want to situate the practice of contemplative silence, which will be taken up further on in the study, and creatively graft it onto this structure. I shall carry this moment forward as I proceed with the study. For the most part, Dauenhauer is claiming that most forms of silence are of indeterminate intentionality. That is to say that they do not ask to be satisfied, and they are not referring to a determinate object of discourse. Finitude prevents contemplative silence from being purely nondeterminate. Even the highest form of silence in contemplative silence is still aware in a determinate way of its own lack of absolute nondeterminateness, because any awareness of something is an awareness of some determinate (some x as opposed to non-x). So awareness of pure x would be a return to subject-object, and would be divine awareness. I may be able to think the thought that God's awareness occurs through my own, but I am aware that it is not my own, and contemplative silence cannot return entirely to the realm of originary silence. In other words, any awareness of x is determinate because it implies awareness of non-x, and is determined by the awareness of non-x. There would be a return to a subject-object unity without losing awareness, which is impossible, because if I lose it, it would not be human, but would be divine. It would be a different type of intellect. In the end, silence is not focally determinate; and, it cannot perfectly manifest nondeterminate consciousness.

The Ontological Significance of Silence

Silence and discourse are two irreducible ways for the human to express life.[77] Human expression is always by way of the world. Dauenhauer's ontological claim is that the human and the world do not counter one another; they are simply different from one another.[78] Being is understood as "interplay."[79]

There are three domains that constitute active intentional performances and are "three irreducibly distinctive ways" whereby humans mediate their encounter of the world.[80] They are as follows: (1) "the fabricational domain," (2) "the actional domain," and (3) "the signitive domain" that includes constitutive silence.[81] The fabricational domain has to do with the person embodying effort to produce a permanent product that, in the end, continues to exist without having to engage in further modification of it. With action, there is no product that is produced. However, action transforms the relationship of myself with the world, albeit indirectly, through transforming the relationship I have with others and with myself. I change the way in which I mediate my encounter so as not to fall into habitual or routine ways of doing business, so to speak. The signitive domain is constituted by the play between silence and discourse, and has primacy over the other two domains, while silence itself has primacy over discourse.[82] Silence clears a way for the mediation. In the play between the determinate and the nondeterminate, that there is a priority of the nondeterminate means that silence has priority.[83] I want to note here the important parallel between Dauenhauer's argument for the priority of silence, and the ontological priority that Ricoeur argues for in his theory of discourse.

The human has to mediate and carry out mediational performances. Engaging in mediational activity is a response inasmuch as one has to listen before one speaks, or acts, or makes anything. When one listens in silence, the way is opened for the occurrence of discursive performances. Listening is required to check answers as well as questions.

It is in the form of originating silence and terminal silence that silence discloses the preeminence of the human as nondeterminate. With originating silence, a distancing occurs from what has been immediately encountered.[84] There is an opening provided for mediations which bring forth into the world the human's determinations. Terminal silence discloses that the human is not preeminently a determiner, but nondeterminate as a being who wonders while performing those determining mediations. Terminal silence has need for a sustenance that comes in a subsequent discourse, which implies that human being is "*enroute*," one whose Being is on the way.[85] When one walks that path, the human will follow it as well as break it.[86] I now have in place the third essential element that comprises capable human. That is, I can make the assertion that capable human understands the relation between silence and discourse. I turn now to a discussion of the fourth element that constitutes capable human.

THE HERMENEUTICAL SELF

The hermeneutical self is the fourth key element in my explanation of capable human. I can say that the recognition of feeling lost and abandoned points to the nothingness of the human being who in humility stands before the reality of the Word. Prior understandings always yield to new and deeper understandings. This is what it means for me to be on the way. Further, it appears that human being has a propensity for spiritual and ethical growth through reflexively understanding itself as situated in the world; human being discovers a relation with itself as other. This is the sixth step of the argument. What follows is an exposition of several types of identity that together constitute the hermeneutical self.

Personal Identity

Recall that Ricoeur increasingly and constitutively connects personal identity with the idea of the other and relation between self and other in *Oneself as Another*. This work can be understood as a reflection that has to do with the self, which is, in hermeneutical terms, different than the I. He gives priority to reflective mediation in which mediation occurs with regard to the self or subject rather than simply positing a subject. The being of the self is relationality. To say "I am this one here" is a relational view. The goal of the reflection is to give primacy to the being of the subject who is an "I" engaged in thinking. I can say as an individual, "When I think, I am understanding and interpreting." I am involved in carrying out a relationship. Selfhood is the focal point of his work, insofar as he asks in a variety of ways "Who is a self?"[87] A hermeneutics of the self, in maintaining consistency with how his thought proceeds, takes the way of a detour in the form of an analysis in which I examine the language that is used to discuss the self.

Ricoeur distinguishes between two meanings of identity in reference to the word "self" in the title of the work, by using the Latin equivalent for "identical," which can be either *ipse* or *idem*. The equivocity associated with "identical" is connected to temporality—the primary trait about the self. Two dialectics are set up to establish personal identity. First, there is a dialectic between two aspects of selfhood: *idem*-identity and *ipse*-identity. *Idem*-identity is sameness. It has to do with temporality in terms of permanence in that I have a physical body that perdures through my physical life span. *Ipse*-identity is selfhood or ipseity. It has to do with temporality in terms of a constant, insofar as I possess character. His thesis throughout the study is "that identity in the sense of *ipse* implies no assertion concerning some unchanging core of the personality."[88] Further, *"ipse*-identity includes a dialectic that is complementary to the one of sameness and selfhood, which is a dialectic between self and other than self. If I remain within the confines of sameness-identity," he says, "the otherness of the other than self offers nothing original."[89] However, in pairing together the terms "otherness and selfhood," there is a type of otherness not merely a result of a comparison, which is constitutive of this selfhood. For Ricoeur, *Oneself as Another* involves "a comparison (oneself similar to another)" as well as "an implication (oneself inasmuch as being other)."[90]

He therefore gradually reveals a threefold hermeneutics of the self that includes, first of all, a detour by way of philosophically analyzing the language that I use to talk about the self. I can say that I am other unto myself. For example, I am me, that is, a body, and yet, I refer to or talk about my body. Second, there is dialectical movement between selfhood and sameness. That is, I commonly share in my humanity with all other human beings, but I have a different story in the form of a narrative to contribute. Third, there is dialectical movement between selfhood and otherness. That is, I have the experience of inner truth arising out of my thought. In the end, a hermeneutics of the self involves a description of the self, on the one hand, and the experience of selfhood, on the other hand. Movement occurs between third person, on the one hand, and first or second person, on the other hand. What is important to keep in mind here is that there is no attempt to return to immediacy; I am in the realm of hermeneutics.

It is essential to note for the argument of this study, that Ricoeur suggests there is an ontology of the lived body, which is intermediary between the action and the agent, or a body (that owes allegiance to physical bodies) which is my body (that also owes allegiance to persons).[91] This is his phenomenology of the "I can" in relation to an ontology of a lived body, that is, my own. The notion of capability and the capacity to act are at the heart of his philosophical anthropology.[92] The hermeneutics of the self is inclusive of the capacities of the "I can."[93] Ricoeur employs the "I can" in four ways: "*I can speak, I can do things, I can tell a story, and I can be imputed. . . .*"[94] These capacities are moral powers that can be exercised.

Narrative Identity

Narrative identity emerges out of the problematic of personal identity. Narrative identity introduces change into the notion of character. It prepares the ground for moral identity. There are two models Ricoeur offers—that of character as well as keeping one's promise. Character has to do with sameness and perseverance. Keeping one's promise has to do with constancy about the self who promises. He reinterprets character as having to do with lasting dispositions that are acquired, and that enable a person to be recognized, which brings in its temporal dimension. In the case of keeping one's promise, the self does not stay the same throughout the course of time; time is challenged, and the change time effects and brings about is resisted. To keep a promise serves to safeguard language and entails a certain responsivity to a trust that I have in the faithfulness of the other, where selfhood persists in spite of change.

Narrative identity is the mediating notion and is disclosed in this dialectic between sameness and selfhood. Character constitutes one pole in the lasting set of dispositions which hold across time, while the other pole is constituted by self-constancy represented in the form of a commitment that once having been made is then kept.[95] Emplotment allows the character to preserve its identity throughout the course of the story, and is correlative to the story. Diversity and discontinuity, for example, are integrated into permanence through time. Plot is a unifying feature of elements that are disparate. It is the plot as a dynamic identity that constructs character identity. Also, emplotment passes from action, now, to characters in the narrative as distinguished from the character that comprises the individual.

Moral Identity

Moral identity is expressed in the statement, "Here I am," in the recognition of the self as a subject of responsibility and imputation. These two oppositional identities are transformed into a fruitful tension that cuts to the heart of commitment. An ethical ambiguity arises when selfhood is deemed a relation of ownership between a person, on the one hand, and that person's thoughts, actions and feelings, on the other hand.[96] The narrative imagination suggests a dialectic between ownership and dispossession, between care and carefreeness, between self-affirmation and self-effacement. But the self of imagined nothingness can quickly become an existential crisis.[97]

It should be noted that Ricoeur distinguishes between the ethical and the moral, and gives primacy to ethics—privileging "the aim over the norm," and the "'ethical intention' as *aiming at the 'good life' with and for others, in just institutions.*"[98] Ethics has to do with the aim of the accomplished, particular life, while morality is an articulation of the aim in norms that claim universality. In relation to selfhood, the ethical aim corresponds with self-esteem, and the deontological moment corresponds to self-respect.[99] The narrative unity of a life brings together judgment of particular actions with an evaluation of the persons who carry out those actions. When I interpret the text of an action, I am interpreting myself. There is a self-interpreting process that turns into self-esteem.

Insofar as I live the good life, an ethical life, feelings are evoked by another's suffering and the moral injunction emanating from that other—feelings that are spontaneously directed at the other—which Ricoeur refers to as solicitude. Solicitude reveals an unfolding of the dialogic aspect of self-esteem.[100] The unfolding has to do with a break or cut in both life and discourse whereby the conditions are created such that both solicitude and self-esteem must be reflected upon and experienced together.[101] Solicitude assumes the standing of benevolent spontaneity, and is a mutual exchange of our self-esteems.[102] Solicitude also adds to self-esteem (as the reflexive moment of wishing for a good life), the aspect of lack insofar as I am in need of friends in order to be a self. Hence, solicitude affects self-esteem such that in reaction, the self will perceive itself to be another among all others.[103]

Ricoeur identifies three elements of reciprocity—reversibility, nonsubstitutibility, and similitude—as constituting perception in this ethical relationship of mutual friendship (Aristotle's "each other"). First, reversibility involves reversible roles that a speaker and listener have and the equality of their capacity for self-designation.[104] When I address another person as "you" that person understands herself as "I" and the opposite holds as well. Second, nonsubstitutibility allows for the different, unique persons in a relationship.[105] In an action, agents and patients are involved in relational exchanges that combine the reversibility of roles with the nonsubstitutibility of those persons. Solicitude contributes the aspect of value in that each person I encounter is irreplaceable in terms of my affection and my esteem; nonsubstitutibility of persons is lifted to the same level as irreplaceability. Third, similitude goes beyond the first two terms and is the fecund effect of an exchange in that I esteem myself and have solicitude for others: "You, too," are capable of beginning something, of taking reasoned actions, of ordering your priorities, of evaluating the results of your actions, and having accomplished this, of regarding yourself with esteem as I regard myself with esteem.[106]

He also expresses this notion as the reality of attestation, the primary means by which I can know the possible, when I recall the four ways of employing "I can," as mentioned above.[107] The moral challenge is to connect the phenomenology of "being able" to ethical events of knowledge (attestation) and responsibility (imputability).[108] The import of this thinking is that persons who have been stripped of their rights or of the exercise of their capacities, such as those who are incarcerated, mentally ill, or in some way impaired or challenged are deserving of respect by virtue of the sheer possession of these capacities that are, in fact, possibilities.[109] That is, the self must be worthy of esteem based on its capacities rather than on its accomplishments.

Feelings are affects that are combined into a course of motivation (an inner disposition for Aristotle, or to tend or incline toward). It is the suffering of the other person, and a moral injunction emanating from the other person which reveal feelings to me. I also come to understand my own lack or weakness. Solicitude undergoes a supreme test on the occasion of unequal power that discovers recompense in the authentic exchange of reciprocity. Equality will be reestablished through a shared acknowledgment and affinity regarding our human fragility and mortality.

Similitude is a fruit of an exchange occurring between self-esteem and the solicitude I hold for an other. The ethical feelings that have to do with a phenomenology of "you too" and "like myself" result in a paradox of an exchange at the locus of what is irreplaceable. Ricoeur says that "fundamentally equivalent are the esteem of the *other as a oneself* and the esteem of *oneself as an other*."[110] One final point should be made: Ricoeur makes a distinction between the agent's power and the power of a community. This second capacity is opposed to relations characterized by domination that result in political violence such as torture, for example.[111] Solicitude is thoroughly affirmative and original and fuels the rejection of any indignities that may be inflicted on other human beings.[112]

Aesthetic Identity

I want to extend Ricoeur's discussion to include and develop the notion that the hermeneutical self has an aesthetic identity as well. The hermeneutical self, who understands the relation between discourse and silence, has an aesthetic identity in the depth of receptivity out of which the felt sense perception of admiration arises, along with awe and wonder, in the face of the miracle of existence. This felt sense perception involves both a sense of moral worth and the continual transformation of mood by the self who is situated in the world; it is an ongoing fluctuating component of the existential structure, inasmuch as there is consciousness of existence. While it is personally felt in the movement characteristic of its structure, beatitude is directing the striving for the beautiful toward the shared experience of personally embodied universal reason, or *logos*.

In the fragile synthesis that characterizes respect, there is a mediating activity that goes on in understanding the relation of silence to discourse. My aesthetic identity, I contend, is formed in direct proportion to the degree that I remain receptive in embracing what is other in my life, in the twofold sense of the self as other, that is, in terms of the relation I have with myself, and in terms of the self in my relation to the other person. It is in this way that I transcend myself in a finite sense, by continually being receptive to what is other, which is synonymous with the ongoing transformation of self. Receptivity involves purposefully letting myself be and letting others be. It is an action insofar as there is deliberateness involved. The letting something be can be seen to be a striving for the beautiful inasmuch as I behold the other in the manner of a gaze, which is to say, I lovingly participate in (the structure of) existence; there is a seeing and a being seen at work here. To lovingly participate in existence is to lovingly participate in language and silence that goes beyond my individual existence, as such, and points to ultimate meaning. I am intermedial, on the way, not only between finitude and infinitude, but between language and silence as well. Awareness of the mediating activity between silence and discourse is grounded in the practice of contemplative silence. I have now covered four essential elements that constitute capable human. The final task in this chapter is to explain the concept of recognition, which is integral to the process of transformation associated with reflexive consciousness.

RECOGNITION

The capacity to undergo a transformation of reflexive consciousness, and the concomitant transformation of my being, has to do with the moment of self-recognition. I previously established the groundwork for recognition. Here, first of all, I briefly adumbrate Ricoeur's structure of recognition—identification, self-recognition, and mutual recognition. Identity, otherness, and the dialectic between that of recognition and misrecognition constitute *The Course of Recognition*. The practice of contemplative silence may choose to focus on moments of recognition. Second, I will explain the conceptual work of the moment of recognition, and how self-recognition works. In the active voice I can recognize something, and in the passive voice I seek to be recognized.

Recognition as Identification

The first three forms of recognition below can be subsumed under the first kind of recognition in Ricoeur's structure—that of recognition as identification. The first form of recognition is the apprehension of sense manifold in intuition. Sensation is the domain of immediacy, which is not yet mediated by thought. I am given modifications of my own state through mediating a series of sensations into a perception.

The second form of recognition is the recognition of a concept in intuition, or the concept in perception.[113] Kant claims that knowledge is a justified synthesis between a concept and an intuition. Consider this example: I see something growing in my garden, and I say, "This is a flower." "This" denotes the sense perception, the intuition, and "a flower" is a concept. "Is" marks the synthesis that produces objectivity. The synthesis is performed by the transcendental imagination. With it, I recognize what I see in my garden as a flower. When I think "this is a flower," I subsume the sense perception under the concept. Ricoeur explains "that the unity of consciousness produces itself in the concept in order to *recognize* itself in it."[114] I unite the percept and concept in thought. The thought, as expressed in language, is either true or false. The truth or falsehood of the sentence must be determined by an independent act of verification.

Change as well as temporalization constitute the circumstances for the events of identification and recognition. As a result of change and temporality, recognition can turn to misrecognition, and beyond, to nonrecognition. Change and temporality can accompany situations having to do with perception and recognition such that someone is unrecognizable. Or, it may be that someone, despite the lapse of years and much change in physical appearance, for example, is still recognizable. Lived experience provides an illustration of the threatening aspect about both change and time, which gives to the concept of recognition the emotional dimension. This idea is explored next.

Recognition of the other person over time is the third form of recognition.[115] Consider this example: I go to meet a friend at the airport whom I have not seen in a few years. As he steps off the airplane, I can say "There he is! I recognize him!" I may remark to my friend, "You look the same! You haven't changed!" Change happens, although in a certain regard my friend has not changed.[116] Consider once more the example of meeting my friend at the airport. This time, however, it has been twenty-five years since we last met. My friend has undergone much life experience, and his appearance has changed, to be sure, with the graying of hair and the deepening lines in the face; however, there are the familiar gestures and expressions, the facial features and definite personality traits that enable me to recognize this person once more as my dear friend.

Finally, in drawing from the work of Proust, Ricoeur discusses the kind of recognition in which the reader is summoned in the reading to become a reader of herself.[117] This occasion provides the opportunity for the reader to discern something in herself that perhaps never would have been able to be discerned were it not for the text. The veracity lies in the very recognition on the part of the reader in herself about what it is that the text says.

Self-Recognition

Identity is still an issue when it comes to self-recognition.[118] The self as a capable human can recognize herself in her capabilities. To the "I can's" Ricoeur adds the unfolding of the temporality of the self with regard to the past—memory, and the future—promises. Both memory and promises carry negative opposites that threaten them in their capacities as such, and constitute part of their meaning—forgetting accompanies memory, and betrayal accompanies promises. Further, these opposites help form their meaning insofar as when I remember I do not forget, and when I keep my promise to someone I do not break it. There is also a connection between attestation and recognition in that when a person says, "I am confident that 'I can,' I attest to it, I recognize it."[119]

Mutual Recognition

There is, too, a question of identification with mutual recognition. There is both a struggle waged against being misrecognized by others, as well as a struggle to be recognized by others. In the case of misrecognition, there is an original asymmetry between self and other, which the mutual reciprocity of the giving and receiving associated with the exchange of gifts, for example, cannot eliminate. Even in the celebratory exchange of gifts, the other is always inaccessible in terms of her alterity such that she, as other, remains unknown. Here the recognition has to do with misrecognizing the asymmetry in the relation between two persons. The dissymmetry serves as a reminder of the intrinsic value of each and every person who is utterly irreplaceable. The concept of mutuality is also protected from my conceiving of it in terms of something like a fusional union. To keep a just distance in a relationship serves to integrate respect into the intimacy that is characteristic of the relationship.

Recognition of the self in the other is the fourth form of recognition and has to do with mutual dependence.[120] It is recognizing the sameness and difference in the relationship between the self and other. I would like to alter the terms used to characterize this relationship slightly, however, and consider a relationship of friendship. While it can be true that one of these two selves can appear to be domineering with regard to the extent to which the one asserts and maintains itself, this distinction depends ultimately on their essential identity. The truth is that the two selves are identical; this identity is the more comprehensive and perfect realization of each self in the other. The accord is superior and more significant than any difference that exists. Even so, the contention and clash has to be experienced so that this effect is brought to the fore. Consciousness discovers its own self-existence in the other's self-existence. And, "They recognize themselves as mutually recognizing one another."[121]

The fifth form of recognition is the recognition of the otherness of the other.[122] This recognition is different from that of seeing the self in the other, because it involves recognition of the transcendence of the other. For Levinas, the "face of the other" summons us, elicits our response, and places a demand on us to extend hospitality in welcoming the other; the self as other is infinitely transcendent.[123] His claim is not that the other is a formal inbreaking, but rather that the face of the other says specifically, "Thou shall not kill."[124] The face is directly apprehended such that the other demands recognition in its otherness.[125] There is the abjectness of the seeing of ourselves, and our own miserable deeds and fault in the light of the other. We affirm the freedom of the other in letting the other be.

I want to note here that Ricoeur brings to the surface a difficult enigma in relation to the work of Levinas.[126] The writer-philosopher who is the third party to his work has to engage in a comparison between what are incomparables—the pole of the other and the pole of the "I." There has to be justice among the incomparable ones, and justice is a comparison between these incomparable ones. In considering the original asymmetry between the other and the "I," whichever pole it is that one starts from, the question is one of comparing incomparables, and therefore "of *equalizing* them," he notes.[127] The point is that Levinas cannot coherently elevate otherness over sameness.[128]

The sixth and final form of recognition is theological recognition. Theological recognition can be recognition of the divine in the human, or of the human in the divine. In the final chapter of *Memory, History, Forgetting*, Ricoeur says that forgiveness happens, and is the ground from on high of the way in which the admittance of wrongdoing emerges from the impenetrable profundity of the self.[129] Forgiveness can signify seeing the divine in the non-divine. Forgiveness can signify that there is an infinite, mysterious depth to my humanity, and that I cannot definitively understand myself or others. Forgiveness can signify a rich and vast reality by teaching me to be open to its possibility.

In the moment of self-recognition, the two movements, recognition of the self and other, and recognition of the other as other (the fourth and fifth forms of recognition), are important. To illustrate this point, I want to deviate slightly from Ricoeur's structure; these forms, as has been shown, belong under mutual recognition. As I take up just one side of the relationship in the discussion that follows, these forms will be considered as part of the moment of self-recognition. Imagine that while practicing contemplative silence I remember a recent altercation I had with a friend. My friend made a rash comment and said something hurtful. I experience a moment of illumination.

In remembering and rethinking the lived experience, I recognize that immediately prior to that rash comment, I made a statement that could have been taken the wrong way. In this moment, I recognize the vulnerability of my friend, but in acknowledging the vulnerability of the other, I also experience a moment of self-recognition in experiencing my own vulnerability in relationship as well. I understand at a new level our mutual dependence. I have made a connection between my insensitivity and the other by thinking the concept of fault: "I was insensitive, and I am to blame." Our friendship is strained—there is an awkwardness in our relationship now. I may feel unworthy.

In the practice of contemplative silence—the focus of the next chapter—I can practice what Ricoeur refers to as "an idle forgetting" that is analogous to memory, insofar as it is "a concerned disposition established in duration."[130] I can carry a kind of purposeful forgetfulness of this past action within the context of memory. Thus, in the case of our friendship, I become aware that I can graciously extend the benefit of the doubt to the other and speak words of forgiveness to clear the space between us. There is a transformational quality of appropriating this moment of recognition by opening up the space of hermeneutical activity for transformation. This space is the dimension of a new relationship that I have with myself and the other.

In the example of friendship above, recognition of the self and other occurred in the moment in which I recognized my own vulnerability as well as the vulnerability of my friend. Recognition of the other as other occurred when I did not expect words from the other. The other was remembered in freedom. The transformational quality of the moment of recognition occurred in extending the benefit of the doubt, and for the sake of the sheer joy of friendship, I spoke words of forgiveness. This space can become the origin of the new relationship that both I and the other are brought into. A new relationship (relational reality) commences in self-recognition so that there is a transcendent possibility embedded in recognition. At the very least, the hope of community and being together is possible. Minimally, there is the transformation toward we, as I consider new motivations and intentions for acting, in relationship with others, and maximally toward the awareness of the wholeness of being and possibility of new being. There is a disclosure of a new possibility for the lighting process, i.e., the illuminating process. This process is not only the opening of intelligibility, but also is the appearance of something brought about in the world, and that appearance can be a symbol of God. This is theological recognition. Moments of self-recognition open me to the possibility of transcendence in my relational realities and open up new and fresh ways of living in the world.

NOTES

1. Ricoeur, SE, 356.
2. Ibid.
3. Ibid. Ricoeur quotes from the "Charmides" of Plato here: "The God [at Delphi], by way of salutation, says to them, in reality: *Be wise:* but, as a soothsayer, he says it in enigmatic form. *Be wise and Know thyself* are fundamentally the same thing, . . . *Nothing too much* and *To stand surety for someone invites misfortune.* . . ." See Plato, "Charmides," *Plato: The Collected Dialogues including the Letters*, eds. Edith Hamilton and Huntington Cairns (Princeton, NJ: Princeton University Press, 1989), 99. The arrogant self-assurance that accompanies certitude is a quality abhorred by the Greeks, and is to be avoided. The subject of the "Charmides" is "What is sophrosyne?" which the editor explains cannot be translated into English in merely one word. According to Hamilton, the word means "*accepting the bounds which excellence lays down for human nature, restraining impulses to unrestricted freedom, to all excess, obeying the inner laws of harmony and proportion.*"
4. Ricoeur, SE, 356.
5. See Blundell, 70. See also Hans-Georg Gadamer, *Truth and Method*, 2nd rev. ed., trans. Joel Weinsheimer and Donald G. Marshall (New York: Continuum, 2000) and *Philosophical Hermeneutics*, trans. and ed. David E. Linge (Berkeley, Los Angeles, London: University of California Press, 1977).
6. Ricoeur, SE, 349.
7. Klemm, HTPR, 70.
8. Ibid.
9. Ricoeur, "The Hermeneutics of Symbols: II," 319.
10. Ibid.
11. Ibid., 330.
12. Blundell, 140.
13. Mark I. Wallace, *The Second Naiveté: Barth, Ricoeur, and the New Yale Theology* (Macon, GA: Mercer University Press, 1995), xv.
14. See Paul Ricoeur, "Philosophical Hermeneutics and Biblical Hermeneutics," *From Text to Action: Essays in Hermeneutics, II*, trans. Kathleen Blamey and John B. Thompson (Evanston: Northwestern University Press, 1991), 101. See also Paul Ricoeur, "The Hermeneutical Function of Distanciation," *Philosophy Today* 17 (1973): 129–69. Finally, see Paul Ricoeur, "Toward a Hermeneutic of the Idea of Revelation," *Harvard Theological Review* 70, no. 1–2 (January–April 1977): 29.
15. Ricoeur, "Philosophical Hermeneutics and Biblical Hermeneutics," 100.
16. My thanks to David E. Klemm for this point.
17. Ricoeur, IT, 7.
18. Ibid., 8.
19. Ibid., 3. Here Ricoeur follows the work of the linguist, Ferdinand de Saussure.
20. Ricoeur, IT, 3 and Klemm, HTPR, 75.
21. Ibid.
22. Klemm, HTPR, 77.
23. Ricoeur, IT, 9.

24. Ibid., 10.
25. Klemm, HTPR, 77.
26. Ricoeur, IT, 12.
27. Ibid.
28. Klemm, HTPR, 78.
29. Ricoeur, IT, 14.
30. Ibid., 15–16. See also Edmund Husserl, "The Appresentation of the Other," *The Essential Husserl: Basic Writings in Transcendental Phenomenology*, ed. Donn Welton (Bloomington and Indianapolis: Indiana University Press, 1999), 149. According to Husserl, I cannot actualize for myself the "hylectic" sense data of what has already been appropriated by another person in my own primordial, spatio-temporal position. This is all to the good: See John Durham Peters, *Speaking into the Air: A History of the Idea of Communication* (Chicago and London: The University of Chicago Press, 1999), 31. He states that "Ralph Waldo Emerson and William James struck the right note: acknowledging the splendid otherness of all creatures that share our world without bemoaning our impotence to tap their interiority. The task is to recognize the creature's otherness, not to make it over in one's own image and likeness."
31. Klemm, HTPR, 78.
32. Ricoeur, IT, 18.
33. Ibid.
34. Ibid., 19.
35. Ibid. This is a distinction originally made by Gottlob Frege whose work Ricoeur cites.
36. Ibid., 20 and Klemm, HTPR, 79.
37. Ibid.
38. Ricoeur, IT, 20.
39. Ibid., 21–22.
40. Ibid., 22.
41. Ibid., 29–30.
42. Ibid.
43. Blundell, 38.
44. Ibid.
45. Ibid., 35.
46. Ricoeur, IT, 12–13; Klemm, HTPR, 77.
47. Ricoeur, IT, 13.
48. Ibid.
49. Klemm, HTPR, 81.
50. Ricoeur, IT, 42.
51. Ibid.
52. Klemm, HTPR, 82.
53. Ibid., 26.
54. Martin Heidegger, *Being and Time, A Translation of Sein und Zeit*, trans. Joan Stambaugh (Albany: SUNY Press, 1996), 468.
55. Ibid., 273. He cites Max Scheler.

56. See Bernard P. Dauenhauer, *Silence: The Phenomenon and Its Ontological Significance* (Bloomington: Indiana University Press, 1980).
57. Ibid., 60.
58. Ibid., 5.
59. Ibid., 4.
60. Ibid., 5–6.
61. See Dauenhauer, 8. For example, the particular intervening silence of A' that lies between the given sound phrases A and B contains something of a sense of not only sound phrases A and B that frame it, but all of the sound phrases that are part of the utterance. Otherwise, there would be no unity to the utterance except in retrospect. Dauenhauer explains that "The first moment of intervening silence A' is heavily freighted, but not exhaustively filled, with the retained sense of sound phrase A. As A' perdures, a 'running off' of the retained sense of A 'empties' A' of some but not all of the retained sense of A. A' could not be totally emptied of A without destroying the unity of the utterance. Correlated to the emptying, there is the filling up of A' with the protended sense of sound phrase B. But again, A' is never exhaustively filled with the sense of B. Thus, there is always in A' something of the senses of both A and B." See also Edmund Husserl, "A Phenomenology of the Consciousness of Internal Time," *The Essential Husserl: Basic Writings in Transcendental Phenomenology*, 186–212.
62. Dauenhauer, 15.
63. Ibid., 17–24.
64. See Ibid., 33–49.
65. Ibid., 52.
66. Ibid., 48.
67. Ibid., 62.
68. Ibid., 77; 65–74. The title of this section is named to follow the temporal structure that Dauenhauer assigns to the appearance of silence in connection with discourse. See also his section on the development of the interpersonal dimensions of silence in relation to discourse.
69. Ibid., 69–70
70. Ibid., 73.
71. Ibid., 75.
72. Ibid.
73. Ibid.
74. Ibid., 77.
75. Ibid., 79.
76. Ibid., 80.
77. Ibid., 90. The title of this section follows the title of Part II of Dauenhauer's analysis, which is also the sub-title of his study.
78. Ibid., 142.
79. Ibid., 143.
80. Ibid., 148.
81. See Ibid., 146–52 for discussion of these domains.
82. Ibid., 151.
83. Ibid.

84. Ibid., 173.
85. Ibid., 161.
86. Ibid.
87. See Ricoeur, OA, 16 for the following discussion.
88. Ibid., 2.
89. Ibid., 3.
90. Ibid.
91. Ibid., 111.
92. Ricoeur, "Ethics and Human Capability: A Response," 280.
93. Paul Ricoeur, *The Course of Recognition*, trans. David Pellauer (Cambridge, MA and London: Harvard University Press, 2005), 151 (hereafter CR).
94. Ricoeur discusses his work in this regard in "Ethics and Human Capability: A Response," 280. See also Ricoeur, OA.
95. Reagan, 85.
96. Ricoeur, OA, 168.
97. Ibid.
98. Ibid., 171–72.
99. Ibid., 171.
100. Ibid., 180.
101. Ibid.
102. Ibid., 221.
103. Ibid., 192.
104. Ibid., 193.
105. Ibid.
106. Ibid.
107. Paul Ricoeur, "The Power of the Possible," *Debates in Continental Philosophy" Conversations with Contemporary Thinkers*, ed. Richard Kearney (New York: Fordham University Press, 2004), 45. See also Richard Kearney, "Capable Man, Capable God," 52n11.
108. Ricoeur, "The Power of the Possible," 45.
109. Ibid.
110. Ricoeur, OA, 194–95.
111. See Reagan, 90. See also Ricoeur, OA, 225.
112. Ricoeur, OA, 221.
113. Kant, *Critique of Pure Reason*. See the section, "On the Deduction of the Pure Concepts of the Understanding," in the division entitled the "Transcendental Analytic."
114. Ricoeur, CR, 46.
115. Ibid., 67.
116. Ricoeur, OA, 117.
117. See Ricoeur, CR, 68.
118. Ibid., 21.
119. Ibid., 250.
120. Ibid., 171–86. Ricoeur engages in an extensive discussion of Hegel and his interpreters here.

121. See Hegel, *The Phenomenology of Spirit (The Phenomenology of Mind)*, 88.

122. See Ricoeur, CR, 259–60. This form of recognition has to do with what Ricoeur refers to as the alterity of the original asymmetry existing between persons that is characteristic of mutual relations involving mutual recognition and misrecognition.

123. See Emmanuel Levinas, *Totality and Infinity: An Essay on Exteriority*, trans. Alphonso Lingis (Pittsburgh: Duquesne University Press, 1969), 75; 77; 194.

124. Ibid., 66; 297.

125. Ibid., 75.

126. Ricoeur, CR, 161.

127. Ibid.

128. See David E. Klemm, "Levinas' Phenomenology of the Other and Language as the Other of Phenomenology," *Man and World* 22 (1989): 403–26. See also Blundell, 127. Blundell, too, discusses Ricoeur's critique and explains that "While the collapse of the self/other dialectic is a perennial grave danger, collapsing it in the direction of the Other is not a viable solution." Moreover, he says that "The Other can still be 'the necessary path of injunction' without overwhelming the Self."

129. Paul Ricoeur, *Memory, History, Forgetting*, trans. Kathleen Blamey and David Pellauer (Chicago and London: The University of Chicago Press, 2004), 467 (hereafter MHF).

130. Ibid., 504–5.

Chapter 4

The Practice of Contemplative Silence as a Historical Phenomenon

I formulated a response to the question, How is the practice of contemplative silence possible? by fashioning a philosophically determined explanation of a structure of human being that appropriates the philosophical anthropology of Ricoeur. From a theoretical perspective, I explored the notions of fallibility and capability within the capacity of finite existence. Further, I presented the ontological structure that provides the condition of the possibility for the practice of contemplative silence. That is, I determined the philosophical and theoretical context for the practice. The task in this chapter is to determine the religious and theological structure so that what it is that makes the practice of contemplative silence possible is, in the end, sufficiently explained. My goal is to reach the point in the study where I can discuss what ought to be—that the actualizable possibility for the transformation of reflexive consciousness is, in fact, a part of human reality. Moreover, it is an ethical and spiritual task that warrants explanation and interpretation.

There is a long tradition of historical writing about the practice of contemplative silence that gives witness to this tradition by telling what it is. It is in this sense that these writings can be regarded as primordial texts. The texts also provide an image of contemplative silence. This image allows me to form the practice around it. While the term "contemplation" has been accorded a variety of meanings throughout history, in religious terms, it is consistently employed in a manner which has to do with a deeper awareness of a divine presence. This awareness can be thought of as unitive in that all of reality is regarded as being united. Accordingly, I am closest to this reality when I hold polarities or oppositions and paradoxes together, as in nondual thinking. While solitude and simplicity are hallmarks of the practice of contemplative silence, action and activity resonate and flow forth from the practitioner, as well. Contemplation as understood in the Eastern and Western tradition of Christianity has its roots in the ancient Greek philosophy of Plato and Aristotle.[1] Philo and Plotinus also exercise influence on the tradition. Select frames of the tradition will be captured to convey what the practice of contemplative silence entails according to some of its leading exponents.

I present historical material in this chapter by focusing on particular authors who, through their written texts, articulate paradigmatic ways of understanding the practice of contemplative silence, and so are considered representative of the tradition. These authors are significant in that they exert enormous influence on succeeding generations of practitioners, who in epitomizing and appropriating the practice in their own right, nevertheless understand the core essence of their practice to be consonant with this tradition. Particular, but not exclusive, attention will be given to the Carmelite school of spirituality and its leading exponents, who with their roots firmly established in the Song of Songs tradition of textual interpretation dating back to Origen, probe deeply the mystery of human existence. Then, in Chapter 5, the figure of Edith Stein will be lifted out of this historical spiritual trajectory as her work comes into sharper focus and ultimately assumes prominence. It is her thought, and what she has in common with the other Carmelites, especially John of the Cross, which will crystallize and then move us into the contemporary world of hermeneutics so that eventually I may shape a hermeneutics of contemplative silence. Before presenting this history, however, I want to describe two sets of terms that are integral to describing the practice of contemplative silence: first, cataphasis and apophasis, also known as the cataphatic and apophatic ways, and second, contemplation and action, or the unitive way of life which ends in silence, although silence is the ground both of speech and action on the way to and from the realization.

THE CATAPHATIC AND APOPHATIC WAYS

At the heart of the contemplative tradition lie two fundamental and diametrically opposed, but complementary ways of viewing the relation with ultimate reality. They are most accurately and fruitfully depicted as being in correlation to each other. The cataphatic way or cataphasis is the way of knowing—of light and affirmation in approaching the divine. The apophatic way or apophasis is the way of unknowing—of darkness, denial, and negation, or the *via negativa* in approaching the divine.[2]

According to the cataphatic way, also referred to as the affirmative way, there is a similarity between the divine and all of created reality, such that while this similarity is emphasized, it must be understood within a greater dissimilarity existing between the two.[3] The divine is affirmed by noting certain characteristics of experience to be considered as perfections of the divine in the human. Exercising compassion, loving tenderly, carrying out familial relationships such as parenthood, living in humility, and promoting peace and justice through the faithful living out of these attributes are but a few of the ways in which human experience is thought to provide an opening or glimpse into ultimate reality. In terms of philosophical theology, the divine is made known in and through human life, specifically through the natural light of reason.[4] In terms of speech about the divine, the divine is also made known among things in the world in the affirmation and predication of all attributes to the divine. In terms of contemplative ascent, the divine is considered to be all in all in that humans and all creatures are expressions of the divine fecundity.[5] And, according to the biblical perspective, given the Creator/creature correlation, the divine immanence is made known through the creature. There can be no wholly cataphatic or affirmative way as there is always imperfection that has to be purified in the spiritual life.

With the apophatic way, there are no words, thoughts, ideas, or symbols that can attain the divine as the divine is in reality.[6] This is the way of darkness in that the activity of thinking and all concepts have to be set aside, as unknown reality is entered into solely through love. While there are attestations in the tradition that provide evidence of knowledge that is imparted through this way, it is generally referred to as a knowing that one does not know, a conscious not-knowing, or an unknowing insofar as the typical ways of cognition in which one comes to know something are abandoned for a knowing that is dissimilar, foreign, and unusual in every way. It is considered difficult, if impossible, to pronounce what, if anything, is imparted in the apophatic way. Nevertheless, in the end, words are used in the tradition to talk of and about it. Pseudo-Dionysius refers to a brilliant darkness, while John of the Cross writes of silent music as they articulate darkness using oxymoronic expressions. In terms of philosophical theology, the divine is considered transcendent, wholly other, and cannot be known through human thought.[7] In terms of speech about the divine, imperfections emerging as a result of human finitude are not of the divine, and so are denied with the negative way. Finally, with regard to a contemplative approach to the divine, with the negative way, all perceptions and understandings are abandoned, and conscious attentiveness remains.

From the time of Augustine and Pseudo-Dionysius on, the idea in Medieval Christianity is to be able to account for both knowledge of God and the naming of God using language that does justice to the divine transcendence, and yet also points to the self-revelation of God that is inclusive of creatures.[8] This is a dueling act of the mind of sorts in finding a way to point to what is, in the final analysis, inarticulate and yet, enunciate something. Also noteworthy and distinctive is the approach of Gregory of Palamas in the Orthodox tradition, which is based on Eastern monastic spirituality. He is in a line of continuity with Gregory of Nyssa and Pseudo-Dionysius: Going both beyond knowing and beyond unknowing, this experience of God is situated higher than negation. While this experience does not rely on the senses or the intellect, it nevertheless is an embodied experience of the Spirit, but one that transcends human cognition. This is the realm of contemplative experience that transfigures the mind and body of human beings such that they are transformed by those divine energies that were communicated "in the light of the transfiguration on Mount Tabor."[9] Apophasis is not merely synonymous with the negative way, but rather, there is an overflow, a surplus, of positivity of experience that remains embedded in silence. Apophatic union with God reaches fruition in the works of the Carmelites, Teresa of Avila and John of the Cross. In Meister Eckhart, God is the negation of the negation, or the non-other, however, absolute difference cannot be distinguished from identity or oneness at this level so that "In the end, identity and difference alike are not definable or sayable. It is only the different *approaches* to this in-difference that resolve into clear distinctness."[10]

An experiential dimension, or what can be referred to as a mysticism of love appears in the anonymous text, *The Cloud of Unknowing*, which follows in the tradition of Pseudo-Dionysius. There is a darkness about the mind in this practice. It is both the darkness and the cloud that stand between the human and God, which can lead to frustration because of the mind's inability to grasp God and the heart's inability to relish God's love; however, the author urges humans to "learn to be at home in this darkness."[11] If love is fixed on God, then the human will be brought to a deep experience of God. The two faculties of knowing and loving—known as powers—are active in the human; but it is love that can fully grasp God.[12] However, this knowing by love is depicted in terms of an unknowing in human experience. The work of contemplative love is what heals the human. The author gives a short explanation of contemplation and says, "I prefer to abandon all I can know, choosing rather to love him whom I cannot know. Though we cannot know him we can love him. By love he may be touched and embraced, never by thought."[13] Affectivity takes precedence over any keen intellectual endeavor such that language falls short and is inadequate.

CONTEMPLATION AND ACTION AS THE UNITIVE WAY OF LIFE

The second task is to explicate the relationship between contemplation and action by drawing from the texts of Teresa of Avila in the Carmelite tradition. While I formally introduce her life and work below, here discussion of union and contemplative awareness captures the dynamics that are at work in the unitive way of life. While Teresa does not explicitly use the language of the three Ways, she does reference this path in her *Life*.[14] She further sets out the biblical figures of Mary and Martha and says they can work in tandem to bring contemplation and action together. Mary represents interiority while Martha represents exteriority, as two parts of the soul.[15]

Teresa leads an extremely busy and active life as she travels around to establish religious communities. She instructs her spiritual daughters to fulfill the duties associated with obedience and charity. Exterior matters are just as important to tend to as interior matters.[16] Further, it is good to follow orders that reveal the human condition. One day in which I learn humble self-knowledge is better than spending several days in prayer, as "the true lover loves everywhere and is always thinking of the Beloved!"[17] Obedience is the true path for subjecting the will to reason.[18] Loss of self-will is the sign that the will is united to God. There is no knowledge that humans are, in fact, recollected in solitude and awareness without experiencing actual situations and circumstances in life that call for patience and humility.[19] Whether one is engaged in contemplation, caring for the sick, or carrying out mundane chores, these tasks are all ways to serve.[20] Detachment and humility are necessary for both active service and contemplation.

Mary and Martha work closely together. Teresa writes on the cohesion of the prayer of quiet and divine union such that contemplative awareness and the active life are in unison. She writes that "Although a person's life will become more active than contemplative, . . . Martha and Mary never fail to work almost together. . . . For in the active—and seemingly exterior—work the soul is working interiorly."[21] These actions have vast influence in benefiting many people as Mary and Martha share in one activity. The performed works share in the commonality of having been done for God rather than strictly out of self-interest.

There seems to be some sort of division in the soul, however, insofar as Martha complains that Mary is enjoying "quietude" at pleasure, "leaving her in the midst of so many trials and occupations. . . ."[22] Nevertheless, Mary and Martha, as distinct figures, represent the unitive way of contemplative awareness. The ordinary way of knowing and the mystical way of knowing are held together in the two of them. Together they form a unique dynamic in which identity and difference are held together. Here, awareness of God and awareness of the soul in union result in a mature relational awareness. Loving service flows out of the intense interior activity of the relationship of spiritual marriage that Teresa discusses in the seventh dwelling place of *The Interior Castle*.[23] She concludes this text for which she is well-known with the platitude, "we shouldn't build castles in the air."[24] After all, it is not the greatness of the work, but the love with which the work is done—the way in which it is accomplished—that counts in the final analysis. To conclude, I have established a context for the presentation of a history of the tradition by introducing and explaining the basic dyadic framework of apophasis and cataphasis, and the unitive way of contemplation and action, against which the practice of contemplative silence can be described. I turn now to that history.

The history of the religious phenomenon of the practice of contemplative silence has to do with a loving awareness of a divine presence who is considered always present, and who accordingly can be apprehended in love. In etymological terms, contemplation derives from the Latin *contemplatio* and *templum*.[25] *Templum* is a diminutive of *tempus*, meaning "time" or "a division or section of time."[26] *Templum* was a place in the heavens, or sky, partitioned off, and therefore, considered sacred space, for an augur, for example, to use devices to attempt to determine favorable or unfavorable times, or to watch the flight of birds, and read the omens or, for a soothsayer to discern what was "the design of the gods" on behalf of the client.[27] *Templum* or the temple was a dwelling place for the gods, and the place in which one could be in the presence of the gods. Also, included in the word, *contemplatio,* is the word, "template" which means a blueprint or a pattern. Hence, contemplation can mean to gaze attentively and thoughtfully at, or to inspect this blueprint or pattern. The temple served as the location for persons who were considered sacred to examine the internal parts of these birds, the entrails, in order to ascertain divine meanings and the goals and aim of life. Contemplation delineates examining the inside of reality in order to see that in its depth, reality is nothing in and of itself. At the same time, however, a source is discovered at the heart of reality that is considered, in the tradition of Christianity, to be origin and ground. That source is identified as "God." To gaze or look at this source is to look at God.

Some of the Greek patristic writers used the Greek word, *theōria*, which approximates the Latin, *contemplatio,* coming from the verb *theōrein*, meaning to scrutinize closely or to concentrate on something intently for a specific purpose, to describe a kind of "natural" contemplation whereby traces of the divine could be found among created things.[28] The Greek word, *theologia*, describes the highest form of contemplative awareness, which refers to a complete and immediate oneness with the divine.[29] I am now in a position to distill the heart of the practice according to its individual practitioners.

ORIGEN (CA. 185–255)

The description begins with Origen of Alexandria who as a hermeneut is one of the most important of the early Greek patristic writers. He is a great scholar and theologian known for his biblical exegesis as well as for his philosophical training. He is thought to have been taught by the Platonist, Ammonius Saccas, who was also the teacher of Plotinus.[30] The prior work of Clement, who is of the Alexandrian school as well, exerted significant influence on his writings. Origen's important work, *On First Principles,* is considered to be an exercise in hermeneutics. However, Bernard McGinn comments that Origen is less interested in determining the meaning of the biblical text, than in the spiritual education that accompanies this encounter in which the aim of life is to be achieved.[31] Material creation provides a means of education for humans to find their way back through their intellects to a perfect vision of the divine. Everything flows out from and returns to the divine. In the process of interpretation, Origen sets out to comprehend the grammatical sense of the words, as well as to obtain knowledge of the historical reality of the specific biblical passage. What has been termed the "theological poiesis" of Origen has to do with an interpretive process whereby religious experience occurs in and through the assimilation of the biblical language, which is transformed at the deepest affective level into a kind of language of the soul.[32]

Origen considers the process of the threefold way to be a return to God. He tiers the three biblical books of Proverbs, Ecclesiastes, and the Song of Songs into different levels that progressively lead to greater depth of understanding. They instruct as to how to live out the respective stages of what was the tripartite philosophical education of the Greeks—moral, natural, and contemplative silence.[33] Origen understands biblical texts to have the same depth that a human being has with the inner meaning hidden yet revealed through the grace and gifts of the Spirit.[34] The first stage, the purgative way, involves moral clarity, whereby I have to exert moral effort to rid myself of any attachments that may impede me from exercising a deeper commitment and involvement in the process. Reform has to occur in relation to intentions, attitudes, behavior—all aspects of thought, action, and feeling in reference to human existence—and be inclusive of the world.

The second stage is the illuminative way in which through a kind of natural contemplation, the individual reaches an understanding that every created thing in the world is of the divine. This stage denotes proficients on the journey. The prayer of infused recollection together with the prayer of quiet are the means for the faculties of the intellect and the will to be conformed to the incarnate Word.[35] The dynamic at work in the prayer of union—conforming love—embraces the whole person who is brought into a divine relation of greater depth.[36] The experience of the prayer of quiet is refreshing and results in everyday tasks being performed with renewed interest. The imagination as well as the memory undergo the integrative process that the intellect and the will previously did. Woundedness as a result of human weakness is healed.

The third stage is contemplation—the unitive way—and a transformation of the individual into the divine. Origen understands the repair to be in the image of God. A person is hereupon open to the divine initiative with an awareness of the divine as being the depth of reality. Divine absence and presence mirror the purgative and illuminative work, and together constitute a life in conformity to the divine life. Infused contemplation and an intellectual vision of divine relational life are characteristic of the third stage. For Origen to proceed from *praxis*, in which virtues are cultivated, to *theōria*, in which the world is seen in a new way, to *theologia*, in which the world echoes the divine, means to have a greater capacity to experience the divine.[37]

For Origen, the Book of the Song of Songs is a wedding song, or an epithalamium in the form of a play illustrative of divine love for humanity at a personal level within the context of community. Human love is a metaphor for divine/human love. McGinn describes this hermeneutical experience in that the search for the correct "understanding of the erotic language of the Song is the exemplary exercise by which these higher and finer 'senses' of the fallen, dormant intellect are awakened and resensitized by the spirit" so that the hermeneut is capable of the inflow of transcendental experience, which is a presence of the Word.[38] Origen also discusses this complex spiritual journey in his *Homily XXVII on Numbers*. He says that the rational nature is nourished by true food, which is "the Word of God."[39] There must be found both "perfection of faith and knowledge, but also that of deeds and works."[40] In this way, he holds in union contemplation and action which together comprise a singular completion of perfection.

GREGORY OF NYSSA (CA. 335–395)

Gregory is known as one of the three Cappadocian Fathers in Eastern Christianity, together with his older brother, Basil the Great, and a friend known as Gregory of Nazianzen. In *The Life of Moses*, Gregory two times over tells the story of Moses whose life he regards as a pattern of beauty. The first part of the work is a history in the form of a narrative. The story is one of ongoing striving to live a virtuous life and thereby attain a life of perfection—an ascent to the divine. The second part is *theōria* or contemplation on the life of Moses in which there is a retelling of the story in order to contemplate its hidden meaning. The practitioner of contemplative silence passes through what the early ascetic tradition refers to as *apatheia* (passionlessness), or "purity of heart" in the monastic tradition, and true knowledge of the divine,[41] which leads to freedom and the presence of the divine in love.[42]

The passage moves from light to darkness. Accordingly, Gregory emphasizes three forms—light, cloud, and darkness—through which the divine reveals itself using the biblical text of the Book of Exodus. Moses moves close to a darkness wherein the divine is to be found.[43] Movement and direction are essential for eternal progress. Moses never ceases in his ascent nor sets a limit for his own growth. Rather, he continues to climb a ladder, always rising higher because he is always able to discover a higher step.[44] In his thirst, he requests to attain not with respect to his capacity, but in accordance with true being. This experience seems to belong to those who love that which is beautiful. Gregory teaches that there is a way in which "hope always draws the soul from the beauty which is seen to what is beyond, always kindles the desire for the hidden through what is constantly perceived."[45]

The request of desire is to enjoy Beauty not reflected, but rather, face to face. The voice of the divine granted the request precisely through the denial of it, displaying in just a few words a profound depth to thought. For the generosity of the divine agreed to fulfill the desire of Moses without promising that the satiety of desire would cease. Thus it is that the true sight of the divine consists in the fact that one who searches for the divine never gives up that desire. What Moses longs for is met by that which remains unsatisfied in terms of his desire. There is an expansion of the desire for what is yet going to come in terms of the Good. The ascending occurs by way of the standing, as "the firmer and more immovable one remains in the Good, the more he progresses in the course of virtue."[46] The good follows good rather than looking it in the face. Here Gregory teaches the notion of *epektasis*: to continuously pursue the divine is what it means to delight in the divine presence.

PSEUDO-DIONYSIUS OR DIONYSIUS THE AREOPAGITE (CA. 500)

Pseudo-Dionysius remains a mysterious figure and scholarship indicates that he was a Syrian monk. He regards the divine as ordering human and cosmic activities. There is an earthly hierarchy and celestial hierarchy, both of which are structured into tripartite systems, so that the pattern emerges of purgation, illumination, and perfection. He defines a hierarchy as "a sacred order, a state of understanding and an activity approximating as closely as possible to the divine."[47] The beauty of the divine in its simplicity and goodness remains untainted by dissimilarity and reaches out to grant beings a share in light, harmony, and peace. It also bestows form on those who set out on the path. What humans refer to and know as "the beatitude of God" would be something that is untainted by dissimilarity inasmuch as it it filled with "a continuous light."[48]

His cataphatic theology is dependent upon the use of reason, while in terms of apophatic theology, he discusses different ways of apprehension that exceed reason. The divine is, however, beyond assertions and denials, or the positive and negative ways, which is how his work, *The Mystical Theology*, comes to a close.[49] He employs paired opposites which are sometimes negated and sometimes affirmed. McGinn notes that such a use of language is reminiscent of the first and second hypotheses of the *Parmenides*.[50] Mark A. McIntosh describes the final stage for Dionysius to be a silence not void of all meaning, but silence that can be characterized as embrace, or union with God "who unspeakably comes forth from divine life in order to draw what is not divine into divinity."[51] Mystical theology accordingly becomes a matter of discerning a hidden presence, as the theological community proceeds beyond concepts and enters into a "supra-conceptual form of understanding, *relationship with the other*."[52]

The Divine Names is a cataphatic work insofar as Dionysius looks to the biblical text for revealed names of the divine, which are positive attributes that have to do with the divine as creator. He inserts, however, a negative theology into the work making the apophatic way superior in which all names of God and symbols of God are denied.[53] Dionysius, in *The Mystical Theology*, discusses the mystery surrounding the divine word which lies in a simple and "brilliant darkness of a hidden silence."[54] Moses is able to be liberated "from what sees and is seen," and plunges into a "mysterious darkness of unknowing."[55] There is a renouncing of anything that may be conceived by the mind. One here "knows beyond the mind by knowing nothing."[56] The more there is upward movement in the spiritual life, the more prevalent that words are limited to the notions that humans have the capacity to form. But in the plunge into the darkness beyond the intellect, it is discovered that beyond "running short on words" humans are rendered "speechless and unknowing."[57] As this argument rises, language falters such that the argument turns silent in its oneness with the divine as indescribable.[58] Dionysius, in depicting the movement and directionality of darkness, articulates the identity of word and silence.

Yannaras discusses, in conjunction with Dionysius, how apophaticism in the Greek East consists not only of negations but of affirmative natural knowledge and an abandonment of the claim to objectify truth in the employment of any conceptual designations. The semantics of knowledge (or conceptual designations) is a beginning point "for realization of an empirical *relationship* with the designated reality."[59] Further, the human capacity to approach reality through apprehension occurs through the coordination of many factors connected with each particular event of knowing including "sensation, understanding, judgement, imagination, abstraction, reduction, emotion, intuition, insight, etc."[60] When the human comes to the realization of such a relationship of knowing, "the many-sidedness" of the faculty of apprehension is preserved, in addition to the otherness of the respective approaches, as well as the freedom of approach, to the point of excluding any predetermination.[61] Further, apophaticism is the "active *abandonment* of the consolidation of knowledge in conceptual categories, [and it] leads to . . . a conferring of meaning on both the subject and the reality facing it, independent of . . . *a priori* necessity."[62]

It should be noted that Yannaras believes that Heidegger's nihilism insofar as it is "respect for the unrestricted limits of questioning" can be equated with apophatic abandonment in Dionysius, although they differ in terms of presuppositions and consequences that comprise the ontology of the person—the connecting of apophaticism to the existential notions of freedom and otherness.[63] Whereas natural knowledge with its conceptual certainty in the Areopagitical writings presupposes individual verification (and therefore individual doubt), and befits the human condition, apophatic knowledge of God is synonymous with personal communion and personal relationship.[64] Hence nature and knowledge are brought into a kind of harmony.[65]

BERNARD OF CLAIRVAUX (1090–1153)

Bernard of Clairvaux is a Cistercian abbot. As a monastic, Bernard follows *The Rule of St. Benedict* under which the community lives. Humans can begin to attain humility in this life.[66] The love that emerges is gradual and occurs in steps through relation with the Word as incarnate by bringing human experience into dynamic relation with the biblical text. Cultivation of the intellect is just as important as love in order to reach the goal of the spiritual life. There is a deep connection between love and contemplation in his texts. He writes with a certain amount of freedom as he draws from the foundational work of Origen. He tiers the biblical texts of Ecclesiastes, Proverbs, and the Song of Songs, the latter which he regards as contemplative discourse.[67] Likewise, he desires, as Origen does, to "advance by degrees."[68] He refers to these three stages or levels of growth in love as penitential insofar as sins are forgiven, grace-filled as a result of the good deeds that are performed, and finally, the contemplative gift.[69]

The kiss takes on a life of its own in Bernard's text, as it becomes a symbol of deeper interiorization of the spiritual life: The kiss as the "living, active word" is dynamic, probing the hearts of all those who open to its power.[70] The use of bodily imagery and the activity of the kiss in the text mirrors that of the Song of Songs.[71] The text, as interpreted by Bernard, serves as an affirmation of the human body as a vehicle, that is, having the capacity for the divine. The three types of kisses that symbolize the human relationship with the divine are "kissing the feet," "the kiss on the hand," and "the kiss of the mouth."[72] These kisses correspond to the practices of confession, devotion, and contemplation and signify deepening levels of participation in divine life. He depicts three stages of contemplation, whereby the divine becomes more present through love. Souls can, through spiritual marriage, give birth both by preaching the word, and by birthing spiritual insights by meditation, whereby the mind is enraptured by the Word.[73]

Bernard says that "Love exists in action [*actus*] and feeling [*affectus*]."[74] Ordered love, or the proper relation between love and knowledge, brings about right relation between contemplation and action. One of the forms of ordered love is that between active love of others and contemplative love of the divine—the latter of which is always considered higher—yet it must give way to action.[75] Contemplation, or what is primarily divine activity, and action, or what is primarily human activity, are correlated such that there is cooperation between them.[76] Finally, contemplative love is always for the sake of loving activity, as Bernard explains in relation to the biblical figures of Mary and Martha, for "as often as she falls away from contemplation she takes refuge in action, from which she will surely return to the former state as from an adjoining place, with greater intimacy, since these two . . . live together: for Martha is sister to Mary."[77]

BONAVENTURE (1217–1274)

Rigorous philosophical speculation and mysticism coincide in the work of Bonaventure. He adheres to a theory of exemplarism. He uses the structure of a journey of ascent to express the idea of growth in the spiritual life. Archetypes or exemplars are first and foremost in the divine mind, and therefore structure God's creation in the world. That is, they are principles of being. Here I want to develop the idea that by virtue of my human thinking (given the 2-in-1 structure), then for me it is thinking and being. There is a dialogical nature to thinking. It is solitary but not lonely because thinking is a dialogue I carry out in that it instantiates a 2-in-1 structure: When I am thinking I am unitary, because the dialogue with the ego and its activity, thinking, is its being. So when I am thinking I divide into two. To contextualize this notion, Plato said this insofar as he viewed thinking as a conversation of the soul with itself. Heidegger regards thinking as a thanking, which is what it is to engage in responsive thinking and therefore makes the move from *denken* to *danken*. Kant's ideas are a break from exemplarism and are ideas of pure reason and not in the divine mind. Absolute idealism recovers exemplarism as in the work of the German romantics, Novalis and Schelling. In Bonaventure's words, he explains that "These creatures, I say, are exemplars or rather exemplifications presented to souls still untrained and immersed in sensible things so that through sensible things which they see they will be carried over to intelligible things which they do not see. . . . ."[78] The divine is present in rational creatures through the powers and capacities of the human mind in memory, understanding, and will. Note the Augustinian thinking here. As eternal and present, the divine enters duration—what persists in time—"as if it were at one and the same time its center and circumference," that is, everywhere and nowhere.[79] As a sphere of intelligibility the divine is "within all things, but not enclosed; outside all things, but not excluded; above all things, but not aloof; below all things but not debased."[80]

Bonaventure divides the journey into stages, with the seventh and final level culminating in ecstatic rapture as he describes the source and summit of contemplation: "it now remains for our mind, by contemplating these things, to transcend and pass over not only this sense world but even itself."[81] What distinguishes this level from the other six levels is that affection has, in its entirety, passed into the divine.[82] He invokes the Song of Songs in his discussion of the importance of affective experience.[83] The first six levels of contemplation are a refinement of the three stages that represent the major kinds of religious consciousness. His treatise outlines three practices—meditation, prayer, and contemplation—that through integration, lead the mind through the three stages into the divine.[84] He says that the mind has "three principal perceptual orientations": (1) through sensuality it is oriented "toward external material objects," (2) through spirit it is oriented "within itself and into itself," and finally, (3) because it is oriented "above itself," it is "designated as mind."[85] I want to focus here on Bonaventure's thought. At the first and second levels, I can say that there is movement of subjectivity beginning with meditation on sensory experience. The first stage is perception, and is characterized by passivity, while the second stage is conception, and is characterized as activity. The contemplative practitioner looks to the divine to ascend; however, this is, in fact, accomplished "below" by means of discovering the divine in creation. At the second stage, there is introspective meditation or prayer whereby the divine is contemplated first through the natural power of reason by virtue of having been created in the divine image, and then by the working of grace deep within the human that reforms the image through intellectual illuminations as the spiritual capacities of memory, intellect, and will are exercised in the third and fourth levels.[86]

At the third stage, the mind is raised to the divine light of Truth, which is contemplated both in the fifth and sixth levels. Here, the human comes to understand two modes of contemplating divine light: By the Cherubim in the Book of Exodus, it is understood that there is first, "the unity of the divine essence" in considering the essential attributes of God and second, "the name of goodness," or "the Good" is proper and attributed to "the most blessed Trinity"—the tripersonal God.[87] The third stage is reason—ideas, archetypes of unity in difference of subject and object, percept and concept.

At this level, I can say that the thinking activity of searching for the concept that illuminates a percept ends in the perfect unity of the two. Activity comes to a rest, a *stasis*. This is contemplation. Hence I refer to these three stages as (1) sensing, (2) thinking, and (3) contemplation—intuition as a union of sensing and thinking.

TERESA OF AVILA (1515–1582)

Both Teresa of Avila and John of the Cross are important Carmelite figures of the Roman Catholic Reformation in Spain. While Teresa is the primary focus of this section, and John is the primary focus of the next section, where appropriate, they are both considered. Teresa enters the Monastery of the Incarnation in Avila in 1535, and eventually becomes its prioress in 1571. She lives a life of interior solitude despite the extensive travel and incessant communication required of her position. It is with great fervor and a sense of humor that she forges ahead to reform religious communities and establish religious foundations. Along the way, she meets John and convinces him to assist her. He eventually becomes chaplain and confessor at the Incarnation. Teresa is denounced to the Inquisition in 1575. In 1577, she writes her masterpiece, *The Interior Castle*.

She, too, builds upon the Song of Songs tradition with its bridal mysticism in her discussion of contemplation. Human capacities are intensified through the activity of becoming fully aware of the spiritual, or depth dimension of human life. Teresa says that there is an unfathomable depth to the human soul, which is spirit.[88] She writes with expansiveness and a sheer exuberance that takes the reader along on the journey traveling to what she calls the center of the soul where the divine dwells. She describes seven dwelling places: The first three dwelling places have to do with meditation. Then, beginning with the fourth dwelling place, there is a transition to contemplation as she distinguishes between spiritual consolations (*contentos*), which begin in the person and end in the divine (meditation), and spiritual delights (*gustos*), which originate in the divine, are freely given, and in which the person participates (contemplation).[89] The fifth, sixth, and seventh dwelling places are a progressive journey into deeper loving union with the divine, followed by spiritual espousal, and culminating in transforming union or spiritual marriage wherein one lives the beatitudes. She speaks to the marvelous capacity of the soul.[90] In the transforming love of the seventh dwelling place, there is the continual awareness of the presence of the divine.[91] One will enkindle and awaken in others a desire to grow in love of the divine as well.[92] The growth in love that occurs has an exterior correlative in the growth in love for others.

The distinction between contemplation and action is considered by many to be a false dichotomy in the tradition. Kieran Kavanaugh explains how in the writings of John and Teresa, "Action flows into contemplation and contemplation pours over into action."[93] John, whose principal source for the *Canticle* is the Book of the Song of Songs, writes that "the cavalry at the sight of the waters descended."[94] Through the use of poetic metaphor, he depicts the merger of contemplation and action. And Teresa describes how the flowing that she refers to as a spiritual marriage "is like what we have when a little stream enters the sea, there is no means of separating the two."[95] Thus, the smaller entity has become part of the larger, all-encompassing entity, and moreover, participates in the life of the larger entity to such an extent that there is no longer any sorting out and distinguishing between the two. She makes explicit what the purpose of this spiritual marriage is in that it is for "the birth always of good works, good works."[96] In the final analysis, contemplation and action are united and deeply integrated for this engaged, worldly person, as well as for her companion, John, to whom I now turn.

JOHN OF THE CROSS (1542–1591)

After making his profession to the Carmelite Order in 1564, John studies the philosophies and the arts, at a time when Italian art and poetry are being introduced into Spain. He enrolls in art courses for three years at the University of Salamanca. John becomes aware of the tradition whereby secular love poetry is taken and transformed into religious poetry. He thereupon studies theology for one year (1567–68) and is ordained a priest in 1568. It is during this time that he first meets Teresa. After serving for five years as confessor at the Incarnation, as previously mentioned, where Teresa is prioress, he is kidnapped and taken to Toledo where he is held in the monastery prison under harsh conditions. After nine months, he escapes. Some of his texts are composed when he is imprisoned.

John is an apophatic theologian in his approach to the practice of contemplative silence, but it is for the sake of life and light and love. His poem, *Dark Night*, and the two incomplete commentaries on the poem, entitled *The Ascent of Mount Carmel* and *The Dark Night* describe the work of the divine as the practitioner of contemplative silence moves from meditation to contemplation.[97] Dark night is considered contemplation, or the flow of divine love into the recipient.[98] Contemplation is knowledge in love.[99]

He employs lyrical poetry in his masterpiece, *The Spiritual Canticle* (poem and commentary), which falls squarely within the Song of Songs tradition. The text uses the bridal imagery of the Song of Songs tradition to describe the relationship with the divine, which culminates in this life with the spiritual marriage, wherein union in love with the divine, or transformation occurs.[100] The soul must learn how to love in order to progress to the spiritual marriage.[101] This important text, which is considered in Chapter 7 as well, mentions three ways that divine presence becomes known: "The first is ... presence by essence," whereby the divine is the ground providing humans with "life and being."[102] The second type of presence is by grace, which signifies the pleasure that the divine takes in the soul. The third type of presence is through spiritual affection, whereby one is refreshed and even gladdened. John's work is filled with lyrical passages in which he describes the flow of divine presence.[103] Ultimately, there is the possibility of unlimited growth for the soul, as whatever one knows of the divine can always be deepened because of the divine incomprehensibility. The theme of divine incomprehensibility can be traced back to Gregory of Nyssa and Pseudo-Dionysius.

Near the end of John's *Canticle*, in the stunning poetic commentary on Stanza 36, the soul rejoices over the love made manifest in contemplation and action, thus, indicating the intimate nature of the relation between the two.[104] He depicts an open, free flowing movement between the interior affective act of the will and exterior works performed in service of the Beloved, in what he calls a divine union.[105] There is a likeness of the soul to the divine beauty of the Beloved in the free flowing movement between contemplation and action. With captivating lyricism, John expresses in his writing his experience and his hope of the continuity of living in eternal beauty.[106] He attempts to lead the reader into a deep engagement with and affective experience of the words through his writings. He achieves this affectivity, in part, by conveying movement. He uses nouns and reduces the use of adverbs and adjectives. He simplifies the syntax, and frequently uses alliteration. The result is an experience of reading profound poetry, which can result in an opening of new places within a human being in much the same way that hearing the music of Mozart, Bach, or Beethoven can affect one.

THÉRÈSE OF LISIEUX (1873–1897)

Marie-Françoise-Thérèse Martin, in what is a very brief life, practices contemplative silence (along with three of her birth sisters), in the Carmelite monastery at Lisieux, France. *The Story of a Soul* is an autobiographical account of the contemplative life she lives there. The text eventually becomes a bestseller. She teaches the "little way" of spiritual childhood, or doing the ordinary daily tasks of life in love with absolute trust in the divine.[107] She makes her profession of vows at the age of seventeen in 1890. She emerges at the age of eighteen with a mature spirituality in which she refers to the divine as friend, spouse, and lover.[108]

On the one hand, Thérèse takes a positive approach to relation with the divine, which she learns from John's writings. Her way of love is founded on trust and confidence. She describes how love consumes what is displeasing to the divine.[109] She says that the divine "has . . . need . . . only of our love. . . ."[110] She also uses the metaphor of an elevator to convey the notion of being lifted up to the divine where she must, however, "remain *little* and become this more and more."[111] This passage is reminiscent once again of John as her notion of littleness can be compared to his notions of emptiness, nakedness, and spiritual poverty.

When Thérèse enters the Carmel at Lisieux, she does so in order to live a life of solitude, and to fulfill what she believes to be her vocation of love. She uses the word "desert" to describe this place, as she says that "I felt that Carmel was the *desert* where God wanted me to go also to hide myself."[112] This term refers to the work of Cassian who writes his *Conferences* and *Institutes* for those living in the monastery cloister, in part, so that ascetic wisdom from the desert abbas could be passed on from master to disciple, as well as to impart wisdom concerning the practice of contemplative silence.[113] She discusses the darkness and spiritual dereliction that she suffers during what is the last period of her life. Thérèse, by now, is well aware of John's description of the dark night wherein the divine is perceived to be absent. She depicts this state as the very thickest of darkness in what is struggle and torment for her. She finds it difficult to describe this state as she explains that the image she wants to present "of the darkness that obscures my soul is as imperfect as a sketch is to the model. . . ."[114] She is coming to grips with, in her own words, "a night still more profound, the night of nothingness."[115] Nevertheless, she discusses how she has continued to carry out good works, in spite of the intense darkness and feelings of abandonment and divine absence.

Thérèse is a fascinating figure in that immediately upon her death, she attracts a great following. While many people are drawn to her descriptions of her contemplative piety and the sweetness of her "little way" (she is fondly and popularly known as the Little Flower in the wake of European Romanticism), some reduce or dismiss her spirituality as being too ordinary and commonplace. And yet, she is a giant among modern literary contemplative religious figures, in that she expresses to the very end of her life the darkness that engrosses her without losing steadfast hope.

EDITH STEIN (1891–1942)

Edith Stein is the last figure to be considered who has Carmelite ties. Her initial higher education takes place at the University of Breslau for two years, from 1911–1913. While enrolled in a psychology seminar studying problems associated with the psychology of thought, she repeatedly comes across references to the work of Husserl.[116] She is given the second volume of his *Logische Untersuchungen* and reads it. She thereupon decides to pursue the study of phenomenology as "I was convinced even at that time that Husserl was *the* philosopher of our age."[117] Given what she learns of phenomenology, it thus far "fascinated me tremendously because it consisted precisely of such a labor of clarification and because, here, one forged one's own mental tools for the task at hand."[118]

She transfers to Göttingen and studies there during 1913–1914 under Husserl. Stein recounts the influence of Max Scheler, too, which transcends the subject area of philosophy.[119] She studies the philosophy of Theodor Lipps, which includes concepts in aesthetics, ethics, and social philosophy, as well as theory of knowledge, logic, and metaphysics. Stein writes, "For the first time, I encountered here what was to be, repeatedly, my experience . . . books were of no use to me at all until I had clarified the matter in question by my own effort. This excruciating struggle to attain clarity was waged unceasingly inside me, depriving me of rest day and night."[120] Her studies are interrupted by the outbreak of World War I, when she takes time off to tend to wounded soldiers. Eventually, she returns to her studies and earns her Ph.D. in 1916, from the University of Freiburg where Husserl now held a position.

She is received into the Roman Catholic Church in 1922. She teaches at a Dominican girls' high school and teachers' training institute, St. Magdalena's in Speyer. She also lectures extensively throughout Germany, Austria, and Switzerland for several years. In 1932, she holds a position as a lecturer at the German Institute for Scientific Pedagogy in Münster, although it is short-lived. Due to a Nazis decree that is issued in 1933, she is prevented from holding an academic position because of her Jewish roots. She enters the Carmel at Cologne and eventually receives her chosen name, Sr. Teresa Benedicta of the Cross at her acceptance ceremony as a novice in 1934, followed by first vows in 1935, and then final Profession of vows in 1938. Because of the growing threat in Germany, she later transfers to the Carmel at Echt where she continues her scholarship until she is taken into custody by the Nazis.

Stein is a philosopher, a philosophical theologian, and a philosophical hermeneut through and through, as well as a practitioner of contemplative silence in the Carmelite tradition.[121] In drawing from her variegated experience in *The Science of the Cross*, she expands upon and explicates the spiritual teachings of John, and in so doing, outlines a philosophical and theological anthropology of the human person who engages in contemplation. I begin here with her discussion of "night" as a symbol. "*Night*," she says, "is the necessary *cosmic expression* of St. John of the Cross's mystical worldview" in the original mutuality as well as the objective correspondence between *"cosmic"* and *"mystic night,"* as sensory knowledge reveals spiritual knowledge.[122] The *"cosmic night"* affects us in that what is harsh or glaring is now muted, and even soothed, with characteristic traits disclosed that do not appear in the light of day.[123] She believes that John is especially sensitive to the tonalities of the cosmic night from without as he spends many nights either gazing at the landscape through a window or outside. The *"mystical night"* produces effects interiorly in terms of "loneliness, desolation, and emptiness," hindering the functioning of faculties.[124]

There is, however, also a *"nocturnal light"* that discloses a fresh interior world of depth.[125] It illumines the external world from deep within so that what is outer is returned as completely transformed. The dark night is the contemplative journey which prepares one for union with the divine. In dark contemplation, the soul does not possess knowledge of its object, and is humbled through the surrender of the spiritual faculties of intellect, will, and memory (she notes an agreement with Augustine here).[126] In opening to the process of purification and renunciation, the old self dies and suffers in union with the divine. As this surrender continues, the divine infuses love and wisdom into the soul, or knowledge of the divine, as the will is conformed to the divine will. Hence, there is a union in likeness, with the soul becoming divine through participation. Stein's writings on divine union, based primarily on the teachings of John, are further explored in Chapter 5.

THOMAS MERTON (1915–1968)

Thomas Merton, the prolific writer and Trappist Cistercian monk, is the final figure to be considered as part of the line of religious practitioners of contemplative silence. His seminal work on contemplation, *New Seeds of Contemplation*, begins with asking the question, "What is contemplation?"[127] He asserts that contemplation is the very highest expression of the intellectual and spiritual life. Cognition and affectivity are brought together into a higher awareness of reality that is the source of life. Contemplation goes beyond everything that a human being is, even beyond natural understanding. It is the sole meaning of, and fullness of human existence. It is compatible with, the fulfillment of, and yet it transcends aesthetic intuition, art, poetry, philosophy, and speculative theology; it seems to supplant as well as deny all of them.

In the dark night of faith there is a passing from meditation or active mental prayer to contemplation. Contemplation is "a deeper and simpler intuitive form of receptivity" whereby one passively receives light with loving attention and awareness.[128] Prayer prepares the person "so that God's action may develop this 'faculty for the supernatural,' this capacity for inner illumination by faith and by the light of wisdom, in the loving contemplation of God."[129] Merton explains that "The unitive knowledge of God in love is not a knowledge of an object by a subject, but a far different and transcendent kind of knowledge in which the created 'self' that we are seems to disappear in God and to know him alone."[130] There is no longer knowledge of ourselves apart from knowledge of the divine. Contemplation is an awakening to a deeper state of consciousness.[131] In a letter, he remarks that contemplation has to do with penetrating one's own silence and advancing "into the solitude of your own heart, and risk[ing] the sharing of that solitude with the lonely other . . . then you will truly recover the light and the capacity to understand what is beyond words and beyond explanations because it is too close to be explained. . . ."[132]

The practice of contemplative silence brings one to an awareness of the contingent reality of human being as received. He also describes contemplation as a response to a call from the divine who does not have a voice and yet, who nevertheless speaks in the depths of human being. In the essay, "Is the Contemplative Life Finished?" Merton discusses how it is important in conjunction with the practice of contemplative silence to rethink aims, motives, as well as ends. However, he says "If our rethinking is valid it is also a re-living."[133] He says that one cannot simply think now and live later. Contemplation and action are deeply integrated in his approach to life. In his essay entitled "Is the World a Problem?" he speaks poignantly of the human condition and of his own humanity in light of his role as a citizen of the world: "That I should have been born in 1915, that I should be the contemporary of Auschwitz, Hiroshima, Viet Nam and the Watts riots are things about which I was not first consulted."[134] He continues, "Yet they are also events in which, whether I like it or not, I am deeply and personally involved."[135] He goes on to explain that the world is not an abstraction but is made up of a myriad of oppositional dyads such as loves and hates, fears and joys, hopes and greed, cruelty and kindness, and trust and suspicion. He believes that if war results because of the lack of trust between people, it is partly because of his own defensiveness, suspicion, and lack of trust.[136] Merton captures the essence of the relational struggle that plays out within self, and the interconnection of self, other, and world.

NOTES

1. For a contemporary account of the practice of contemplative silence, which includes a rich account of the Eastern Orthodox tradition as practiced at Mount Athos in Greece, see Christopher Merrill, *Things of the Hidden God: Journey to the Holy Mountain* (New York: Random House, 2005).

2. See Christos Yannaras, *On the Absence and Unknowability of God: Heidegger and the Areopagite*, ed. and intro. Andrew Louth, trans. Haralambos Ventis (London and New York: T&T Clark International Ltd., 2005), 60. He explains that "[t]he apophatic way or position presupposes the prior acceptance of the methods of philosophical epistemology—the acceptance, for instance, of both the way of affirmations and the way of denials—as potentialities for attaining knowledge. It is precisely the emphasis on the *possibility* of knowledge that sets apophaticism apart from any *positivism* about knowledge, that is to say, from any form of absolutizing of the rules or presuppositions needed for ascertaining the validity of any formulation of knowledge."

3. See Harvey D. Egan, s.v. "Affirmative Way," in *The New Dictionary of Catholic Spirituality*, ed. Michael Downey (Collegeville, MN: The Liturgical Press, 1993), 14–17.

4. Ibid.

5. Ibid.

6. See William H. Shannon, s.vv. "Contemplation, Contemplative Prayer," in *The New Dictionary of Catholic Spirituality*, 211.

7. See Harvey D. Egan, s.v. "Negative Way," in *The New Dictionary of Catholic Spirituality*, 700–4.

8. See William Franke, ed., *On What Cannot Be Said: Apophatic Discourses in Philosophy, Religion, Literature, and the Arts*, vol. 1, Classic Formulations (Notre Dame, IN: University of Notre Dame Press, 2007), 29.

9. Ibid., 31.

10. Ibid., 32.

11. William Johnston, ed., *The Cloud of Unknowing and The Book of Privy Counseling* (New York: Doubleday, 1973), 48.

12. Ibid., 50.

13. Ibid., 54.

14. Teresa of Avila, "The Book of Her Life," 2nd rev. ed., vol. 1, The Collected Works of St. Teresa of Avila, trans. Kieran Kavanaugh and Otilio Rodriguez (Washington, D.C.: ICS Publications, 1980), XXII.1 (hereafter Life). See also Edward Howells, *John of the Cross and Teresa of Avila: Mystical Knowing and Selfhood* (New York: The Crossroad Publishing Company, 2002) for a rich discussion of the epistemology and the anthropology of Teresa and John.

15. See Teresa of Avila, Life, XVI.1; XVII.4.

16. Teresa of Avila, "The Book of Her Foundations," vol. 3, The Collected Works of St. Teresa of Avila, trans. Kieran Kavanaugh and Otilio Rodriguez (Washington, D.C.: ICS Publications, 1985), V.8.

17. Ibid., V.16.

18. Ibid., V.11.

19. Ibid., V.15.

20. Teresa of Avila, "The Way of Perfection," vol. 2, The Collected Works of St. Teresa of Avila, trans., Kieran Kavanaugh and Otilio Rodriguez (Washington, D.C.: ICS Publications, 1980), XVII.6.

21. See ibid., "Meditations on the Song of Songs," VII.3.

22. See ibid., "The Interior Castle," VII.1.10 (hereafter IC).
23. Ibid., VII.2.9.
24. Ibid., VII.4.15.
25. See William H. Shannon, s.vv. "Contemplation, Contemplative Prayer," 209–10.
26. Ibid.
27. See Keith J. Egan, s.v. "Contemplation," in *The New Westminster Dictionary of Christian Spirituality*, ed. Philip Sheldrake (Louisville, KY: Westminster John Knox Press, 2005), 211–13. This entry is an excellent, succinct source that spans the history of the tradition of contemplation.
28. William H. Shannon, s.vv. "Contemplation, Contemplative Prayer," 210.
29. Ibid.
30. Bernard McGinn, *The Foundations of Mysticism: Origins to the Fifth Century*, vol. 1, The Presence of God: A History of Western Christian Mysticism (New York: The Crossroad Publishing Company, 1991), 108.
31. Ibid., 111.
32. Ibid., 116n147. Bernard McGinn uses and cites the phrase "theological poiesis" from the work of Patricia Cox.
33. Ibid., "The Prologue to the Commentary on the Song of Songs," 231.
34. Origen, "On First Principles," *An Exhortation to Martyrdom, Prayer and Selected Works*, The Classics of Western Spirituality, trans. and intro. Rowan A. Greer, pref. Hans Urs Von Balthasar (Mahwah, NJ: Paulist Press, 1979), 2.3.
35. Thomas D. McGonigle, svv. "Illumination, Illuminative Way," in *The New Dictionary of Catholic Spirituality*, 529–31.
36. Ibid.
37. William H. Shannon, svv. "Contemplation, Contemplative Prayer," 209–14.
38. McGinn, *The Foundations of Mysticism: Origins to the Fifth Century*, 121.
39. Origen, "Homily XXVII on Numbers," *An Exhortation to Martyrdom, Prayer and Selected Works*, 27.1
40. Ibid., 27.6
41. See Jeremy Driscoll, "*Apatheia* and Purity of Heart in Evagrius Ponticus," *Purity of Heart in Early Ascetic and Monastic Literature*, eds. Harriet A. Luckman and Linda Kulzer (Collegeville, MN: The Liturgical Press, 1999), 156. Driscoll comments how the enlarged heart is frequently referred to by Evagrius Ponticus: In addition to being purified, the heart is enlarged and lifted up as a result of receiving knowledge of many kinds in contemplation.
42. See Columba Stewart, "Introduction," *Purity of Heart in Early Ascetic and Monastic Literature*, 8. Stewart explains that there is "a textual archaeology of the traditions underlying [John] Cassian's choice of purity of heart as his premier definition of Christian and monastic perfection. Cassian borrows much of his teaching on this theme from his master, Evagrius Ponticus. Evagrius, however, had synthesized the theological, philosophical, and ascetical traditions under the Stoic label *apatheia* . . . rather than the biblical 'purity of heart.' Cassian's shift of terminology from *apatheia* to *puritas cordis* shows both a keen appreciation of biblically-based pedagogy and a recentering of Evagrius' understanding of Christian perfection. By using the phrase familiar from the Matthean beatitude, 'Blessed are the pure in heart, for they shall

see God' (Matt. 5:8), Cassian highlighted the interplay of moral worthiness, physical integrity, and psychological balance in the process of attaining Christian maturity."

43. See Keith J. Egan, s.vv. "Darkness, Dark Night," in *The New Dictionary of Catholic Spirituality*, 247–48. This entry is an excellent source for an overview of the theme of darkness in the Western mystical tradition. See also Gregory of Nyssa, *The Life of Moses*, The Classics of Western Spirituality, trans., intro., and notes Abraham J. Malherbe and Everett Ferguson (New York, Ramsey, Toronto: Paulist Press, 1978), II.252–54.

44. Gregory of Nyssa, *The Life of Moses*, II.219. See also II.227n309. The theme of the ladder comes from Plato and Plotinus.

45. Ibid., II.231. See also II.231n312.

46. Ibid., II.243.

47. Pseudo-Dionysius, "The Celestial Hierarchy," 3.1.

48. Ibid., 3.2.

49. See Denys Turner, *The Darkness of God: Negativity in Christian Mysticism* (Cambridge and New York: Cambridge University Press, 1995), 44–45. Turner explains that the language of "similarity" and "dissimilarity" fails of the divine according to Dionysius, "and that means that our language fails and is known to fail to an unutterable degree. This, then, is what Denys means when he says that the Cause of all is 'beyond assertion and denial.'" Furthermore, he comments "that what falls away are both our affirmations and our negations, whose inadequacy is demonstrated in the necessity of affirming both, in what I have called the characteristically apophatic 'self-subverting utterance,' the 'negation of the negation.' It is on the other side of both our affirmations and our denials that the silence of the transcendent is glimpsed, seen through the fissures opened up in our language by the dialectical strategy of self-subversion."

50. See McGinn, *The Foundations of Mysticism: Origins to the Fifth Century*, 176n228; 176n229. See also Pseudo-Dionysius, "The Mystical Theology," *The Complete Works*, The Classics of Western Spirituality, trans. Colm Luibheid with Paul Rorem, pref. Rene Roques, intro. Jaroslav Pelikan, Jean Leclercq, Karlfried Froehlich (New York and Mahwah, NJ: Paulist Press, 1987), 5 (hereafter MT), for examples of the *negation* of paired opposites in which he explains that "It is not . . . greatness or smallness, equality or inequality, similarity or dissimilarity. . . . It falls neither within the predicate of nonbeing nor of being." Finally, see Pseudo-Dionysius, "The Divine Names," *The Complete Works*, 9.1 (hereafter DN), for examples of the *affirmation* of paired opposites, as he explains that "Greatness and smallness, sameness and difference, similarity and dissimilarity, rest and motion—these are all titles applied to the Cause of everything. . . . His similarity is adverted to in the context of the fact that he is the subsistence of things similar and is responsible for this similarity of theirs. Yet he is also dissimilar to all in that 'there is none quite like him' . . . ."

51. Mark A. McIntosh, *Mystical Theology: The Integrity of Spirituality and Theology* (Malden, MA, and Oxford: Blackwell Publishers, Inc., 1998), 55.

52. Ibid., 56. For a provocative discussion of mystical theology, see also William Johnston, *Mystical Theology: The Science of Love* (Maryknoll, NY: Orbis Books, 1995).

53. Pseudo-Dionysius, DN, 7.3. See Bernard McGinn, ed., *The Essential Writings of Christian Mysticism* (New York: Random House Publishing Company, Inc., 2006), 283. See also McGinn, *The Foundations of Mysticism: Origins to the Fifth Century*, 159.

54. Pseudo-Dionysius, MT, 1.1.

55. Ibid., 1.3.

56. Ibid. See also Turner, *The Darkness of God: Negativity in Christian Mysticism*, 46. Turner comments "that such an unbalanced emphasis on union at the expense of the distinct identity of the soul can claim no support whatever in the dialectics of Denys' apophaticism. On the contrary, what those dialectics specifically show is that in the description of the soul's oneness with God we have no language, because that union transcends it, in which it would be possible to contrast the union of the lovers with their distinctness of identity. For the achievement of that union is possible only at the point where the mind has surpassed all discourse in which to state the contrast. Hence, if our language of distinction fails, so too has our language of union. Denys himself says precisely that, for in that union, all that the mind may conceive 'being renounced,' Moses does indeed 'belong completely to him who is beyond everything.' But here, not only Moses, but any person who climbs the same mountain of negation, is *'neither oneself nor someone else.'*"

57. Pseudo-Dionysius, MT, 3. See also Turner, *The Darkness of God: Negativity in Christian Mysticism*, 47. Turner explains that "Denys' 'cloud of unknowing' [is not] a vehicle for an anti-intellectualism, for a displacement of the role of intellect, at least ultimately, in favour of that of love in the making of the ecstatic union of the soul with God. Rather, in Denys, it is the immanent dialectic of knowing and unknowing *within* intellect which governs the pattern and steps of its own self-transcendence to a union, principally, of *vision*. Denys' is a mysticism which, as the psalmist puts it, 'seeks the face of God' (Ps. 24, 6), but under the condition imposed by Exodus: 'no one may see me and live' (Exod. 33, 20). That 'death' which is the condition of 'seeing' is Denys' 'cloud of unknowing': a death in an apophatic darkness which will rise in the knowing-unknowing vision of God."

58. Pseudo-Dionysius, MT, 3.

59. Yannaras, *On the Absence and Unknowability of God: Heidegger and the Areopagite*, 71.

60. Ibid.

61. Ibid.

62. Ibid., 71–72.

63. Ibid., 72.

64. Ibid., 91.

65. Ibid.

66. Benedict, *The Rule of St. Benedict*, ed. Timothy Fry (Collegeville, MN: The Liturgical Press, 1982), 7.7.

67. Bernard of Clairvaux, *On the Song of Songs I*, Cistercian Fathers Series 4, trans. Kilian Walsh, intro. M. Corneille Halflants (Kalamazoo, MI: Cistercian Publications, Inc., 1971), 1.2–3.

68. Ibid., 3.4.

69. Ibid., 4.1.
70. Ibid., 2.2.
71. See Song of Solomon 1:2,10,13,15, 2:6,14, 4:1–3,11, 5:2–3,5,14–15, 7:1–2,4 (NRSV).
72. Bernard of Clairvaux, *On the Song of Songs I*, 3.3.
73. Bernard of Clairvaux, *On the Song of Songs IV*, Cistercian Fathers Series 40, trans. Irene M. Edmonds, intro. Jean Leclercq (Kalamazoo, MI: Cistercian Publications, Inc., 1980), 85.13.
74. Bernard of Clairvaux, *On the Song of Songs III*, Cistercian Fathers Series 31, trans. Kilian Walsh and Irene M. Edmonds, intro. Emero Stiegman (Kalamazoo, MI: Cistercian Publications, Inc., 1979), 50.2.
75. See McGinn, *The Essential Writings of Christian Mysticism*, 525. McGinn explains that "Where Bernard advances beyond his sources is in rooting this teaching in his theology of charity, with its two forms of love of action and love of feeling based upon the Song of love. . . ."
76. Bernard of Clairvaux, *On the Song of Songs I*, 18.1. Bernard employs the terms "infusion" and "effusion" to denote contemplation and action. See also Bernard McGinn, *The Growth of Mysticism: Gregory the Great through the 12th Century*, vol. 2, The Presence of God: A History of Western Christian Mysticism (New York: The Crossroad Publishing Company, 1994), 221–22.
77. Bernard of Clairvaux, *On the Song of Songs III*, 51.2.
78. "Bonaventure, "The Soul's Journey into God," *The Soul's Journey into God, The Tree of Life, The Life of St. Francis*, The Classics of Western Spirituality, trans. and ed. Ewert Cousins, pref. Ignatius Brady (Mahwah, NJ: Paulist Press, 1978), 2.11.
79. Ibid., 5.8.
80. Ibid.
81. Ibid., 7.1.
82. See ibid., 7.3.
83. See ibid., 4.3. He cites verses 3:6; 6:10; and 8:5.
84. McGinn, *The Essential Writings of Christian Mysticism*, 151.
85. Bonaventure, "The Soul's Journey into God," 1.4.
86. See ibid., 3.1–7; 4.1–8.
87. Ibid., 5.1–2; 6.1.
88. Teresa of Avila, IC, VII.2.3.
89. Ibid., IV.1.4; IV.2.3; IV.2.4.
90. Ibid.
91. Ibid., VII.2.4.
92. Ibid., VII.4.14.
93. Kieran Kavanaugh, "Contemplation and the Stream of Consciousness," *Carmelite Prayer: A Tradition for the 21st Century*, ed. Keith J. Egan (New York and Mahwah, NJ: Paulist Press, 2003), 118.
94. See Kavanaugh, "Contemplation and the Stream of Consciousness," 118. See also John of the Cross, "The Spiritual Canticle B," *The Collected Works of St. John of the Cross*, trans. Kieran Kavanaugh and Otilio Rodriguez, rev. and intro. Kieran Kavanaugh (Washington, D.C.: ICS Publications, 1991), 40.5 (hereafter SC).

95. See Kavanaugh, "Contemplation and the Stream of Consciousness," 118. See also Teresa of Avila, IC, VII.2.4.

96. Ibid.

97. See Keith J. Egan, s.vv. "Darkness, Dark Night," 247–48. See also John of the Cross, "The Ascent of Mount Carmel," *The Collected Works of St. John of the Cross*, 2.13.2–4 (hereafter Ascent) and John of the Cross, "The Dark Night," *The Collected Works of St. John of the Cross*, 1.9.2–8 (hereafter DN).

98. See John of the Cross, Ascent, 1.2. See also Colin Thompson, *St. John of the Cross: Songs in the Night* (Washington, D.C.: The Catholic University of America Press, 2003), 187. Thompson notes the sense-spirit polarity that John of the Cross establishes and explains why he refers to the transition as "night." Thompson explains that "it is called night because of its point of origin: the soul must abandon her pleasure in worldly things, and this negation is night to the senses. It is also night because of the road which must be followed, faith, which is dark as night to the intellect. It is night too by virtue of its goal, God himself, who is a dark night to the soul in this life. The symbol therefore covers the whole journey, its human and divine aspects, from start to finish; . . ." Hence "night" refers to the purification of the senses and spirit as well as to union with the divine. In the end, recall that "night" in John of the Cross is always for the sake of greater life and light and love.

99. See John of the Cross, Ascent, 2.8.6. John refers to contemplation as that "by which the intellect has a higher knowledge of God." In this passage he also says that contemplation "is called mystical theology, meaning the secret wisdom of God. For this wisdom is secret to the very intellect that receives it."

100. John of the Cross, SC, 12.8; 1.1; 20; 21.1

101. Ibid., 14; 15.2; 18.1–8; 19.6; 20; 21.1–3; 27.8; 28.10.

102. Ibid., 11.3.

103. Ibid., 24.5; 24.7; 17.6; 26.7.

104. Ibid., 36.2–5. See also 36.4n2.

105. Ibid., 36.4.

106. Ibid., 36.5.

107. Keith J. Egan, "Thérèse of Lisieux, St. 1873–1897," in *Encyclopedia of Monasticism*, ed. William Johnston, vol. 2 (Chicago and London: Fitzroy Dearborn, 2000), 1268–70.

108. Thérèse of Lisieux, *Story of a Soul: The Autobiography of Saint Thérèse of Lisieux*, 3rd ed., trans. John Clarke (Washington, D.C.: ICS Publications, 1996), 179 (hereafter Story of a Soul). Thérèse explains, "Ah! how many lights have I not drawn from the works of our holy Father, St. John of the Cross! At the ages of seventeen and eighteen I had no other spiritual nourishment. . . ."

109. Ibid.

110. Ibid., 189. See also 194, as she exclaims "that LOVE COMPRISED ALL VOCATIONS, THAT LOVE WAS EVERYTHING, THAT IT EMBRACED ALL TIMES AND PLACES. . . . IN A WORD, THAT IT WAS ETERNAL!" She then cries out to the divine, "MY VOCATION IS LOVE!" Finally, see 195, as she remarks in relation to the divine that "love is repaid by love alone, and so I searched and I found the way to solace my heart by giving you Love for Love."

111. Ibid., 208.

112. Ibid., 58.

113. See John Cassian, "Ninth Conference: The First Conference of Abba Isaac: On Prayer," *The Conferences*, Ancient Christian Writers 57, trans. and annot. Boniface Ramsey (New York and Mahwah, NJ: Paulist Press, 1997), 323–63. See also John Cassian, *The Institutes*, Ancient Christian Writers 58, trans. and annot. Boniface Ramsey (New York and Mahwah, NJ: The Newman Press, 2000). Certain contemporary theologians have turned to spirituality and the practice of contemplative silence as a theological resource for thinking. For one such excellent source, see David Jasper, Chapter 3, "The Desert Fathers: Wanderings and Miracles," *The Sacred Desert: Religion, Literature, Art, and Culture* (Malden, MA and Oxford: Blackwell Publishing, 2004), 25–41.

114. Thérèse of Lisieux, Story of a Soul, 213.

115. Ibid.

116. Stein, Life, 217.

117. Ibid., 219.

118. Ibid., 222.

119. Ibid., 260.

120. Ibid., 277.

121. Ibid., 502n184.

122. Edith Stein, *The Science of the Cross*, vol. 6, The Collected Works of Edith Stein, trans. Josephine Koeppel (Washington, D.C.: ICS Publications, 2002), 41–42 (hereafter SC).

123. Ibid., 40.

124. Ibid., 41.

125. Ibid.

126. Ibid., 114–15; 121–22; 128.

127. Thomas Merton, *New Seeds of Contemplation* (New York: New Directions Books, 1961), 1.

128. Thomas Merton, *Contemplative Prayer*, intro. Thich Nhat Hanh (New York and London: Doubleday, 1996), 44. This text was also published as *The Climate of Monastic Prayer*, fwd. Douglas V. Steere (Spencer, MA: Cistercian Publications, 1969).

129. Ibid., 45.

130. Ibid., 75–76.

131. See William H. Shannon, Christine M. Bochen, and Patrick F. O'Connell, s.v. "Contemplation" in *The Thomas Merton Encyclopedia* (Maryknoll, NY: Orbis Books, 2002), 79–84. They cite the essay Merton wrote entitled "The Gift of Understanding," the source of which they have been unable to locate.

132. Lawrence S. Cunningham, ed., "A Letter on the Contemplative Life," *Thomas Merton: Spiritual Master: The Essential Writings*, fwd. Patrick Hart, pref. Anne E. Carr (New York and Mahwah, NJ: Paulist Press, 1992), 426–27; 421. Lawrence Cunningham explains that Merton received a request to help draft a letter on the contemplative life for the bishops' synod that was to be held in Rome in October, 1967,

and this was his response—"as such it is a letter within a letter." The letter is dated August 21, 1967, and it was written at the Abbey of Gethsemani.

133. Thomas Merton, "Is the Contemplative Life Finished?" *Contemplation in a World of Action*, fwd. Robert Coles (Notre Dame, IN: University of Notre Dame Press, 1998), 223.

134. Thomas Merton, "Is the World a Problem?" *Contemplation in a World of Action*, 143.

135. Ibid.

136. Ibid.

Chapter 5

Edith Stein and the Carmelite Tradition: Blazing a Prophetic Path in the Light of Love

This chapter completes the historical description of the practice of contemplative silence. Initially, I want to establish the context for situating Stein more deeply in the contemplative tradition by addressing the topic of Carmelite spirituality. Then the focus will shift to what she has in common with other Carmelites. The remainder of the chapter has a twofold purpose: First, spiritual union is addressed in the texts of Stein. This discussion privileges the work of John of the Cross. Second, the dynamics of contemplation and action are depicted as contemplative awareness becomes an operative force for good. There is ample evidence of this integrating movement of embodied awareness in her letters.

CARMELITE SPIRITUALITY

The Carmelite tradition, which takes its name from the mountain range of Mount Carmel, is considered to be a school of spirituality. It is also referred to as a "school of contemplative prayer."[1] The tradition dates back over eight hundred years, to around 1200 or so, when a small group of men formed a religious community near a spring, "the fountain of Elijah" at the canyon or wadi, "ain es-Shiah" on Mount Carmel, approximately three miles south of present day Haifa, Israel.[2] The original group formed a lay community of penitent hermits, somewhere between the years of 1206 and 1214, who were the recipients, from Albert, the Patriarch of Jerusalem, of a formula of life, which came to be known as the Rule of the Carmelites.[3] The formula of life prescribed for its adherents an ascetic life of simplicity, solitude, silence, attentiveness, and prayer in the spirit of the early desert fathers and mothers.

The hermits occupied individual cells that were situated close to a chapel dedicated to Mary. The biblical prophet, Elijah, who appears "in the northern kingdom of Israel in the ninth century BCE," was considered the first monk and model of the religious life *par excellence*, having lived on Mount Carmel for some sixteen years.[4] Soon, there were lay women who associated themselves with the men, though they remained at home even as they led a religious life.

Dating from 1238, the Carmelites left Mount Carmel for different parts of Europe, after having been in the area for a number of years.[5] Eremitic living in Europe was difficult. Eventually with papal approval from Innocent IV, the formula of life was transformed into its final form in 1247, when it officially became the Rule (*Regula*) of the Carmelites.[6] Hence these friars as mendicants could live now in towns, in addition to wilderness areas. By the end of the thirteenth century, the Carmelites had migrated to such places as Sicily, Cyprus, England, as well as southern France, and established themselves at major university centers such as Cambridge, Oxford, and Paris. The issuance of a papal Bull in 1452, *Cum Nulla*, would officially authorize the Carmelites to allow communities of women affiliates.

While Mary is not cited either in the Carmelite Rule or in the *Rubrica Prima* of the 1281 Constitutions, there are "early traces" of her in the history of the Order.[7] The 1294 Constitutions are the first to make reference to Mary as patroness, as it becomes a requirement that on the occasion of a formal inquiry concerning either the Order or the name of it that "Mary" be invoked.[8] At the time of the 1324 Constitutions, the *Rubrica Prima* discusses the dual Elijan and Marian origins of the Carmelite Order.[9] At the end of the fourteenth century, Felip Ribot, a provincial from Catalonia, tells the story of Carmel in a fresh way that draws together different strands in the Order—associated with the tradition of Elijah and Mary—and provides a foundational myth which brings together myriad themes as well as the values associated with them.[10] What eventually emerges is an early document of the tradition, *The Institution of the First Monks*, which is thought to have been circulating among the Carmelite order from 1390.[11] This document today is second only in importance to the Rule in terms of the evolution of Carmelite spirituality.[12] In many ways, "the *Institution* claims to be the history of the origin of the Carmelite Order. . . ."[13] The Marian and Elijan traditions are united in the *Institution* in that God reveals four mysteries to Elijah that are associated with the life of Mary. Devotion is to Mary as Patroness of the Order. This "synthesis" of traditions, in the end, provides two figures for Carmelite spirituality, both of whom witness to "a contemplative attentiveness and availability to God."[14] Elijah is portrayed as a "mediating human being" who changes his ways upon receiving a divine call.[15] Mary is prayerfully obedient in submitting her will to the divine will. The pattern of summons and response is part of the spirituality of the tradition. Stories such as those told about Elijah are paradigmatic for medieval Carmelites, for example, as they had mechanisms that allowed them to scrutinize their own ways.[16]

Solitude and community, or person in community, is the paradoxical hallmark and reality of Carmelite spirituality.[17] A Carmelite community is comprised of persons who come together in freedom and responsivity, and desire and love, to live their lives in conscious companionship with one another and in solidarity with humanity. The pursuit of intellectual activity and spiritual solitude and silence leads to an increasingly integrated life of the mind and spirit for many Carmelites.[18] A grounding in community life provides the basis for encounter with other persons and the divine. Solitude prepares the way for contemplation. This solitude "has always been for the sake of inner solitude, a habit of deep inner mindfulness of the presence of a loving God. Physical solitude is for the sake of solitude of the heart . . . for the sake of poverty of spirit, an emptiness to be filled by God's love."[19] Love and desire propel the Carmelite in the quest for self-knowledge and knowledge of God and are characteristic of that which lies at the heart of Carmelite spirituality. Whether it be living in an actual desert or attentiveness to living in the desert inscape of interiority, there is a preference for aridity of environment in order to pursue a divine-human love story—a relationship with a mystery that dwells at the center of human life. Listening and loving attentiveness to this mystery as well as a desire for simplicity and silence are essential in terms of exteriority as well as interiority.

What is other is meant to be pursued in relational encounter, whether it is the deepest self or the divine. In the *Institution*, it has been noted that "it is grammatically impossible to separate statements about the love of human beings for God from those that describe the love of God for human beings (1:7)."[20] The true self enters reality through self-knowledge, a notion that both Teresa of Avila and John of the Cross testify to in their writings.[21] Teresa and John are paradigmatic figures for expressing what constitutes authentic human personhood in that it is "a process of divinization, a participation in the knowing and loving of God."[22] They believe that graciousness exists at the center of life, an Otherness, which as a transcendent source nurtures and guarantees personhood inasmuch as a new identity issues forth. A person discovers that she has been named. Personality dysfunction results when life is not centered on the divine as a transcendent source. Divine love is healing and freeing for the person who waits in hope. The divine, although beyond name and image, is nevertheless pursued in a natural process through the world—a world that is full of words as well as images. Forms of spiritual life such as prayer, religious imagery, and sacramental ritual are central to Carmelite spirituality; nothing can take the place of God.[23] Some of the most renowned

Carmelite writers draw attention in their texts to the importance of the activity of God as experienced in contemplation.

Contemplative prayer is intended to be a spiritual discipline that liberates a person from any attachments and compulsions so that the world may be enjoyed without possessiveness.[24] Human effort has limits but divine life does not. Contemplative prayer is in service to the world. To pray is to have an awareness of the divine presence. Prayer and life cannot be separated. The contemplative orientation is a human journey within to discover the loving presence of God. No amount of human effort, however, can access the deepest part of the self that is divine. Without divine union, there is an inner depth to human life that remains inaccessible. To have a loving heart is to have a heart that has been freed so that it may love God and others; stillness and quiet are requisite. There is awareness and solidarity through prayer with those whose lives are endangered in any way. A Carmelite prays without ceasing.

Darkness manifests in spiritual life, whether it be through poverty of spirit, contemplation, or openness to divine transforming love. Carmelites listen to and accompany others on the spiritual journey such that they are encouraged to be themselves. That is, empathy is valued over issuing advice and admonishment. It is how one serves others that is important, which is to say one should serve lovingly. The quality of life in community indicates the authenticity with which one prays. It can be gleaned from John's writings, for example, that he esteems rather than judges the other members of his community, even on those occasions when he is treated unfairly. There is allegiance to the incarnate Word through the trials and tribulations of life. Finally, Carmelite spirituality entails a continuum between human and divine life—life on earth and life upon physical death. Contemplation is a way of learning to see this continuity.

STEIN AND THE CARMELITE TRADITION

Stein's texts provide a window into her position on a range of issues having to do with philosophy, theology, spirituality, formation of mind, education, and pedagogy. There is deep continuity in her thinking both prior to and following her long-anticipated entry into the Carmelite monastery. Her philosophical works on being, humanity, individuality, and community are all subjects that lend themselves to meditative reflection in academic circles as well as in religious community. Her letters provide especially rich insight into what she has in common with the Carmelite tradition. Moreover, it is evident from her letters that she is well on the path to becoming a Carmelite for many years before her entry.

She writes in a letter that she has learned that religion cannot be compartmentalized and on occasion spurned, but rather it should inform one's entire life, even the life of someone who chooses to engage in scholarly research.[25] She goes on to explain what a life of integrity entails and has clarity as to the purpose of living a contemplative life. Immediately prior to and for a time after she enters the church, she explains how she believed that in order to live a proper religious life, she had to forego any secular interests and be completely absorbed in thoughts having to do with the divine. Eventually, though, she says she reached the understanding that she was being challenged to maintain a deep relation with the world from her position in the middle of the world even as she pursued a contemplative lifestyle. In fact, she believes that the deeper one feels drawn into the divine, the more that that divine life requires one to engage with the world, and in so doing, that life is brought into the world.[26]

She is concerned with what is the real in life as illustrated in a letter in 1927 in which she responds to the academic work of Dr. Maria Brück whose dissertation she has just finished reading. She critiques the manuscript and explains that in the conclusion of the study, in the attempt to make understandable the real, she should go further and thinks it not extreme enough in its current iteration; she suggests moving this discussion to the beginning of the work, thus making it more prominent so that it can serve as the premise for the whole argument.[27] She further suggests that she is certain that if Brück continues to pursue systematic philosophy that she will soon understand the necessity to pursue a course of study that transcends it.[28] It is as if, in the letter, she is drawing from her own experience and mirroring the course that her own life is taking at the time, as she gives this advice. In fact, during the same year, in a letter written to another friend, the philosopher Roman Ingarden, she strongly asserts her position that while it is unnecessary to correctly prove religious experience by the time of death, what is necessary is that one should make a decision either for the divine or not, which is the wager that is demanded of a life of faith: The proper order is faith first and then understanding will follow rather than the reverse.[29]

A few years after having completed her doctorate, she had already informed Fritz Kaufmann, a member of her circle of fellow phenomenologists that she was working on an analysis of what constitutes the person.[30] And much later, on the eve of her entry into Carmel, to her good friend, the philosopher, Hedwig Conrad-Martius, she discusses how she has been holding lectures on philosophical anthropology for the semester and wants to pursue the problems she faces also from a theological perspective.[31] She expresses her interest in working with people in other academic areas of study in order to develop a pedagogy in the Catholic tradition and writes of the desire to discover common ground together.[32] During the summer semester of 1932, when she is initially appointed as a lecturer in Münster, she engages the concept of individuality for a series of public lectures she presents.[33] She explains that "There is a correspondence between the uniqueness of the individuality and the suitable activity to which she is called. . . ."[34] It should be the goal of education to develop that individuality and cultivate its uniqueness. What is particularly needed is for one to have faith and courage in one's own being, and the faith to follow an individual calling. If one is to help facilitate the development of individuality in others, then one must lead them to trust in divine providence and be ready to recognize its signs and follow them.[35]

While she had long been interested in living a formal religious life dating back to the time of her entrance into the church, the time she spends living with a Dominican community while teaching at Speyer serves also as preparation for entry into vowed contemplative life; she essentially lives as a member of the religious community during this period. Once she becomes a Carmelite nun, she continues to pursue the questions that had occupied her thought although they are pursued now from a theological perspective. In a letter to a nun from another religious order, she writes that Teresa of Avila understood a vocation to Carmel to be synonymous with a vocation to contemplative life: Stein writes, "I think there is more security in doing all one can to become an empty vessel for divine grace."[36] She also makes reference in the letter, within the context of writing about divine union, to "Our holy parents in the Order"—Teresa of Avila and John of the Cross—as this is how the members of the Carmelite community regard their spiritual teachers in the Order who have preceded them.[37] Stein is one of their spiritual daughters. She quotes a "Maxim" of Teresa in the same letter and refers to her as "our Holy Mother."[38] The spiritual masters of the tradition, as Teresa and John are, continue to form members of the community through spiritual reading and meditation on their life and texts.

For Stein, hagiographic writing is a meaningful, formative exercise and a way of appropriating the wisdom imparted by the saints of the tradition. She writes meditations, spiritual reflections, and poems, sometimes for special feast days in the liturgical church year. In addition, she pens pieces that deal with the history and spirituality of Carmel, and the spiritual significance of the liturgical and Eucharistic prayer of the church. Two writings, in particular, stand out in this regard: First, there is one on Teresa that is entitled "Love for Love: The Life and Works of St. Teresa of Jesus," and second, there is one on John entitled "Love of the Cross: Some Thoughts for the Feast of St. John of the Cross."[39] In the lengthy essay on Teresa, Stein methodically works through the different phases of Teresa's life and also treats of different aspects of interiority in the piety of a contemplative. She describes the practice of contemplative silence according to the stages or levels from Teresa's texts and sometimes comments on them. It is in this way that Stein appropriates her work as she is spiritually enriched and further formed in the contemplative life. She, in turn, provides spiritual guidance and reading material for the members of her community to reflect upon in the process.

Stein's meditation on John is a sign of her increasing interest in writing about his spiritual life and thought. Recall how she writes *The Science of the Cross* based on John's work, which is the focus below. In the other piece, she explores the foundation of identification for John, for all Carmelites, including herself, and for Christians, in general, as being in the burden of the Cross. She opens by proclaiming that all John desired to do was "to suffer and be despised," and states that "We want to know the reason for this love and suffering."[40] She goes on to write about the contemporary state of the world as she knows it, and discusses how when one sees with spiritual eyes, then one can understand how there are supernatural correlations of events that occur in the world. She concludes the piece by exhorting that "to laugh and cry with the children of this world and ceaselessly sing the praises of God with the choirs of angels—this is the life of the Christian until the morning of eternity breaks forth."[41] Union with the divine allows that one may suffer and yet, be happy through it all.[42]

She looks to the close study of John's texts, in the end, as a form of spiritual exercise and guidance for living out her contemplative vocation. She explicates his teachings and expands upon them such that they take on additional meaning. Once again, it is much like holding a mirror up to her spiritual life and thought. She lives out what ultimately becomes her formal vocational vows by placing her giftedness in the form of her heartfelt intellectual work at the service of the religious community, the larger church, and the world. In this way, Stein comes to deepen her roots in the Carmelite spiritual tradition. Her richest and most meaningful life experience, which is for her a living mysticism, becomes identified with, indeed, is one and the same as a life lived in conscious solidarity with humanity. For her, love of all humanity is based on the specificity of action and in this respect her thinking approaches rabbinical thought.

UNION

When seen through the eyes of faith, the nature and life course of a person are the work of God, so that it is God who calls a person to a particular vocation. In a scriptural sense, God calls people to be the *imago Dei* that they are created to be. Stein recounts the different ways that the human can receive this call. The divine speaks in the biblical text, the call is inscribed in the very nature of the human, history can serve to illuminate this matter, and finally, the times in which a human lives can advance an urgent message.[43]

She details the spiritual journey of union and the teachings of her spiritual father in *The Science of the Cross*. She personalizes John's theological anthropology by bringing the language of her philosophical anthropology to bear on his work and lends clarity and modernity to the interpolation of his text. She also presents the reader with an outline of the work. She is concerned with meaning at the outset of the study in the introduction which she entitles "Meaning of the Science of the Cross and the Essentials of its Origin."[44] She pursues the living truth of his life, and in so doing, pursues her own as well. She says that to speak of a science of the cross is not to talk about the usual meaning of science in terms of a theory and body of propositions. Neither is it to deal with a structure consisting of ideas with reasoned steps. She then interprets the meaning of the science that she proposes to address: She says she is dealing with living truth that is impressed upon the soul and which dictates what it does and does not do, and in its effulgence is recognized in the activity of what it chooses to do or omit. It is in this way that one can refer to "a science of the saints" and she is going to "speak of a science of the cross," which is both a living form and a strength in the inmost depths of a human being.[45] One's life perspective and image of God and world emerge from this center so that it is expressed "in a mode of thinking, in a theory."[46] Further, there is a development of the idea-image of the cross in both the life and thought of John. She refers to this integrated activity as *"Holy realism,"* as an inner receptivity in the soul original to itself that joyfully permits itself to not only be led but molded by the very thing that was received.[47]

After initially presenting the message of the cross, she sets out John's doctrine of the cross and the dark night of the senses. Active entrance into the night is described as a following of the cross, while the passive night is depicted as a crucifixion. The night of the spirit follows, which is comprised of the active night, the night of faith, described as the way to union, and the passive night marked by faith, dark contemplation, and detachment. The spirit can be understood to mean the intellect as well as the heart. She follows John's *Ascent of Mount Carmel*, in which he speaks of a higher form of meditation. Her philosophical training in phenomenology becomes apparent as she explains that a vibrant spirit engages its intellect to probe "the truths of faith," so that an interior dialogue proceeds in which all sides of thoughts are systematically investigated and intrinsic connections are discovered in the process.[48] The human spirit feels itself to be held by a superior power that enlightens it in such a way that it seems that it has altogether stopped its own activity and is now receiving instruction by means of divine revelation.[49] When the intellect and heart—knowledge and love—are thus integrated, then the spirit resembles that of two humans who have lived together for many years in an intimate and trusting relationship. They have no need to gather additional information concerning one another or further reflect on each other to reach mutual comprehension and a deeper love. Words are scarcely needed as new awakening and love increases as a spontaneous result of the relationship.[50] When this kind of relational dynamic is applied to the relationship with God, this is known as acquired contemplation insofar as the soul no longer has to engage in meditation to love and to know God. Prayer is peaceful, loving surrender in silence to the presence of God.[51] Without images and concepts, detached from powers, and living in unity and simplicity, life is at one and the same time not only love and knowledge, but remembrance as well, which she refers to as a threshold for the transformation that occurs in the night of the spirit—or mystical life.[52] Now, the main task is to resist what is not of God in the active night of the spirit.[53]

Stein asserts that a person who seeks after truth lives principally from the heart with an actively engaged intellect.[54] This person, rather than collecting knowledge for its own sake, perhaps lives closer to the divine as Truth and to its own inmost center than it is consciously aware of.[55] For both John and Stein, this is an experience both of yearning and suffering for the divine—ascent and descent—as the capacity for the divine grows so that the soul perceives the difference between a superior, spiritual part and a lower and sensory part.[56] She describes the soul in contemplation as being structured as a spirit such that there is opposition between what is internal and what is external.[57]

Spiritual life rises up out of the depths of the primal life of the unconscious: Rising movements known as "thoughts of the heart" (not thoughts in the usual sense), become something that can be interiorly perceived with the result being that spiritual faculties "split off" and form conceivable structures or active spiritual energies of thought (such as knowing and loving), of the movements of the mind, and the impulses of the will.[58] Whatever is allowed an entrance does so at a proper depth level. The created spirit who only wants to do the right action, has placed its will in the divine will. If such a spirit is uncertain as to whether it is a good action, then discernment is lacking and points to the fact that the deepest center is not yet open.[59]

Stein, for the most part, follows John as she describes indwelling as threefold: First, there is the indwelling "which sustains all things in existence," by which "God dwells substantially in all created things. . . ."[60] Second, there is "the indwelling of God in the soul through grace. . . ."[61] And third, there is "the transforming union through perfect love that divinizes the soul."[62] She follows John in that "between the second and third kinds, there is only a difference in degree."[63] She follows both John and Teresa in that the indwelling through grace "differs from the presence common to all creatures by which he maintains their existence."[64] Finally, she once again follows John in saying that the third indwelling of "the union of love differs from that [of the first indwelling] which sustains all things in existence."[65]

She refers to divine life as tripersonal life.[66] While only a small number of people perceptibly experience this reality, she explains that the larger number of people have enlightened faith and therefore, a living knowledge of the indwelling, and are in loving communion with the tripersonal God in faith alone.[67] Further, she explains that "faith is a dark night, but also . . . it is a *way*: the way . . . to union with God."[68] The way involves dying to the natural faculties of the senses and the intellect in order to reach the goal of supernatural transformation and thus learn what faith has to teach.

Her concern is primarily with the deepest indwelling that is personal life and which flows in only where the divine is freely admitted; John refers to this state as "transforming union through perfect love that divinizes the soul."[69] This "being-within-each-other" can only transpire in the interior being of one who is genuine.[70] In this indwelling, she says that "both sides must have an inner being, that is, a being that contains itself interiorly and can receive another being within itself" so that while "ceasing to be independent, a unity of being comes into existence."[71] A spiritual being is penetrated inasmuch as the capacity of the recipient allows. The divine meets the personal life of the other in this inmost region of the soul. When the mystical marriage is consummated, there is a complete interpenetration of the divine life. She sees light rather than darkness now, as the divine continually renews her, which enables her to return both love and light. The darkness is luminosity.

The soul in loving union judges no thing as bad. To love and serve the divine are the terms for this equality in friendship. Suffering is divine wisdom, as it purifies and gives more depth to the interior being, which results in a deeper knowing—the knowledge of which results in a purer, exalted joy as the knowing is from deeper within.[72] To derive benefit from everything that happens in life, one must come to realize that all persons are instruments. Certain objects carry both knowledge of the divine and an energy of encountering the other; however, one must learn how to listen in order to have a sense of the other. One will know that a spiritual transformation is occurring in this experience of relationship motivated by love, as the capacity to receive and give love freely, for the sake of God—the highest action one comes to—grows in human experience and is related to the search for truth as knowledge of reality grows. This act of knowing involves human freedom in the realm of the spirit and is a gift of the contemplative life. Mystical marriage entails union with the tripersonal God. She also discusses divine union in *Finite and Eternal Being*, and the importance of the soul who is summoned to be the image of the divine in a wholly personal way since the divine wills for the soul eternal participation in the tripersonal divine life—that is, eternal being.[73] In the final analysis, the human person must discover itself anew in terms of a dual sense in that "It must *learn to know* itself, and it must *come to be* what it is destined to be."[74]

CONTEMPLATION AND ACTION AS A SEAMLESS UNITY

There is textual evidence of the existence of the transformed, unitive consciousness, or the seamlessness of contemplation and action in Stein's writings. For example, in a meditation she discusses how spirits and hearts are to be free for the divine.[75] When a person lives in divine unity, she explains that whether one rests or engages in activity, is silent or speaking, everything is unified and one.[76] Moreover, throughout Stein's texts there are examples that illustrate a certain fluidity—a harmonious flow—of the integration of contemplation and action in her life and thought. She writes a letter from the Cologne Carmel and exclaims, "You just cannot believe how active our contemplative life is."[77] She expresses the unity of thought and action as she instructs in an essay that words should lead to action, otherwise, they are simply rhetorical and conceal empty or even illusory feelings or opinions.[78]

She also recounts in her autobiography how as a teen she first became aware of a hidden depth of mystery within her inasmuch as she claims she "could not act unless I had an inner compulsion to do so. My decisions arose out of a depth that was unknown even to myself. Once a matter was bathed in the full light of consciousness and had acquired a definite form in my thoughts, I was no longer to be deterred by anything; indeed I found it an intriguing kind of sport to overcome hindrances which were apparently insurmountable."[79] She understands this interiority in herself and others to be closed off to human understanding: What is innermost and most authentic about a human being, that is, what is understood as a depth principle is, in this life utterly dark and mysterious, even ineffable.[80] After all, she writes that what one thinks one understands concerning the soul is merely a "fleeting reflection" of what is God's secret, and lest one become discouraged and grow impatient about what is perceived, one must go about life having faith in a secret history and rely on that for strength.[81]

She applies what she knows of the contemplative vocation and communicates it to a group of working women as well who live according to a religious rule. She writes an instructional letter to them in 1932. She says that "What we can and must do is open ourselves. . . ."[82] The practice of contemplative silence has to do with rendering love, and enkindling love in others in daily life whatever one is doing and with whomever one is engaged.

Stein makes a distinction concerning the spiritual life, which is the genuine region of freedom. Free acts are ones in which the I can choose the content and direction to take in relation to its own being, and in having chosen that experiential content, then in that sense it can be said that it generates its own life. However, to generate my own life is not the same thing as being the creator of my own life: She says that "The I has *received* the freedom of self-determination as a gift."[83] The power of enduring is received, with each free act a response as well as a grasping of that which has been proffered. A free act has a distinguishing feature known as "self-engagement" [*Selbsteinsatz*], which is authentic personal life.[84] Spiritual life and free acts are based in matter that is at the disposal of the intellect and will in order that the human may be enlightened and formed.[85] This dark, mysterious ground in its bodily sentience is the foundation for the emergence of personal life in all of its integrity. The human spirit in freedom has to work to illumine the ground such that a more and more personal form is revealed through communication and disclosure. The personal I now moves around freely in the soul, at the center of personal life; this is the locus of sense and spirit. Grace, freedom, and nature work together so that one comes to know itself as one is known by the divine, which is a personal life of responsivity—of call and response.

I conclude this section by emphasizing three points that serve to reinforce the image of the practice of contemplative silence which I hope to convey in this study. First, there is an exceedingly rich textual tradition, comprised of biblical exegesis, commentary, sermons, prose, poetry, autobiography, and letters, through which the practice is passed down. The Song of Songs tradition lies at the heart of the textual tradition. The Song of Songs tradition is uniquely suited to accompany this practice, as it combines intellectual pursuit and the eliciting of affectivity, which are brought together through hermeneutical activity. In other words, language and silence and the creative art of being are brought together. Second, while the history presented occurs through a line of men and women who live out their lives primarily in the confines of the religious cloister, it becomes evident from what they have to say about the practice that cultivation of depth and meaning in human life is a life-giving capacity that human beings possess—that all humans have the capacity to bring about new life—whether it be to begin something new or to begin again as in start something over. Finally, they strive, while it is for the most part within the confines of the cloister to be sure, to integrate contemplation and action. They are aware that the practice is for the sake of the work of living an increasingly properly ordered life in right relation with others, however narrow or wide that circle may be. That is, there is an ordinariness about this practice, which is not necessarily meant to be esoteric, whereby daily life with its tasks, interaction, and communication can be lived with deeper value and meaning.

NOTES

1. See Keith J. Egan, "Carmel: A School of Prayer," *Contemplative Prayer: A Tradition for the 21st Century* (Mahwah, NJ: Paulist Press, 2003), 7–8.
2. See John Welch, *The Carmelite Way: An Ancient Path for Today's Pilgrim* (Mahwah, NJ: Paulist Press, 1996), 1; 6–7. See also Egan, "Carmel: A School of Prayer," 8. Finally, see Keith J. Egan, s.v. "Carmelite Spirituality," in *The New Dictionary of Catholic Spirituality*, 117–25.
3. Welch, 9.
4. See Jane Ackerman, *Elijah: Prophet of Carmel* (Washington, D.C.: ICS Publications, 2003), 1. See also Welch, 54–55.
5. Welch, 9.
6. Ibid., 10.
7. Ibid., 57.
8. Ibid.
9. Ibid.
10. Ibid., 51–52.
11. Ibid., 52. See also Ackerman, 141.
12. Welch, 52.
13. Ackerman, 144–45.
14. Welch, 58.
15. Ackerman, 177.
16. Ibid.
17. Keith J. Egan, "The Solitude of Carmelite Prayer," *Carmelite Prayer: A Tradition for the 21st Century*, 39.
18. Ibid., 59.
19. Ibid., 41.
20. Ackerman, 178.
21. Welch, 96.
22. Ibid.
23. Ibid., 98.
24. Ibid., 97.
25. Stein to Sr. Callista Kopf, OP, February 12, 1928, Letter 45, in SPL, 54.
26. Ibid.
27. Stein to Maria Brück, July 31, 1933, Letter 149, in SPL, 152.
28. Ibid.
29. Edith Stein, *Self-Portrait in Letters: Letters to Roman Ingarden*, vol. 12, The Collected Works of Edith Stein, trans. Hugh Candler Hunt, intro. Hanna-Barbara Gerl-Falkovitz, ed. and cmts. Maria Amata Neyer, notes prepared in collaboration with Eberhard Avé-Lallemant (Washington, D.C.: ICS Publications, 2014) (hereafter Letters to Roman Ingarden). Stein to Roman Ingarden, November 20, 1927, Letter 117, in Letters to Roman Ingarden, 263. She quotes Anselm of Canterbury here.
30. Stein to Fritz Kaufmann, March 10, 1918, Letter 21, in SPL, 23.
31. Stein to Hedwig Conrad-Martius, February 24, 1933, Letter 135, in SPL, 134.
32. Ibid., 135.

33. Stein, Woman, 201.
34. Ibid.
35. Ibid., 202.
36. Stein to Sr. Callista Kopf, OP, October 20, 1938, Letter 277, in SPL, 286.
37. Ibid.
38. Ibid.
39. See Edith Stein, *The Hidden Life: Essays, Meditations, Spiritual Texts*, vol. 4, The Collected Works of Edith Stein, trans. Waltraut Stein, ed. L. Gelber and Michael Linssen (Washington, D.C.: ICS Publications, 1992), (hereafter HL).
40. Ibid., 91.
41. Ibid., 93.
42. Ibid.
43. Stein, Woman, 60.
44. Stein, SC, 7.
45. Ibid., 9–10.
46. Ibid.
47. Ibid., 10–11.
48. Ibid., 116. See also John of the Cross, Ascent, 2.29ff.
49. Stein, SC, 116.
50. Ibid.
51. Ibid., 117.
52. Ibid., 118.
53. Ibid.
54. Ibid., 163.
55. Ibid.
56. Ibid., 143; 145; 151.
57. Ibid., 153.
58. Ibid., 158.
59. Ibid., 165.
60. Ibid., 171; 167.
61. Ibid., 167.
62. Ibid.
63. Ibid.
64. Ibid., 168.
65. Ibid., 171. Stein is making an important distinction here between Teresa and John, and follows John in that what Teresa experienced in the prayer of union differs in form from the indwelling that is common to creatures without exception.
66. Ibid., 169.
67. Ibid.
68. Ibid., 59; 46.
69. Ibid., 168–69.
70. Ibid.
71. Ibid.
72. Ibid., 267–68.
73. Stein, FEB, 504.

74. Ibid., 430.
75. Stein, HL, 100.
76. Ibid., 16.
77. Stein to Hedwig Dülberg, October 31, 1938, Letter 280, in SPL, 290.
78. Stein, Woman, 104.
79. Stein, Life, 152.
80. Stein, FEB, 505.
81. Stein to Sr. Maria Ernst, OCD, May 16, 1941, Letter 320, in SPL, 331.
82. Stein, Woman, 143.
83. Stein, FEB, 372.
84. Ibid.
85. Ibid.

Chapter 6

The Practice of Contemplative Silence as a Transformative Spiritual and Ethical Activity

I have shown how human being as intermedial being is intermediate between the finite and the infinite, and between discourse and silence. Spiritual joy is the hoped for gift of a life humbly dedicated to living in the truth. To live in truth entails both expressing what is the truth with love, as well as loving in a truthful way. The conceptual framework that spans the history of the tradition of Christianity provides a way to think about the progression of growth that occurs in the spiritual life. Contemplative reality is an intermedial way. Inasmuch as it is a spiritual itinerary, through conforming one's life to the threefold way there is a sought for congruence so that the content of life (as the means of spiritual transformation), and the form of life (as the end of spiritual transformation), may assume a growing dynamism. It is in this way that they come to more closely coincide and mirror each other such that the depth of being is disclosed. While many writers depict the threefold way in terms of a linear progression, it is also characterized in terms of a spiraling dynamic.

To begin to understand the transformation involved, a theme that will continue to be discussed throughout the remainder of the study, I identify and explain five levels of awareness ingredient in the phenomenon as potentialities—immediate, objective, reflective, reflexive, and contemplative awareness are presented. While at one level this explanation involves the creative arrangement of thought, at another level, what emerges, finally, is a contribution to an original development of the idea of a hermeneutics of contemplative silence. With the explanation of the practice of contemplative silence and the five levels of awareness in place, these aspects round out discussion of the capable human.

The heart of this chapter then lies in the task of adumbrating these five crucial levels of meaning-creating consciousness that are ingredient in the phenomenon of the practice of contemplative silence. I want to connect the intentionality and practice of contemplative silence to the heart of meaning in language. In this way, lived experience and language can be brought into a dynamism that gives expressive voice and clarity to the mode of being that is connected to contemplative silence. The mode of capable being of one who engages in the practice of contemplative silence, in all of its depth, is an exceedingly rich and intense form of consciousness in which the individual subject experiences a release in which she is reflexively aware of being with being, and is simultaneously aware of the reflexive awareness. Contemplative silence is practiced by persons who live a disciplined religious life not only in the cloistered settings of monasteries and convents, for example, but in the midst of ordinary, everyday life, as well. This mode of being is also highly sought after and valued as an aesthetic experience by writers and artists, and other creative and committed individuals from a variety of walks of life who inhabit many different settings. That is, in any place where the human search for the heart of meaning is carried out, it is possible that the practice of contemplative silence accompanies this search. Communities of discourse can be the locus of this practice, too. Persons who participate in such communities express contemplative silence in language whenever there is the spontaneous experience of shared understanding such that a complete and pervasive stillness is imparted and communicated. The first task is to engage in a brief analysis of the meaning of the practice of contemplative silence.

AN ANALYSIS OF THE MEANING OF THE PRACTICE OF CONTEMPLATIVE SILENCE

Recall how silence can be thought of as surrounding, suffusing, and permeating discourse. Recall, too, the three irreducible moments of silence—originating silence, pervasive silence, and terminating silence. Thus explained, silence can be defined as a kind of "break" or "cut" in discourse, or as a transition point in time. I also established that the locus of the practice of contemplative silence is within the third moment—that of terminating silence. Max Picard, in his elegantly written classic, *The World of Silence*, says that "Speech and silence belong together."[1] Further, he explains that "Words that merely come from other words can be hard and aggressive," lonely even.[2] Words require the spacing that silence gives in order that the full meaning can emerge in time. Commas indicate where a pause should be taken in the succession of words, so that meaning can shine through. Words need silence, and language and silence share in an intimate relationship. Silence also provides for language "a natural source of re-creation," which serves to refresh and purify it from the maliciousness that sometimes arises out of language.[3]

Finally, silence donates to word a depth dimension. Words not only rest in that depth, but there is an ongoing dynamic in that words flow out from and return to the great silence.

With regard to the word "contemplative," I need to ask "What qualification of silence is made by the adjective "contemplative?" In response, I can say that "contemplative" refers to the form of silence in which the depth of meaning is held in consciousness amid silence. Here I want to explore two additional definitions of the word as well. I want to set out a philosophical definition of the word according to Aristotle, and a religious definition according to Merton. Aristotle, in his *Nicomachean Ethics*, explains that the summit of a virtuous life is one that is characterized by *theōria*, i.e., contemplation, which is translated as "understanding."[4] He says that I "understand what is fine and divine, by being itself either divine or the most divine element in . . . [me]."[5] For Aristotle, intellectual life—the life of the mind—is the supreme element of human being. The activity of contemplation is supreme because it is engaged in for its own sake. Aspects usually attributed to blessed humans, such as unwearied activity, for example, are features of the activity of contemplation. Humans can live this life because of the presence of a divine element within.[6] Furthermore, to live contemplatively is to live a divine life rather than merely a human life. Cultivating the life of the mind is an opening to the divine, in the human being, for Aristotle. Finally, contemplation is constitutive of the human being. Moreover, contemplation is proper to its nature insofar as "for a human being the life in accord with . . . [contemplation] will be supremely best and most pleasant, if . . . [contemplation], more than anything else, is the human being."[7] If I follow Aristotle, contemplation constitutes the highest mode of being.

Next, I want to expand upon the initial discussion of Merton's thought in Chapter 4, in order to further define contemplation. Contemplation is, he says, "a sudden gift of awareness, an awakening to the Real within all that is real."[8] Further, it is the awareness of the contingent reality that characterizes human life as received. There is a theme of call and response in that humans are words who in responsivity answer and echo the divine in contemplation.[9] Contemplation is "awakening, enlightenment, and the amazing intuitive grasp by which love gains certitude of God's creative and dynamic intervention" in daily life.[10] Finally, contemplation is "a pure and a virginal knowledge, poor in concepts, poorer still in reasoning, but able, by its very poverty and purity, to follow the Word 'wherever [it] may go.'"[11] Merton makes a distinction between meditation as discursive, and contemplation as a simple letting go, and the quiet of resting in the presence of the divine as equivalent to intuition.

As a final task in this section, I want to define the word "practice." I follow Alasdair MacIntyre's definition of practice, which he explains as follows:

By a "practice" I am going to mean any coherent and complex form of socially established cooperative human activity through which goods internal to that form of activity are realized in the course of trying to achieve those standards of excellence which are appropriate to, and partially definitive of, that form of activity, with the result that human powers to achieve excellence, and human conceptions of the ends and goods involved, are systematically extended.[12]

I want to note that "practice," according to MacIntyre's definition, requires deliberation, choice, and a great degree of purposefulness. "Practice," so understood, is the means and end of spiritual transformation. Having defined the basic terms of this study, I move, now, to my discussion of the relation of word and silence within the Word. Recall that several of the terms below have already been introduced and defined. For the sake of coherence, they reappear in the discussion that follows.

THE DIALECTIC OF SILENCE AND LANGUAGE WITHIN THE WORD OR *LOGOS*

Animal life can be characterized as instinct and appetite. Human life can be characterized as animal life plus rationality, or *bios* plus *logos*, which is a struggle. Divine life is the perfected unity of *bios* and *logos*, or the incarnate *logos*. *Logos* is the capacity for rational thinking. *Logos* as abstract meaning in thought is dependent on language. The Greeks idealized *logos*. The tradition of Christianity negated the ideality and transcendence of *logos* to conceive of it as incarnate. Let me proceed by characterizing the relation of silence and language in three ways. First, there is silence prior to language. It is the undifferentiated Divine Word. Word comes out of primordial silence as the potentiality to speak and write, to listen and read. Humans have fallen out of primordial silence by having received the word. Silence prior to language can be referred to as *bios* or animal life, which is instinct and appetite. This level also corresponds to what I refer to in Chapter 3 as originating silence.

Second, there is silence within language. Recall that to think in language requires combining and separating the words in sentences with meaning. The sentence can be regarded as a primary unit of meaning. Because of the activity of combining and separating word-meanings in sentences, language is always punctuated by silence. "Word" means a sign (uttered or written) that carries a meaning (or many meanings). Language can be regarded as the medium of being, because being is the combining and separating. "Language" means a system of relations and rules governing words, plus a lexicon of word-meanings. Thinking is the sheer activity that includes knowing, understanding, imagining, remembering, and all other mental activities. Thinking activities, while dealing with the world of appearances, do not themselves appear. Thinking is a self-removal from the world of appearances into a world of thoughts. I am always conversing with myself in thinking. Thinking is a dialogue of the "I" with itself—an activity that displays the two-in-one structure of human being. Thinking is solitary but not lonely, because of the reflexivity of the thinking ego. Thinking presents sense-objects to the mind in their absence as sense-objects, but in the form of thought-objects, which are universals, concepts, ideas, etc. "Thought" means an abstract, invisible, spiritual, or ideal meaning held in the mind. To think a thought is soundless. Next, "*logos*" refers to the capacity for, and potentiality for, abstract thought; it is the capacity for reasoning, and it is also the resultant rationality. Silence within language can be referred to as *bios* mixed with *logos*, or human life (animal life plus rationality), or *bios* plus *logos*, and is characterized as a struggle. This level also corresponds to what I refer to in Chapter 3 as pervasive silence.

Third, there is silence following language. Language strives toward a postulated silence, which is the plenitude of meaning—a totality of meaning relative to past, present, and future. The silence beyond language is the Divine Word—the fully differentiated Divine Word, or the *Logos*. This silence beyond language, can be referred to as *Logos*, or Divine Life, and is the perfected unity of *bios* and *logos*, the incarnate *Logos*. This level corresponds to what I refer to in Chapter 3 as terminating silence, the locus wherein the practice of contemplative silence is grafted. Finally, I can say that in the silence prior to language, the one is everything. In the silence following language, everything is the one. In the silence within language, one and everything are mixed. Yet in the silence following language, there is nothing to talk about. Thinking ceases. Now that the fundamental terms and their relations are established, I shall proceed to the next step of the argument, and an ancient and yet contemporary example of the practice of contemplative silence.

AN ONTIC EXAMPLE OF THE PRACTICE OF CONTEMPLATIVE SILENCE

I turn now to the practice of contemplative silence to grasp it as the means and end of spiritual transformation. The seventh step of the argument is that human being fashioned a practice of contemplative silence as a transformative practice in order to open itself to and understand more fully the truth of redeeming grace in lived existence—that is, to always be able to look with ever fresh eyes to the world and see the world in a new way. An ontic example of the practice of contemplative silence illustrates how this is so. Human being discovers an infinite capacity to grow in spiritual and ethical maturity through attentive listening and responding to the Word. The practice of contemplative silence is one means or approach to redeeming the fallibility of human being. It is undertaken in a reflexive space of consciousness that involves a dialectic between silence and language within the Word, or *Logos*. With the practice of contemplative silence, there is the possibility that my awareness can be expanded such that I can reach a new understanding of the depth of my connection to all of reality. An empirical exemplification of the practice in the description below derives from a film.

A Still Life Moving Portrait

The film *Into Great Silence*, by Philip Gröning, is an artistic portrayal and a poetic depiction of the practice of contemplative silence. The setting is the apparently austere and magnificently majestic monastery, the Grande Chartreuse, ostensibly tucked away in time in the French Alps. Here, too, daily life is punctuated by periods of personal and communal prayer, reading and study, meals and manual labor, and solitary stillness. Becoming empty and listening are characteristic marks of the monk who prays unceasingly. A distinctive feature of Carthusian life is long periods of solitude spent in the individual cell. Solitary life is supported by the community as a whole. There are spaces that are designated as common, whether it be to receive new members or to care for the infirm. There is also communal activity in shorter increments of time spread throughout the day. Then, in the darkness of the night, the monks vacate their cells, and gather to sing the offices of Matins and Lauds, as the Night Office is prayed together in community. For two to three hours, a prayer ritual is performed consisting of psalms, songs, oration, lectures, and the deep silence of contemplation. Through prayer and song, life itself is transformed in and through the experience of this performance, a performance that plays to a full house—before the presence of the living God. The periods of deep silence are a way of growing closer to the divine. This ongoing practice is embodied in the quiet and steady, pulsating heart of the Carthusian.

The film is punctuated by close-up, still life frames of the individual monks' faces. In this way, each monk assumes the character of an icon. They are icons in living flesh and bone. One by one, as each monk gazes into the camera, I, in turn, gaze back penetrating the resplendent depths of their sparkling, dancing eyes, which mirror my own. I see the contours of their expressions and their facial features, all the lines and twitches that reveal as well as conceal their personalities, as I look for a sign—a sign that would point to and tell me who they really are. One monk explains that it is not signs that are to be questioned, but the monks themselves who are to be questioned. They could be mug shots for all I know, prisoners of time, shut up in a world in which time seemingly goes on forever, with the date of their eternal release known only to God . . . one day unfolds onto another in rhythmic progression, as they vow to live each day out, each monk in his own cell, in everlasting prayer and penitence—in perpetuity *ad infinitum*.

A crystal clear glass of water sitting atop the desk. Sun streaming, gleaming in the window. Sliced apples. A monk who is ill. A monk at the altar reminiscent of a bride at the altar. Flames from a fire. The flame of dawn—a new day. The sanctuary light.

The sun shimmering, glimmering through the window. The haircuts and close shaves. "Behold I have become human."[13] Cleaning—the mopping of the wood floor. The smoke of incense billowing out in the shape of clouds. A monk praying the rosary in the choir stall. The procession: Monstrance and Eucharist. Eucharistic Adoration. The pale blue sky with the puff and billow of gentle white clouds floating ethereally into the celestial realm. A monk praying before ringing the bells that call the community to prayer.

The frost that coats the plants. The still, soft snow. Praying in the cell and the creaking of wood. The monks praying prostrate in their choir stalls. The baguette and the bottled water—the scene filmed from behind as the monk sits at the window and eats. The bowl of fruit on the window sill, and the snow spilling over the rooftops outside—a scene through the window as seen through the window—the monks are letting themselves be found.

The sole of the shoe glued and repaired by the strong soul of a workman. The monks outside with snowshoes, walking and talking in the snow, two-by-two. Sledding and skiing. Winter. "No, why be afraid of death. It's the fate of all humans. One should have no fear of death. For us we find a Father. In God there is no past. Solely the present prevails. He eternally seeks our well-being. I often thank God [that I am blind]. . . . Everything that happens is God's will. God is infinitely good."[14]

Plants growing. Silence. Practicing chant with the small portable keyboard. Silence. The woods. Silence. The unadorned, unaffected monk in his cell praying incessantly, unceasingly. Silence. The posture of the body—the reverential bowing that punctuates the prayer. Silence. The monk who with his eyes shut bids welcome the darkness with prayer and utters the word to close his holy thoughts. Silence. A monk who puts his sandals on, and then looks up and smiles widely. Silence.

Birds flying. Airplanes flying. The mountains and fog. The repetition of the saw in the arm of the monk who cuts wood. Night prayer. The chanting of the Night Office. Chant and antiphonal prayer. The brilliant darkness. The twinkling stars. The dancing flame. The chanting of the *Treatise of St. Basil on the Holy Spirit*: "Reason demands that the singular is separated from the plural."[15] The monks in the choir stalls chanting. They ponder the analogy connected with the sunbeam, insofar as the Spirit is sent to each person, as if that person is the only one.

Bells ringing, calling the community to prayer. The dipping of fingers into the holy water font before going into the church to pray. Walking through the cloister. The monk reading. The monk kneeling, "What do you ask for? Grace. Out of love I ask . . . to be admitted to community life."[16] The desire for the desire . . . the desire for the word . . . the desire for silence . . . the practice of contemplative silence . . . the means and the end of being transformed . . . *Into Great Silence*: "Oh Lord you have seduced me and I was seduced."[17]

My aim shall be to set out the trajectory of philosophical thinking that undergirds each of the five contextual levels of awareness that I have designated. In order to understand this transformation, I must have knowledge of the five levels ingredient in the phenomenon itself. Then all the elements will be present to understand the meaning of capable human.

IMMEDIATE SELF-AWARENESS

The first level of awareness is immediate self-awareness. It is the direct experience of the self, of my being. I have awareness that I am here—the I to whom I ascribe actions. I have the awareness that it is I who am thinking when I think, or that it is I who am feeling when I feel. There is an immediate experience of my own being both in terms of what is, as present and manifest, and to what is, as absent or unmanifest. Immediate self-consciousness is the awareness of my seeing a tree, for example; and if I were not conscious of this, I could not ascribe to myself the seeing a tree—the immediate conviction that it is my seeing. Immediate self-consciousness is the necessary condition of all other acts of consciousness. In it, I am conscious of a modification. The "I" feels itself affected, and I sense my own condition. I have no warrant for the object at this point. There are no objects in immediate awareness. Thus, immediate self-consciousness is not yet objective consciousness; it is subjective consciousness. Feeling or mood enter into the discussion at this level, because I immediately feel "how I am" or "how it goes with me."

At the first level of awareness, being "is" and "is not." One way to think of "being is" in hermeneutical terms is being as what is in understanding its understanding. Heidegger probes the meaning of hermeneutics insofar as it has to do with the interpretation of existence. He makes a fundamental ontological move in *Being and Time* in that he shifts from the Kantian how one knows and critique, to discussion of the mode of being of the person, who, as being, understands the meaning of being. He puts in question the questioner. Understanding is a more primary term than knowing is. In the most elemental sense, understanding means to transfer the meaning expressed in signs, such as verbal, written, and gestural signs, into my mind. The test of understanding is to be able to articulate meaning in my own words. Interpretation is the secondary term, and it works by asking if there is any hidden meaning contained in the signs, that is, whether there may be something not immediately grasped in my mind that takes time to figure out.

Understanding can be considered as a thought-relation to the world. For example, there are three initial thought-relations in the statement, "The sky is blue." (1) I perceive in that I perceive concrete things and have the percept as object, as in the statement, "I perceive the sky." The subject term, "the sky," indicates that a particular something exists as an object of perception. (2) I conceive concepts in that "I conceive the sky as blue." The quality of blueness as designated by the nominative predicate is a universal one. Finally, (3) I understand the connection between percepts and concepts, and thus, render being. That is, I understand being. "Is," as manifestation of being, refers to the connection as well as to the activity of connecting the percept and concept, the particular and the universal, which is an act of being that correlates with understanding. Particulars are given to experience, while universals (such as ideas, concepts, rules, laws, and the like), are thought by the thinking ego; it is between the particular percept and the universal concept that being is. How does being appear? It appears in the medium that is between concept and percept, universal and particular—namely language. Hence being appears in language. When being comes to be apparent in the medium of language in terms of understanding the meaning of a sentence, being is then accessible to the mind.[18] The being could be a symbol, a schema, or an image of contemplation. Something has to occupy this role of a "temporal object" in Husserlian terms, in exactly his sense of object. Temporality, the combination of particularity and universality, and the combination of sensory givenness and abstract thought come together here. When I understand "is," I am understanding the connectedness of things in language. When I reflect, what I reflect on is language. I take up reflection itself at the third level of awareness.

The hope expressed in *Being and Time* was that if I can understand the meaning of being, then I might even be able to understand being itself.[19] Heidegger, however, could not finish the project. *Dasein's* being is care and the meaning of care is temporality. Because of temporality, Heidegger could not move any further with his analysis, and there is a kind of disappearing into the temporality of *Dasein* that occurs. What the human mind cannot think, however, language can sometimes give or donate. That is the notion behind his statement that thinking is a thanking. Heidegger wants to reverse thought from prior epistemological understanding in order to focus on the "being who understands," or an ontology of understanding.[20] Ricoeur points out that any such passing from understanding as a mode of knowledge to understanding as a mode of being must occur within language.[21] Consequently, Ricoeur advocates a long route through semantics and the theory of text, rather than the short route of Heidegger.

Stein expresses being in personal terms as "I am" and "I am not." Human being is immediate self-awareness insofar as there is a living ego; its own life is equated with its own being and that life is continually full of changing contents.[22] That is, life is fresh and wells up altogether new in every moment insofar as being is present.[23] In beginning with the ego, there is a spiritual process of continuous unfolding that opens onto the "Being-Person" [*Das menschliche Personsein*].[24] This unfolding is a temporal process that entails a self-disclosure in its vital activity so that eventually, in terms of the five different levels, there is an unfolding of some new meaning.[25] The God of the Jewish and Christian texts designates itself by the name "I am who I am"; she follows the Augustinian interpretation of the name as "being in person."[26] The human is sustained in its being from moment to moment, and in this limit experience of finitude, is opened to a more expansive meaning of being—the eternal meaning of being.[27] Finite being as temporal being cannot possess its being and has to receive it from moment to moment, while eternal being "must be its very act of existing."[28]

There is an "original naïve attitude of the subject" that is absorbed in human experience without making it an object of my attention or observation.[29] In her comparison of Husserlian phenomenology and Thomistic scholasticism, she states that "Immediacy applies . . . to the experience of our own existence."[30] She believes that Husserl does not deviate in his philosophy from "the intellectual processing of sensory data," whereby humans acquire natural knowledge as she follows Thomas Aquinas.[31] She writes that "All knowledge begins with the senses. . . ."[32] The joining of the percept and the concept in the "is" represents understanding in the human; the human comes to know by "the light of the understanding" as a requirement in order that I come to know my own existence.[33] She also explains that insofar as thought and understanding are correlated in the interpretive process, an empathized interpretation can be at odds with the primordial experience of my inner perception and thus prove to be a deception.[34]

It is important to establish an awareness of the "not" so that it is clear that the aim of this study is a hermeneutical project, and not an onto-theological program. One way to refer to this thinking in hermeneutical terms is of being as non-being in understanding being as not. Heidegger addresses the question of the nothing in regard to being. He refers to the nothing as non-being. The nothing is distinguished from the negative or negation, which is, in turn, an act of the intellect. He asserts "that the nothing is more originary than the 'not' and negation."[35] The ramifications of this thesis are that the act of negation on the part of the intellect, as well as the intellect itself, are in a dependent relationship with the nothing. The nothing is defined as "the complete negation of the totality of beings."[36]

It is in the mood of anxiety that I am brought face to face with the nothing. Heidegger says humans hover with nothing to hang on to in the anxiety which manifests the nothing. In the "clear night" of the nothing an original openness arises for humans in "that they are beings—and not nothing."[37] The meaning of *Dasein* has to do with being extended into what is nothing so that a manifestness of beings is made possible by the nothing. The nothing is an original belonging of the essential unfolding of beings: "In the being of beings the nihilation of the nothing occurs."[38] The nihilation of the nothing is the origin of the manifestation of the "not." The origin of the "not" does not occur through negation. Rather, the ground of negation lies in the "not" that emerges from the nihilation of the nothing. Further, being is not of a qualitative nature that can be brought forth in an objectified manner like an object. Being is completely "other than all beings," and "is that which is not."[39] The nothing is a deep-felt expanse that grants each being the justification to be. Paul Tillich refers to the experience of anxiety in this context as "the courage to be"—namely, the courage to affirm my own being in the face of the nothing revealed in anxiety.[40]

Stein, too, characterizes being as "not." She puts it this way: "My own being, as I know it and as I know myself in it, is null and void [*nichtig*]; I am not by myself . . . and by myself I am nothing; at every moment I find myself face to face with nothingness, and from moment to moment I must be endowed and re-endowed with being. And yet this empty existence that I am is *being*. . . ."[41] She writes a letter to her prioress in which she explains in a spiritual context that "I know that I am a nothing. . . ."[42] However, there is a fullness of being that she claims to be in contact with and rests secure in that knowledge. The duality of being and not-being reveals the notion of pure being in which there is no longer the admixture of the two so that it can be referred to as eternal and not temporal.[43] Further, since it is within the intellect itself that one encounters the ideas of eternal, temporal, and not-being, she concludes that she has discovered a legitimate departure point for a philosophy founded on natural reason as well as natural knowledge.[44]

Finally, I want to mention a retrospective comment Stein makes in her autobiography: She explains how she had been interested in the constitution of the human person in order "to show how the comprehension of mental associations differs from the simple perception of psychic conditions."[45] She thought this distinction an important one to make in terms of studying various topics having to do with the I, consciousness, psycho-physical dynamics of the individual, as well as the personality.[46]

IMMEDIATE OBJECTIVE AWARENESS

The second contextual level of awareness is immediate objective awareness. It involves the way in which I am already immersed in the world. It is the direct experience of being with being, of being with myself. I must discover my being-with being, and therefore come to know myself better. The way I am with things is that I am attuned through my mood. My surrender allows for encounter. My being-with is what makes it possible for others to encounter me. My body is the vehicle through which what I perceive appears, and I am therefore open to the world. Ricoeur explains in his philosophical anthropology that in the first place, I am aligned with and ordered to the world as the correlate to my existence; the world is a complement to my being real and my immediate self-awareness.

Being-with (*mitsein*) is the mood dimension of immediate objective awareness, which is the term Heidegger uses in *Being and Time* to explain how it is constitutive of *Dasein* and my being here and, at the same time, there in the world.[47] My authenticity in the world is at stake. This structure makes it possible for others to encounter me and must be interpreted if it is to continue to be existentially constitutive to my being in the world.[48] Showing genuine concern in being with another is to go out ahead of that other human being to give care back for the sake of other humans in order that those others are disclosed.[49] To know myself is to be grounded in a primordial understanding of being-with. Since concern, though, has to do with dwelling in modes that have to do with my deficiency, this essential knowing myself requires that I get to know myself better.[50]

Stein explains that "The being of persons having minds is essentially *living aware of self and directed to objects.*"[51] She concludes that there is no mind "to which no be-ing would be accessible, that is, to which nothing would be knowable."[52] The human being is constituted for coming to know itself so as to reach a deeper understanding of who it is. The human being also is disposed such that it is capable of being reached by the other and therefore constituted for encounter and relationship.

A relationship that is full of life and energy that is based on being-with is many times dependent upon exactly how much *Dasein* understands itself. It is dependent upon the extent to which my essential being with others has created transparence. My own way of being disappears entirely into the way other human beings are such that I am not my genuine self; I receive pleasure or satisfaction in the same way that other humans do and am inauthentic as I follow the crowd. I rely on others for judgments or decisions and am so dispersed in this world that I must discover myself anew.[53] I am reduced to objective presence.

As a human being, I have existential spatiality such that I am here and also there insofar as I encounter other human beings in the world and disclose spatiality; I am not closed.[54] This is a mode of being in that I am illuminated such that the shining of being as it is in itself as being in the world results in the disclosure of the meaning of truth (*aletheia*) through an openness. While truth as *aletheia* is discussed at the fourth level of awareness, what is important here to note is that the sustaining ground for truth as correspondence at the third level of awareness is herein established. Being emerges from hiddenness and is brought into presence by virtue of a mode of being—of being there through attunement and through understanding.[55]

It is to the idea of attunement to being through mood, the disclosure of how being appears, or being-with (*Befindlichkeit*), that I turn to determine the mood appropriate to the practice of contemplative silence, and the openness with which it is characterized. I am attuned and related to things in the world in a way that they matter according to mood.[56] I must allow a thing—even when I examine something in theoretical terms as that which is only objectively present—to show itself in *theōria* or contemplation and allow it to come to me and simply be with me.[57] Attunement entails a kind of surrender that has to do with encounter such that I am moved and affected in my very being. This attunement to my being through mood is a being-with insofar as there is a disclosure of how my being manifests as well as how I am. This being-with connects the I with whatever is the temporal object.

Stein, in her theory of empathy discusses general feelings and moods as "self-experiencing," and describes them in consciousness as being "visible as 'colorings' of giving acts."[58] They penetrate all levels and completely inundate the I. They are likened to the omnipresence of light. She discusses how "be-ing" is accessible to a finite mind: "A person's way of being is being-there-for-itself [*Für-sich-selbst-dasein*] and being-open-for-what-is-other [*Für-anderes-geöffnet-sein*].[59] A human being is therefore oriented to reality as through and for persons and disposed to a depth dimension of reality. I am present to myself, open to, and constituted for encounter with what is other.

The notion of letting be (*Gelassenheit*), as Heidegger uses it is also significant. He distinguishes between two kinds of thinking in a public address, calculative thinking, which involves computation and scattered thoughts, and meditative thinking, which has to do with contemplating the meaning in all that is.[60] Meaning (*Sinn*) comes to light in awareness or thinking remains open to what meaning there is. Meditative thinking begins with the field within which objects appear—the awareness of a field of awareness that provides given meaning to my thinking. I must learn to be with something in such a way that I bring the depth of my own thinking to bear. The "yes" and "no" to technology is referred to by Heidegger as a *"releasement toward things"* (*"die Gelassenheit zu den Dingen"*).[61] It is noted that the mystic,

Meister Eckhart, uses it in his writings in the sense of a letting go of the world so that one is free to give oneself over to the divine. Releasement as a distinguishing characteristic of the true nature of myself as a human being includes openness and does not fall within the realm of the will.[62] Releasement is very close to the meaning of contemplation, insofar as it is beyond the distinction between activity (thinking) and passivity (perceiving).

Meditative thinking involves an opening of a region in which I may express a resolve for truth that emerges out of inner necessity, which is bestowed as a gift to me as a human being. What it is that is required by me remains independent of me.[63] Heidegger is not, therefore, speaking about making my own subjective truth here. That is, human nature as thinking does not create or impose structure, but rather receives the movement involved in the disclosure or unveiling.[64] Thought opens in turning itself to whatever is given; and what is given approaches the demand of thought that what this is be articulated, and thus become true. Hence this turning toward and opening to the given actually sets whatever is given at a distance, because it is the movement which distinguishes and thus sets thinking apart from the given meaning. Meditative thinking can therefore be thought of in terms of nearness and distance. This movement takes what is given and veiled and makes it into what is unveiled as well as expressed. This movement is characterized as Being. I am now in the middle of the ultimate as I have gone beyond what is subjective—that which is my human perspective.

The way in which I approach thinking is of paramount importance. Chauvet, in his interpretation of Heidegger's work, explains this way as one in which "thinkers learn to serenely acquiesce," a process of "learning to 'let go,'" or *Gelassenheit*, as Heidegger employs the idea.[65] Chauvet says that if I attempt to overcome metaphysics by jumping outside of it I will naïvely repeat it. The task can only progress insofar as there is a stepping backwards on the part of a thinker from the received tradition. There must be a demystification of metaphysical presuppositions.[66] The thinker cannot entertain the prospect of attaining some ultimate foundation. In reversing the direction of thought, the thinker sets off in a new direction in order to begin from what is an uncomfortable non-place whereby the activity of permanent questioning is carried on.[67] The human being is an ecstatic breach and an emptiness that enables humans to reach their truth, which they do by overcoming the barriers of reason having to do with objectifying and calculating activity.[68] I must be attentive in my thinking to the way being is. I am always on the way when I think; this is what it means to think. It is the "way making its way," insofar as there is the speaking way.[69] In echoing Heidegger, he says "what is at stake is to think the truth about being," by way of being.[70] I overcome metaphysics in being always underway, on the way, or on the path toward language.

Language is, primarily, a summons or vocation for me. Rather than my possessing it, I am possessed by language. The saying of language in its primordiality is the coming forth and emergence of being. The way in which I am in my being with being has ethical implications because it includes my relationship to language. The human project is one of learning how to speak well, in the way of letting myself be spoken such that I can express a silence that is appropriate. The appropriation of Being takes place through disappropriation—letting be.[71]

Finally, I want to mention that Simone Weil, in an essay, addresses the notion of attention within the context of studious endeavors, which are understood as preparatory for the kind of attentiveness, waiting, and openness that are characteristic of the second level of awareness. A certain receptivity is essential. She says that "Attention is . . . the greatest of all efforts. . . ."[72] Moreover, the way in which attention works is that I suspend my thought, and detach from it so that I am empty: "it means holding in our minds, within reach of this thought, but on a lower level and not in contact with it, the diverse knowledge we have acquired. . . ."[73] The notion of attention is connected to waiting in that "We do not obtain the most precious gifts by going in search of them but by waiting for them."[74] Weil belongs in this line of gratuitous thought and accentuates the importance of receptivity and patience before the mystery of existence.

REFLECTIVE AWARENESS

At the reflective level of awareness and given the critical thinking that accompanies it, I am aware of objects in the world. Language is the first object that I reflect on. When joining together the concept with the percept, a judgment is produced. Being has to do with understanding and ascertaining the sense in the sign. The sign is twofold. It is the combination of words in a proposition, for example, "This tree is old." When the proposition is understood, I see what sense is in it; and I therefore see being itself as meaning. Second, the sign can be regarded as an appearing object, as when I understand an object, I am ascertaining a connection between what is singular and what is universal ("being as reality"), which is signified in terms of its appearance to the mind.[75] It is this appearance that finds expression in a judgment. The meaning of a judgment can be detected or denied.

Through the process of understanding a proposition, being becomes open and accessible to the mind. The question of truth arises at the third level of awareness, insofar as I can ask if there is correspondence between how truth manifests in meaning and how truth manifests in reality. Being appears in the form of a judgment in language as well as in the world as reality in the connectedness of the universal and the particular. Whereas interpretation strives at clarity of meaning, verification involves making a determination of the truth of what is said. With reflective awareness and the concomitant critical thinking that accompanies it, truth lies in the correspondence between the thought itself and the percept, with the locus of this reflection lying in the judgment that issues forth.

Reflection, or "the self's relating itself to its relation-to" allows me to distinguish between an entity that is a referent in an assertion and an entity as a bearer of essence.[76] In order to make the judgment, "This is a rose," I must add two categories: (1) substance, which is a concept of identity through time, in that the rose is an independent entity, and (2) causality, inasmuch as the rose is a causal nexus and affects other things, and the rose also affects me. The rose also has a cause—something brought it about. These two concepts, substance and causality, are universals in the form of categories as *a priori* concepts. The concept of a rose is an empirical concept. Empirical concepts have no necessity because the objects to which they refer—in this example, a rose—is not necessary because I can imagine a world or a garden without a rose. The empirical judgment is either true or false. I enumerate properties, and if there is correspondence between the empirical concept and the percept, then the statement is true. I can say that there is correspondence between what is said—"This is a rose"—and that it is so.

An object (an acorn as just an acorn, for example) and a symbol (an acorn as the very essence of what an oak tree is) can be distinguished by reflection. An assertion has an object as the referent. The object is what the assertion is about. The object inasmuch as it synthesizes elements that are perceptual as well as cognizable, indicates being as appearing in a specific place, and as indicating an essence; this object is the referent of an assertion and the signifier of yet another referent, as an essence that is embodied there.[77] The essence can be considered as a second referent, and paraphrased in terms of a capacity, which is the meaning that is the being of a thing.

The verification of the assertion about the symbol is different than that of the assertion in regard to an object. In the assertion concerning the symbol, "A tree is this," the thing as a symbol reveals essence. In showing essence, rather than it saying that "This is what is meant by the word or idea 'tree,'" it says, "There I can see what it means for a tree to be a tree at all."[78] The thing as symbol works as the sign that carries the meaning, which in turn indicates the being as the very essence of the thing. Robert P. Scharlemann explains that "To see that the *meaning of an assertion* is the same as the reality of an object is to experience truth upon that object; to see that the *meaning of an object* is the same as the reality of the object (though meaning is distinct from reality) is to experience truth upon a symbol."[79]

The Practice of Contemplative Silence 129

Stein reflects on language and the cognitive value of feeling as it reveals something to her—and to all other human beings as well—who have inimitable access to the fundamental experience of their own immediate self-awareness; this is a spiritual act or conscious perception that can attract the heart.[80] She explains that "If we . . . feel our own essence or nature as well as the essences or natures of others to be thus constituted, and if we feel this 'thus' . . . to be something 'unique,' . . . with the contention of the uniqueness of this 'thus,' we have transcended the frame of an individual experience and have ventured to pronounce a sentence that lays claim to universal validity."[81] Given the distinctiveness of "thus," "we" have gone beyond the structure of the individual experience of a human being and have undertaken to declare a sentence than can be attested to by all, that is, universally. She discusses the meaning of such a pronouncement: The meaning of the proposition is that there are no other human beings that thus compare with this one. This can be explained by the proper make-up of a human being: in the distinctiveness of who the I is as self-aware and who accepts this singularity—that is, one who is different from another human being due to the experiential content in its stream of consciousness—"as its 'very own'" and attributes to all other I's "the same uniqueness and individual *particularity* [*Eigenheit*]."[82] The experiential content that is contained in the thus cannot be perceived and voiced universally. While all humans have in common that they have their own feeling of primordial experience or immediate self-awareness by virtue of being human, the actual content as living experience cannot be directly accessed by anyone else; however, its meaning can be expressed and communicated. Recall how this is an important aspect of Ricoeur's interpretation theory. Her work on empathy and the notion of the appresentation of the other in Husserl's work are evident here. She takes up the mediating function of language dating back to her early theory of empathy. She explains that with foreign experience the communication (of words) expresses something objective and externalizes or announces the meaningful act of the person, in addition to the experience behind the act, which includes perception.[83] The message is communicable in the structure of its meaning. In the end, she moves between percept and thought and then issues a judgment about the "thus" in her reflection. Truth lies in the correspondence between the percept in experience and the thought itself, and between the thought and understanding in terms of hermeneutical inquiry. She accounts for and maintains the connection between uniqueness and individual particularity, on the one hand, and universality, on the other hand, by philosophical reflection on language and experience.

Stein also provides the standard explanation for understanding the issuing of a judgment in language, as was initially discussed in this section. She explains how truth is arrived at in issuing a judgment. She uses the example of the statement, "The rose is red," which is the truth she considers.[84] When

I perceive a rose I grasp it under the concept, or what is the general idea of the rose. It is also perceived as "this" in the sentence and is the subject of the sentence. The process of understanding includes both analytic and synthetic acts. A judgment is issued using the linguistic expression "is" in the statement expressing what is the case in reality.

Finally, she poses the question, What is truth? and in so doing, distinguishes between an infinite Mind and a finite mind. With the absolute, infinite Mind, knowing and knowledge come together and are one, as are being and truth.[85] That is why, she explains, that "the *Logos* [Word] can say 'I am the truth.'"[86] For a finite mind who knows, however, the truth that is reached comes as a result of what is the process of knowing.[87] The process of issuing forth judgments in language is a temporal one, which leads to the next level of awareness.

REFLEXIVE AWARENESS

Temporality is added to truth at the fourth level of awareness. Reflexive awareness has to do with the truth about truth, or reflection on the event of being in truth. Truth has to do with disclosure rather than correspondence in that the awareness of time is brought to this level. In considering the truth about truth, the temporality of being emerges as an event; being is not simply the awareness of being and the appearing of being. Being has a temporal structure in appearing. For Stein, there is a temporal process of knowing for the finite mind who approaches truth in an incremental, infinite process as an ideal goal that can never be reached.[88] Human being can be thought of as a "carrier" of an originality as there is a fullness that one carries and simultaneously one is carried by a deep ground.[89] Because humans are suspended between being and not-being, there is an existential movement in which time is created as space; I experience time as present.[90] The intellect functions in its being as it understands the understandable.[91] Understanding and meaning go together. Meaning is what is understood; understanding involves grasping the meaning. There is a rational process about the understanding as it seeks to investigate "semantic associations" as well as "contexts [*Sinnzusammenhänge*]."[92]

Although humans have no access to immediacy in that it is systematically elusive, the thinking "I" or consciousness itself is immediate. When I reflect on reflecting or think about thinking, which is reflexivity, I have the memory of the event of pain or of joy, for example. When the memory subsides and diminishes into the horizon, I lose the immediacy of the situation that initially generated the pain or the joy, and I thus no longer feel its extent. However, the pain or joy is still registering in time-consciousness, which means that I still have it, albeit in a diminutive form. I can, through the experience of the past, anticipate new experiences of pain or joy. My memory and imagination, and the oscillation between the two, assist me in spanning the gap, and bring me up to the door of immediacy. I have awareness of the one or the other, and an awareness of being neither and I am aware of this awareness. With the event, there is an irreducibility about the subject-object relation.

The symbol, too, can have a reflexive character about it. I can say that the certitude of truth "is the truth that no one possesses the truth."[93] There is a self-relativization entailed here which has to do with an experience that I have of truth that is characterized as both the experience of truth and the experience that places truth in connection with what is its opposite. The truth about truth of the symbol is that a depth can be experienced in that it allows an experience of what is true, as well as what is false. Reflexive awareness therefore sees that reflection carries the capability of being able to see the true as well as the false.[94]

Reflexive awareness is concerned with the truth about truth which is an event insofar as there is an announcement of the meaning of being, and the announcement of being itself. Stein's way of expressing the truth about truth is through an explanation of that which is finite as having two meanings. The first meaning was discussed above insofar as temporal being requires time to achieve being with its being received in the existential movement of the continuous "flashing up" of actuality.[95] The temporal object has a meaning, which is namely a meaning of being. Its meaning reciprocally determines the meaning of my being, and it therefore discloses a mode of being. The second meaning of finite being is that it is something and yet not everything; eternal being corresponds to finite being in that it consists of and is everything with meaning and life entirely one only in the divine.[96] Reflexive thinking takes on spiritual import for her in that when one lives a life filled with meaning its being has a form that is "spiritual [*geistig*]."[97] In a cycle of lectures she emphasizes the importance of proper intellectual training and critique. It is not sufficient to rely merely on the opinion of others when, for example, discussing aesthetics: intellectual critique is essential in the ability to ascertain for oneself why something is good, true, or beautiful so that one develops an ability to distinguish between spiritual truth and spiritual falsehood.[98]

Heidegger develops the mode of being of a work of art, and that of poetic language. First, in the mode of being of a work of art, the opening up of a world and a disclosure of truth are made.[99] This mode of being is religious because it shows me a living universe to which I respond. Heidegger discusses how in the artwork itself, that of a pair of peasant shoes in the painting by Vincent van Gogh, I am gathered into the truth of the life of the shoes.[100] The peasant shoes disclose the way in which they belong to the earth, as well as project the world of the person who wears them, although I cannot learn of everything of that world. Hence it is in this way that I can speak of what is revealed as concealed; this is an originary event. The earthly quality of the earth and the depth of the work quality of work, in its revealing and concealing in the painting, is about what they show—being, and perhaps even the disclosure of being itself. In this way, art opens me up to a new world—the real world in which I live. Art brings me deeper into myself and tells me what it means to be in the world; it is in this sense that truth happens as an event in present time.

Second, in terms of the mode of being of poetic language, Heidegger explores the relationship between language and being. Language, in showing itself from itself, is the voice of being, and is the house of being. I have my being in the speaking of language, which is an articulation out of silence and the poetic world; I disappear as author and language speaks. The word is originary, as the word both reveals and conceals something, just as the artwork did. The thinking of being discloses through the self-disclosure of language itself. The poetic word is able to announce being itself and think according to its own voice the meaning of being. The nature of language is shown in being and silence, as being is disclosed. In this way, the poetic word in the announcing of being itself is an event of truth, the happening of truth. Poetic words announce the truth about truth. Language summons and differentiates being and beings. In the speaking of language, there is a holding together of the world and things—this is the "dif-ference."[101] The dif-ference carries with it pain; there is an apparent loss of unity in the distinguishing of world and things that occurs, but this duality also signals unity at the same time.

Heidegger discusses what it is to dwell poetically as well.[102] This is his approach in order to disclose how language creatively moves in the human being. Language has a way of withdrawing that is not the incapacity for speech, but the silencing, which I oftentimes fail to recognize—or heed. When I dwell, I stay with things, and thus persist through spaces. There is creativity involved in poetically dwelling, as it primarily involves letting things be and letting things show themselves from themselves. Authentic life is an intensification of life by living in the way of understanding, which is a becoming in the "lived experience of lived experience"—at the reflexive level in terms of hermeneutics.[103] Truth is an event of the disclosure of the being of something. Things can show forth both their own being and Being that comes from the ground of total meaning. Thus, *aletheia*—"the uncon-cealedness of beings"—is a happening, a disclosure of truth, an event in the life of being in the world.[104]

Stein, too, explains how one can meet in several spheres of reality the work of the artist. She uses the example of a poet and a musician. When I hear the words of a poem or the notes of a song, I encounter a life that is related to my own on several levels. A poem contains a sequence of words while a melody contains a sequence of sounds and both have a *"meaningful structure [Sinngebilde]"* which takes on life in the depths of a human being such that the meaningful structures are "re-created or copied [*nachbilden*]."[105] The human being bears a meaning because of the possession of "a certain ontological prerogative . . . by virtue of its own 'depth.'"[106] She says an artistic expression is at once "image *(Bild)*" in its presentation and "*structure (Gebilde)*" with the genuine expression also being a "symbol *(Sinnbild)*" in that it emerges out of "that infinite fullness of meaning *(Sinn)* into which every bit of human knowledge is projected to grasp something positive and speak of it. It does so in such a manner . . . that it mysteriously suggests the whole fullness of meaning, which for all human knowledge is inexhaustible. Understood this way, all genuine art is revelation and all artistic creation is sacred service."[107] This mode of being is religious—revelatory—in that I am shown a living universe to which I can respond.

With Ricoeur it is textuality that gives us an indication of where language speaks. Texts are linguistic performances that include words whether they be spoken or written. Texts carry an objective standing in that they serve to mediate between my reasoning capabilities, or thinking, and my reality, or being. Hermeneutics can be narrowly defined as the *"reflexive interpretation of poetic texts."*[108] With textuality, there are three levels that culminate in self-reflexive thinking. At the first level, there is a direct reading of the text. At the second level, I attempt to recover in conceptual terms by way of description or explanation, the primary relation that characterizes the naïve understanding of the text. I also critically ascertain the structure of the text, which indicates the boundary of an ontological world wherein the reflexive interpreter is positioned.

At the third level, there is new subject matter for the reflexive interpreter, as the meaning of being in the aforementioned ontological world is the subject of interpretation. That is, the reflexive interpreter can identify with the initial primary relation, or with a critical relation. The reflexive interpreter realizes that she is not just awareness itself, but that she is a finite, moving subject. The structural analysis designates another dimension of the overall meaning. There is recognition on the part of the "I" of the naïve meaning, the critical disintegration of meaning to one now of immanent signs, and of new meaning that can be opened up through a comparison between them. I also can consider whether my thinking about the reflections about the direct readings of the text carry truth or falsity. The "I" can actualize itself as a unified mark of a subject pole in unfolding a text-world over and against both the text-world that is imaginatively constructed, or an analytically displayed textual structure. Finally, there is a deeper possibility in that the moving reflexive subject through opening to multiple self-understandings can freely judge if one of those self-understandings is a possibility insofar as the text-world so presented provides the context of meaning in which the "I" can be the "I" that it genuinely is. It is in this way that the possibility exists for hermeneutics to lead to self-discovery in and through the texts, which is the event of appropriation. Thought and immediacy are held together, and this movement makes possible the anticipatory re-creation of language of Ricoeur's second naiveté.

The hermeneutical self can adopt imaginative variations through which it potentially can respond to the reality that is expressed in the discourse of literature and poetry, for example.[109] Reason comes together with different modes of being. Grasping and responding to texts gives rise to the acknowledgment of the multiplicity of meanings in life, and the conflict of interpretations. I have shown how reflection must become hermeneutics, because I can only grasp through signs in the world the activity of my existence.[110] Recovery of existential activity becomes the task of appropriating and reappropriating the effort to exist and the desire to be. It is the work of hermeneutics to illustrate that existence reaches expression and meaning through continually interpreting the significations that arise within culture.[111] The awareness of the awareness of being with being, or reflexive awareness is a recapitulation of that openness and reflexive recovery that is the second naiveté, which is the critical appropriation of the primordial silence that sublates reflection into reflexive self-awareness.

In thinking about thinking, the reflexively aware subject is, according to Schleiermacher, the finite "I" in its identity, a unity of thinking and being—a unity of opposites, who in its very being has to unify those opposites.[112] He views "thinking as action," or the being as thought through the thinking process.[113] Hence thinking about thinking separates into thinking, on the one hand, and being, on the other hand. It is part of the primordial structure of thinking to think about being. Thinking is in this sense a mediating activity between an intelligible form that derives out of the intellectual function of human being, which is referred to as "ideal being," and sense content that derives from the organic function of human being, which is referred to as "real being."[114] Further, I can add the dimensions of space and time to the activity of thinking: It mediates, in turn, between thinking, in the strict sense of the term, as temporal activity controlled through an intellectual function, and perceiving, as the activity controlled through an organic function, which joins spatial content.

Schleiermacher concerns himself with the question, How is it possible to think the essence of being, or a thing? Essence is the principle by which a being, or a thing, is determined in terms of both sameness and otherness. Being is, first, a being that is similar to all other beings. Second, being is the same or identical to itself, i.e., what appears is the same in terms of its concept. Third, being is other than what are all the other things in the world, i.e., there is a way in which a being or thing specifically differs from all other things. Fourth, being is other than itself, i.e., there is a way in which appearing being or thing differs in terms of its concept.

In order to be able to relate the different elements of sameness and otherness in concepts or judgments, all the related elements have to originally share the same primordial ground, which means there has to be "an absolute sameness of sameness and otherness" that allows for the possibility of acts of joining and differentiating sameness and otherness in both concepts as well as judgments.[115] The common and primordial ground has to be formulated as a first principle in absolute terms of thinking, in order that thinking be possible. There has to be a "transcendental-logical status" to the first principle in terms of the condition of the possibility of real moments in which the "I" thinks about being; and there has to be a "transcendental-ontological principle" in terms of the concepts that are used as thinking thinks in terms of real beings.[116] Hence original knowing (*ein Urwissen*) is, for Schleiermacher, what it is to postulate the original absolute identity of thinking and being—what is in itself insofar as it originates from itself. The first principle as ultimate "must be the absolute identity of the sameness and otherness of thinking and of being in their identity and difference."[117] This is what divine essence is, or the being of the divine—God. This first principle is also Anselmian in that it is that than which nothing greater can be thought. In addition, in the feeling (*Gefühl*) of absolute dependence, immediate self-consciousness refers to an original unity of thinking and being in the finite self, which mirrors the infinite ground.

In concluding this fourth level, I want to reiterate how in terms of reflexivity and thinking about thinking, Schleiermacher draws a correlation between thinking and being in the finite person ("I") whose identity is a unity of thinking and being. If I apply this correlation symbolically through the appearance of the "not" in my thinking, contemplative silence understands the identity of being in God. The justification for this statement is that (only?) through absolute identity can I understand the "not" as it appears in these different places.[118] To postulate the original absolute identity of thinking and being or the original knowing (*ein Urwissen*), is to postulate the idea of God as the originary locus of the relationship between thinking and being. As a consequence any individual act of thinking reflects the original act (*Urdenken*) that is its ultimate ground. All finite thinking presupposes a first principle that cannot be adequately thought by the human mind; it is the unknowable, infinite, ultimate ground (*Urgrund*), the presupposed Absolute, or "God-term" in regard to the dialectic.[119]

CONTEMPLATIVE AWARENESS

The fifth level of awareness is contemplative awareness. This level adds the awareness of the awareness of the awareness. The awareness is of an instantiated mode of being. I can say that the awareness is of the mode of capable being for this study. The awareness sees the mode of capable being as the manifestation of being itself, and is, in this case, the activity of actively grasping the mode of capable being. At this fifth structural level the initiative is on the side of the mode of being that appropriates me into it, or an "enowning."[120] This enowning is also what Schleiermacher means in terms of his philosophical theology, a second language which makes Heidegger more understandable.

If the manifestation of being is, in addition, seen and understood as a symbol in terms of its givenness, contemplative awareness can call it a symbol of God. For example, take the case of the manifestation of being itself in and through the thinking activity, striking me as a universal phenomenon of illumination—the event in which things emerge from the darkness of unintelligibility and appear in the light of intelligibility as what they really are. If the phenomenon of light takes on symbolic meaning in that way, then I have reinstated the symbol of light as a manifestation of being itself.[121] Light can, in this way, become for me a symbol of God. In other words, consciousness at the fifth level has two forms: The first form is an active one, in which I grasp the being of thinking as a manifestation of the mode of being itself. The second form is a responsive one, in which I can respond to this mode of being as something actual in the world—as a symbol of God. Contemplative awareness is capable of unifying and distinguishing the manifestation of being itself and the symbol of God. The criteria for doing so are: (1) The manifestation of being itself and the symbol of God both intend ultimacy—that than which none greater can be conceived. (2) A symbol of God is distinct from the manifestation of being itself, however, in that it takes the activity of thinking as a concrete particular object in the world to which the viewer responds. In awareness I am assuming the role of what is for Ricoeur suffering, responsive, passive reflection, or I could say interpretation. He sees the mode of being as God itself, and the mode of being as symbol. I understand this mode of being as a manifestation of being itself.[122] But I also trust and believe or respond. Key to believing is "responding to" the mode of being as a symbol of God.

This notion could be taken into the *via negativa* insofar as contemplative silence both manifests and defers the symbol of God. It does that through awareness of the "not" or "non-being." Thus, I am aware that the manifestation of being is not being itself. The symbol of God is not God. The manifestation is not the symbol; this is the last level of entering "not." Nevertheless, the symbol of God is God, being itself is the manifestation of being itself. "Is" and "is not" combine in contemplative awareness. Contemplative awareness understands an onto-theology that incorporates the critique of onto-theology through awareness of the "not" being brought in from the very beginning. This discussion has to do with the overcoming of ontology.

When I am engaged in the act of understanding, I do not merely see the words on a page, but rather, my mind attempts to grasp the meaning that is carried through those words.[123] For example, when I engage in discourse that is intelligible, and hear the word, "rose," within this context, I have an understanding that while the word is different than the object, it has to do with the object, and in this respect is of, and connected to the object. It is precisely this connection of "being-of," while at the same time, "not being," that constitutes a symbol. Words and things are linked together without collapsing the difference between them. My everyday reality of the world as perceptible as well as intelligible is dependent upon maintaining a difference between meaning and the referent—that is between what the text or something says, and what the text or something refers to or is about. This distinction is integral so that that reality can be delineated from what are subjective states of mind. Scharlemann explains that the word "God" is a sign or pointer in that it carries the sense of not being "I," and "not-this." In this way, "God" carries the meaning of the negative that I can instantiate upon both subject and object through the very saying of that word. It is in this way that a word can instantiate a negation by turning

> the subject by which it is spoken or the object to which it is applied into a sign of the subject's or object's own otherness. God appears as the otherness that can be at the place where any subject or object is. . . . [T]he word 'God' always has a referent because the very naming of the word creates a referent out of the thing upon which the 'not,' the intended otherness, is made manifest. . . . [O]ne cannot say 'God' without becoming or indicating the otherness that appears in the negation of the subject or the object or both. 'God' refers to the otherness that is manifested upon the speaking subject or the object spoken of or both. In this way, the word *God* is the reality of God. . . . [T]he word *God* makes it possible for a subject or an object to be the sign-reality that is God's presence, the other that is there in the naming. . . . [T]he meaning and the referent are so intimately fused that the meaning makes the referent and the referent appears only with the meaning.[124]

Further, the referent with regard to the word "God" is given in two ways. First, the referent is given through whatever it is that is instantiated in the actual pronouncing of the word—that is, the subject and/or object can become the sign of whatever is not the subject and/or object, in addition to other than what is the otherness that exists between those subjects and/or objects.

Second, the referent is given in language considered as a phenomenon in the very word as word itself. Hence the word "God" has a double referent. It can refer to an "I" or a "this" whereat otherness appears, as well as refer

> to the other word (namely, the word *word*) for the word *God*, or to that as what God is God. "God is God as the word" asserts that "word" (or language) is the way in which God is the deity God is (namely, as not being God, that is, as other than the word *God*.) God is God, then, as what is other than God doubly (as the word *word* and also as the word *God*); for the otherness that appears upon a word, which is always a pointer-to, is the same as the otherness as which God exists.[125]

Scharlemann says that to include time and negation into deity when thinking about the relation of "God" to being is an opportunity to think in a new way what has not been able to be thought. This is a retrieval in terms of a symbol of an existent deity, "and of its attendant conception of the being of God when God is not being God."[126] It is by using this formula that an object characterized by believing is translated into an object characterized by understanding. Hence a "language of believing" is translated into a "language of understanding."[127]

Finally, he distinguishes between "ontological," "religious," and "theological" texts. An ontological text includes the thought-sense and is the world signified by that sense. A religious text is similar to an ontological text except the unity of meaning is between that of an image, rather than a thought, and the world that is signified by that image. A theological text can be either an ontological or a religious text—one that is overturned such that it is not what it is or it is what it is not.[128] This threefold distinction can be understood in the statement, "The rose is pink," in terms of sense (what the statement says—that the rose is pink), reference (what the statement is about—the rose), and, what the statement is generally all about—(that the rose is the rose it is as the pink thing there). Scharlemann adds this third aspect to round out Ricoeur's work on the first two aspects of sense and reference. Now, when this threefold distinction is brought to a person, then I can say, "I am this one here." What the statement says is the unity of the subject "I" and the place as "here." What the statement is about is the person who is making that statement. What the assertion or statement is "*all about* is the mode of being expressed in the statement that I am myself *as* what is here—I am I *as* 'here'"[129]

What the text is all about has to do with "being as." "Being like" is the phrase Ricoeur uses in his theory of metaphor to designate the unity between being and not being that is characteristic of poetic worlds and worlds such as "the kingdom of heaven" of the parables, for example.[130] Metaphor is a rhetorical process in which discourse liberates the power of certain fictions in order for reality to be redescribed. The copula of the verb "to be" is the place of metaphor. Through the employment of "is" in the metaphorical process, "is" at once signifies "is not" and "is like." A more accurate way to depict that unity of being and non-being so characteristic of constructed poetic worlds is in the phrase "being . . . as not," according to Scharlemann.[131] That is, there is an overturning in the poetic or theological text such that it is not what it is or it is what it is not. This overturning has to do with the degree to which the meaning reveals the negation and the otherness to which it makes reference. He explains the phrase, "the kingdom of heaven," in that when one understands the meaning of a parable one is simultaneously in the kingdom that the meaning refers to. This occurrence is what the kingdom of heaven is. There is not only an ontological relationship here, but an overturning of the ontological "just because the reality to which the meaning refers is the reality of the kingdom of heaven when that kingdom is not the kingdom it is; it is the kingdom of heaven in the time when the kingdom of heaven is not being the kingdom of heaven."[132] If one understands the parable then what is understood is that "what shows the kingdom is not the kingdom, and to be in this kingdom (while understanding the parable) is to be in the world that is not the kingdom of heaven. Hence, the summary phrase for the being of the parable and its referent: 'being . . . as not.'"[133] Importantly, I hold in mind the overturning of the ontological lest I get caught up in a kind of onto-theology.

Stein, too, distinguishes between the literal and metaphorical meaning in language in an essay on Pseudo-Dionysius, as she explains that "We need a key to interpret this image-language, since if it is taken literally it can be grossly misunderstood. . . ."[134] The purpose of image-language is to unveil meaning for those who are striving for deeper meaning and "striving for holiness and [who] have freed themselves from childish thinking. . . ."[135] She thus sets out the first and second naiveté. Transformation is an ongoing process for the theologian who reads the revelatory text such that there are myriad ways of reaching an understanding of the revealed truth: "But this on no account means that he grasps everything in a *living* way. . . ."[136] That is, the reading may fail to grasp the meaning of the words at a certain level, and thus effect no change in one's life. However, Stein explains that "We feel the difference clearly when all of a sudden we see a passage we have often read 'in a new light' . . . ."[137] The theologian must form images of God based on what her awareness of God is.[138]

She takes up the symbol of fire and the experience of Moses in the Book of Exodus who proclaims that God is a consuming fire. Fire, she says, is an image of God and of God's Word as well such that "there is a likeness" between what happened in his experience and "consuming fire."[139] The verb "is" in the metaphorical process at once signifies "is" and "is like." She goes on to explain how it is that the process of understanding works with the metaphor. Something in sense perception represents something different because of an "objective commonness" which allows me "to recognize the one in the other."[140] If I follow Scharlemann here, the word, "God" is a sign insofar as it carries the sense of not being "this." The word "God" instantiates a negation so that "God" carries the meaning of the negative as well. Fire is a sign of God's own otherness. Employing the word "God"—that is, the very naming of the word creates a referent out of the word, fire—the thing upon which the "not" (the intended otherness) is made manifest. To say "God" is to indicate the otherness that appears in the negation of the subject. So the word "God" allows for the possibility for a subject or the object to be the sign-reality that is God's presence (the other that is there in the naming). The meaning of the symbol and the task of understanding bond as symbol and thought are held together.

Stein goes on to explain how the entire thought structure directs attention to something beyond itself and so, one must "disengage a 'type' [*Typus*] from the story—in the sense of a general form—that is to serve as a guide for building a second structure behind the first which will reappear in the same form but with another meaning. . . ."[141] Stein poetically expresses something of the reality of hermeneutical existence in interpreting a sacred text as she employs a metaphor: "The parables present the divine truth in a locked box, as it were. Often it is left up to us to look for the key. Sometimes the key is given in an added explanation or in an inner enlightenment. Moreover, an 'office of the keys,' the gift and task of interpreting Scriptures, may be vested in individuals or states of individuals."[142]

I come finally to revisit the work of Chauvet. When I think about language as an "ontophanous"[143] human reality, freely consenting to the practice of openness in everyday existence, then I learn in humility to recognize by virtue of my continual displacement by the other, what I so richly receive in terms of the largess of human reality bestowed—what I simply "cannot give [myself]. . . ."[144] My genuine presence includes an awareness of absence.[145] Chauvet explains that "The concept of '*coming-into-presence*' precisely marks the absence with which every presence is constitutively crossed out; nothing is nearer to us than the other in its very otherness . . . nothing is more present to us than what, in principle, escapes us (starting with ourselves)."[146] Chauvet's work introduces symbol and sacrament. Initially, I want to present his notion of the functionality connected with symbol. This presentation is followed by a more extensive discussion of sacrament. There are three aspects of sacramentality to explore in connection with his work—otherness, making present what is absent, as referred to above, and the disclosure of my material existence through the natural order and situatedness within a sociohistorical context. Symbol performs a primordial function for language, of summons or challenge, and of communication.[147] It is the symbolic about language that enables what is real to speak. Symbol discloses "the *primary* dimension of language," which is its vocation, to make reality significant; and "its reality is to be immediately a metaphor" for the entire existence of a human being.[148] But symbolic experience is insufficient lest it dissolve into imagination, as it requires cognition and re-cognition so that discourse may emerge. And, when discourse emerges, so, too, do silence and being issue forth.

Chauvet makes three important points about sacramentality. First, he says that when one speaks about God, inevitably one is speaking about humans; and that when one speaks of the relation of humans to God, inevitably one is speaking about the relationships of humans, one to the other.[149] I have shown how in Ricoeur's hermeneutics of the self, the reflexive structure of the self has otherness inscribed within itself, in its very being: I am the same as myself. However, I am also different from myself. There is an otherness about myself that I am always relating to in the being of myself even as I am part of the world. I am also always open to and relating to other selves who are also part of this world. Otherness is a structural feature of the being of the hermeneutical self that I am. I recognize others to be just like me in that they, too, have otherness about them. At the same time, there must be a process of learning to consent to this otherness about everyone. I therefore must hand myself over to myself "by and for the Other."[150] There is reflexivity at work here: I do not hand myself over to the Other. I must hand myself over to myself in order, in turn, to hand myself over to the Other. Hence human autonomy is not full autonomy, as I am always already beholden to otherness as part of my constitutive structure.

Second, what is most spiritual comes forth in what is most corporeal. Symbolism means that I am unable ever to finish the thinking process in which I am engaged. However, the impossibility of completion is precisely what enables me to think. This difference that thinking is, is what allows me to live; this is "the bread of absence [that] nourishes us."[151] He speaks in symbolic terms of the passage of "God" through language, and of the presence of the absence of "God." A theological act as such can come to the truth through a transitive way that the symbol opens up. The Word is expressed in a categorical imperative that includes life as well as action, and privileges justice and mercy in recognition of and out of respect for others.[152]

Third, the body that is my desire, and which includes history and society, and I would add culture, becomes the locus of a disclosure about the truth concerning my word.[153] The body is the locus where "God" can be recognized in the fashioning of a language in which the mystery can be heard. If not the only place, sacraments are the genuine places where the affirmation of both world and body as locus of "God" is verified; these affirmations find primordial expression in them.[154] Sacraments are "events," and are characterized both by language and symbol. The relation between "God" and humans can be characterized as one of otherness insofar as both "God" and humans are in a mode of being that is open.[155] In terms of the incarnate *Logos*, he discusses the idea of "God" whereby the manifestation of "God's" self occurs as "God" in the very act of "refusing to be God."[156] The implications of this act in terms of speaking about "God" are that of a humanity about the divine—"God," which, in turn, entails letting humanity be spoken in accordance with a "transitive way of thinking"; this is sacramental grace for Chauvet.[157] Hence there is dialectical movement between making present an absence, which is the divine depth of all of reality, and a recognition of what is and should be present through disclosure of material existence and being, if not in perfection, then more and more through a natural order about things.

To conclude, contemplative awareness holds together negation, absence, and presence, as well as language—discourse and silence. Contemplative awareness holds the depth of meaning in consciousness amid silence. When contemplative awareness accompanies the practice of contemplative silence, then I can appropriate the meaning of silence that is embodied "now." All five levels of awareness are actualizable possibilities and ingredient in the phenomenon. By appropriating contemplative silence, I can re-create genuine human living, which is to say I can live creatively, and with ethical and spiritual purpose in doing so.

NOTES

1. Max Picard, *The World of Silence* (Wichita, KS: Eighth Day Press, 2002), 36.
2. Ibid.
3. Ibid., 38.
4. See Aristotle, *Nicomachean Ethics*, 2nd ed., trans. and intro. Terence Irwin (Indianapolis and Cambridge: Hackett Publishing Company, Inc., 1999), X.7.1.
5. Ibid.
6. Ibid., X.7.8.
7. Ibid., X.7.9.
8. Merton, *New Seeds of Contemplation*, 3.
9. Ibid.
10. Ibid., 5.
11. Ibid.
12. Alasdair MacIntyre, *After Virtue: A Study in Moral Theory*, 2nd ed. (Notre Dame, IN: University of Notre Dame Press, 1984), 187.
13. *Into Great Silence*, Disc 1, directed by Philip Gröning (Berlin, Germany: Zeitgeist Video, 2005), DVD.
14. Ibid., "Speaking of God," Ch. 20.
15. Ibid., Disc 1.

16. Ibid., "Assimilation," Ch. 4.
17. Ibid., Disc 1.
18. See Robert P. Scharlemann, *The Being of God: Theology and the Experience of Truth* (New York: The Seabury Press, 1981).
19. Heidegger, BT.
20. Paul Ricoeur, "Existence and Hermeneutics," *The Conflict of Interpretations: Essays in Hermeneutics, I*, trans. Kathleen McLaughlin, 10.
21. Ibid.
22. Stein, FEB, 49.
23. Ibid.
24. Ibid., 363.
25. Ibid., 162.
26. Ibid., 57–58; 57n36; 342; 342n22. Stein quotes Exod. 3:14.
27. See Mette Lebech, *The Philosophy of Edith Stein: From Phenomenology to Metaphysics* (Bern: Peter Lang, 2015), 156.
28. Stein, FEB, 61; 59; 263; 373.
29. Stein, Empathy, 88.
30. Edith Stein, "Husserl and Aquinas: A Comparison," *Knowledge and Faith*, vol. 8, The Collected Works of Edith Stein, trans. Walter Redmond (Washington, D.C.: ICS Publications, 2000), 53.
31. Ibid., 42.
32. Ibid., 41; 49.
33. Ibid., 54.
34. Stein, Empathy, 88.
35. Martin Heidegger, "What Is Metaphysics?" *Pathmarks*, ed. William McNeill, trans. David Farrell Krell (Cambridge and New York: Cambridge University Press, 1998), 86.
36. Ibid.
37. Ibid., 90.
38. Ibid., 91.
39. Martin Heidegger, "Postscript to 'What Is Metaphysics?'" *Pathmarks*, 233.
40. See Paul Tillich, *The Courage to Be*, intro. Peter J. Gomes (New Haven and London: Yale University Press, 2000).
41. Stein, FEB, 55.
42. Stein to Mother Ottilia Thannisch, OCD, March 26, 1939, Letter 296, in SPL, 305.
43. See Stein, FEB, 37.
44. Ibid.
45. Stein, Life, 397.
46. Ibid., 502n184.
47. Heidegger, BT, I.IV.120.
48. Ibid., I.IV.121.
49. Ibid., I.IV.122–23.
50. Ibid., I.IV.124.
51. Stein, "Knowledge, Truth, Being," *Knowledge and Faith*, 67.

52. Ibid.
53. Heidegger, BT, I.IV.129.
54. Ibid., I.V.131.
55. Ibid.
56. Ibid., I.V.137.
57. Ibid., I.V.138.
58. Stein, Empathy, 100.
59. Stein, "Knowledge, Truth, Being," 66.
60. See Martin Heidegger, "Memorial Address," *Discourse on Thinking*, trans. John M. Anderson and E. Hans Freund, intro. John M. Anderson (New York: Harper and Row, Publishers, Inc., 1966), 46.
61. Ibid., 54.
62. Ibid., 61.
63. See Martin Heidegger, "The Question Concerning Technology," *The Question Concerning Technology and Other Essays,* trans. and intro. William Lovitt (New York: Harper and Row Publishers, Inc., 1977), 31.
64. Ibid. See also Heidegger, "Conversation on a Country Path About Thinking," *Discourse on Thinking*, 81.
65. Louis-Marie Chauvet, *Symbol and Sacrament: A Sacramental Reinterpretation of Christian Experience*, trans. Patrick Madigan and Madeleine Beaumont (Collegeville, MN: The Liturgical Press, 1995), 53 (hereafter *Symbol and Sacrament*).
66. Ibid.
67. Ibid.
68. Ibid., 53n29.
69. Ibid., 54n30.
70. Ibid., 54.
71. Ibid., 61.
72. Simone Weil, "Reflections on the Right Use of School Studies with a View to the Love of God," *Waiting for God*, trans. Emma Craufurd, intro. Leslie Fiedler (New York: HarperCollins, 2001), 61.
73. Ibid., 62.
74. Ibid.
75. Scharlemann, *The Being of God: Theology and the Experience of Truth*, 48.
76. Ibid., 82.
77. Ibid.
78. Ibid., 83.
79. Ibid. Furthermore, Scharlemann explains that "We determine whether a thing has certain properties ('this is a tree,' 'the leaf is green') by what we can see—with our eyes, our intuitive perception of form, or through some measuring instrument. We determine whether a thing shows the essence, or being, of what it names by what we can understand in view of the object. If, for example, the response to a particular thing is to think or say, 'It makes sense for a tree to have branches if to be a tree means to be able to offer protection and refuge,' then in view of this object we can understand the being of a tree. The essence (in this case, the capacity of offering protection and refuge) is what is shown by the particular object; that capacity is the second referent,

which is contained in the first referent, the perceived object tree, and which we become aware of as an understanding. This is what seeing that the meaning of the object is the same as the reality of the object amounts to."
   80. Stein, FEB, 503.
   81. Ibid.
   82. Ibid.
   83. Stein, Empathy, 82–83.
   84. See Stein, "Knowledge, Truth, Being," 72.
   85. Ibid., 71.
   86. Ibid.
   87. Ibid.
   88. Ibid.
   89. Stein, FEB, 377.
   90. Ibid., 40.
   91. Ibid., 65.
   92. Ibid.
   93. Scharlemann, *The Being of God: Theology and the Experience of Truth*, 178.
   94. Ibid., 179.
   95. Stein, FEB, 61.
   96. Ibid., 61; 380.
   97. Ibid., 380.
   98. Stein, Woman, 104.
   99. Martin Heidegger, "The Origin of the Work of Art," *Poetry, Language, Thought*, trans. and intro. Albert Hofstadter (New York: Harper and Row Publishers, Inc., 1971), 43.
   100. Ibid., 32–36.
   101. See Martin Heidegger, "Language," *Poetry, Language, Thought*, 187–208. In this essay he comments on Georg Trakl's poem, "A Winter Evening."
   102. Martin Heidegger, "Building Dwelling Thinking," *Poetry, Language, Thought*, 155.
   103. See Benjamin D. Crowe, *Heidegger's Religious Origins: Destruction and Authenticity* (Bloomington and Indianapolis: Indiana University Press, 2006), 22.
   104. Heidegger, "The Origin of the Work of Art," 49.
   105. Stein, FEB, 379.
   106. Ibid., 40.
   107. Stein, SC, 12.
   108. See Klemm, HTPR, 107–8.
   109. Paul Ricoeur, "Phenomenology and Hermeneutics," *From Text to Action: Essays in Hermeneutics, II,* 37.
   110. Ricoeur, "The Hermeneutics of Symbols: II," 330.
   111. Ricoeur, "Existence and Hermeneutics," 22.
   112. See David E. Klemm, "Schleiermacher's Hermeneutic: the Sacred and the Profane," *The Sacred and the Profane: Contemporary Demands on Hermeneutics*, ed. Jeffrey F. Keuss (Burlington, VT: Ashgate Publishing Company, 2003), 70–72. See

also Friedrich Schleiermacher, *Hermeneutics and Criticism*, trans. and ed. Andrew Bowie (Cambridge and New York: Cambridge University Press, 1998).

113. Friedrich Schleiermacher, *Dialectic or, The Art of Doing Philosophy: A Study Edition of the 1811 Notes*, trans., intro., and notes, Terrence N. Tice (Atlanta, GA: Scholars Press, 1996), 41.

114. Klemm, "Schleiermacher's Hermeneutic: the Sacred and the Profane," 71.

115. Ibid.

116. Ibid.

117. Ibid., 72.

118. See Robert P. Scharlemann, "The Being of God When God Is Not Being God: Deconstructing the History of Theism," *Inscriptions and Reflections: Essays in Philosophical Theology* (Charlottesville, VA: University Press of Virginia, 1989), 30–53.

119. See Klemm, "Schleiermacher's Hermeneutic: the Sacred and the Profane," 74; 75n24. Klemm argues for a theological modeling as a type of theological hermeneutic, which helps to respond to concerns that hermeneutics is a form of relativism. He explains that hermeneutics "posits logically and ontologically an absolute ground of thinking and being, which completely dispels the possibility that nothing is sacred while preserving the tentativeness, humility, openness and honesty that have come to mark hermeneutical thinking in our time." Further, he comments that Schleiermacher's thought has "deep Augustinian and Anselmian roots" as it is the "elaborate working out of the ontological argument."

120. See Martin Heidegger, *Contributions to Philosophy (From Enowning)*, trans. Parvis Emad and Kenneth Maly (Bloomington and Indianapolis: Indiana University Press, 1999). There is a helpful discussion of Heidegger's notion of "enowning" in the "Translators' Foreward," xix–xxii.

For Heidegger, it is the event of language (*Ereignis*) or his use of *enowning* whereby what is unarticulated or underarticulated is the notion of this event, because it is an event of being as well as of thinking that has an ontic reality. What is in the event is a connection between some particular words which involve silence, and the event of language which is ontological. The ontic opens to the ontological; the mind is open to being in the event (*Ereignis*). This language-event, as Heidegger explains, can be likened to what Schleiermacher means by the religious consciousness: A unity in self-determination shows itself in intuition and feeling as immediate consciousness of the self and world which is ontological (having to do with being) and opened by the ontic (existence).

121. See Barbara O'Dea, s.v. "Light," in *The New Dictionary of Catholic Spirituality*, 600–1.

122. Cf. Scharlemann, "The Being of God When God Is Not Being God: Deconstructing the History of Theism."

123. Ibid., 48.

124. Ibid., 49.

125. Ibid., 50.

126. Ibid., 51.

127. Robert P. Scharlemann, "The Question of Philosophical Theology," *Being and Truth: Essays in Honour of John Macquarrie*, eds. Alistair Kee and Eugene T. Long (London: SCM Press, Ltd., 1986), 16.

128. Robert P. Scharlemann, "Being 'As Not': Overturning the Ontological," *Inscriptions and Reflections: Essays in Philosophical Theology*, 57. See also Robert P. Scharlemann, "The Textuality of Texts," *Meanings in Texts and Action: Questioning Paul Ricoeur*, eds. David E. Klemm and William Schweiker (Charlottesville and London: University Press of Virginia), 13–25.

129. Scharlemann, "Being 'As Not': Overturning the Ontological," 58.

130. See Paul Ricoeur, *The Rule of Metaphor*, trans. Robert Czerny with Kathleen McLaughlin and John Costello (London and New York: Routledge, 1977).

131. Scharlemann, "Being 'As Not': Overturning the Ontological," 59.

132. Ibid., 62–63.

133. Ibid., 63.

134. Stein, "Ways to Know God: The 'Symbolic Theology' of Dionysius the Areopagite and Its Objective Presuppositions," *Knowledge and Faith*, 90.

135. Ibid.

136. Ibid., 109.

137. Ibid., 110.

138. Ibid., 97.

139. Ibid.

140. Ibid.

141. Ibid., 115.

142. Ibid.

143. See Elbatrina Clauteaux, "When Anthropologist Encounters Theologian: The Eagle and the Tortoise," *Sacraments: Revelation of the Humanity of God: Engaging the Fundamental Theology of Louis-Marie Chauvet*, eds. Philippe Bordeyne and Bruce T. Morrill (Collegeville, MN: The Liturgical Press, 2008), 163; 164n22.

144. See Patrick Prétot, "The Sacraments as 'Celebrations of the Church': Liturgy's Impact on Sacramental Theology," *Sacraments: Revelation of the Humanity of God: Engaging the Fundamental Theology of Louis-Marie Chauvet*, 35. See also Bruce T. Morrill, "Time, Absence, and Otherness: Divine-Human Paradoxes Bonding Liturgy and Ethics," *Sacraments: Revelation of the Humanity of God: Engaging the Fundamental Theology of Louis-Marie Chauvet*, 151n40. Here Morrill, in commenting on the moral philosophy of Edith Wyschogrod, explains that "the temptation to think that we know entirely who the Other is, that we can 'write off' that person, for whatever reason, as unworthy of our efforts, betrays what Wyschogrod calls the 'category mistake' of thinking that our language directly applies to (represents) the Other."

145. See Bruce T. Morrill, "Building on Chauvet's Work: An Overview," *Sacraments: Revelation of the Humanity of God: Engaging the Fundamental Theology of Louis-Marie Chauvet*, xviii. Morrill makes this comment with regard to the work of Louis-Marie Chauvet. See Chauvet, *Symbol and Sacrament*, 404. Finally, see Clauteaux, "When Anthropologist Encounters Theologian: The Eagle and the Tortoise," 162.

146. Chauvet, *Symbol and Sacrament*, 404.

147. Ibid., 121.
148. Ibid., 123n14.
149. Ibid., 504.
150. Ibid., 506.
151. Ibid., 533.
152. See Louis-Marie Chauvet, *The Sacraments: The Word of God at the Mercy of the Body*, trans. Madeleine Beaumont (Collegeville, MN: The Liturgical Press, 2001).
153. Chauvet, *Symbol and Sacrament*, 535.
154. Ibid., 537.
155. Ibid., 544.
156. Ibid.
157. Ibid.

Chapter 7

The Meaning of Capable Human

I have thus far addressed how the practice of contemplative silence is possible and what the practice is. I explained hermeneutical, phenomenological, historical, and religious/theological contexts for the possibility of the practice. In the final part of the study, I want to address the following questions: First, I ask, What does the practice mean for the capable human? I propose that the meaning of the practice is the transformation. The practice of contemplative silence is the means and end of the transformation of reflexive consciousness. To understand the meaning of capable human is to understand the transformation that transpires. I want to address the term "transformation," and present its meaning as understood by one theologian below. I further pose the question, Are those transformations real? Second, I ask the question, Does the transformed consciousness exist? The interpretive responses to these questions comprise this chapter, which includes the eighth and ninth steps of the study and the next chapter, which includes the tenth and final move of the argument.

I interpret transformation in a threefold way: First, I reinterpret Ricoeur's four "I can's." Second, I interpret texts of John of the Cross, as the first of two representatives of the Carmelite tradition, inasmuch as they constitute at once spiritual transformation and contemplative action. In working with both Ricoeur and primary texts of the Carmelite tradition, I want to illustrate how the actualizable possibility of the transformation of reflexiveness consciousness is a part of ordinary human reality, and that inasmuch as it is an ethical and spiritual task, it warrants explanation and interpretation. A case is therefore made for the possibility of transformation. As part of the interpretive part of the study, I show how the transformations have been actualized using the language of the Carmelite tradition. Textual evidence for the transformations are brought to bear. Third, in Chapter 8, I return to the work of Ricoeur, and also, in continuing with the Carmelite tradition, I interpret Stein's texts, too, as a performance of the transformation of reflexive consciousness, while acknowledging her theological roots as well. In the end, an interpretation of contemplative human reality is an intermedial way of being on the way.

Bernard Lonergan interprets transformation in terms of what happens to a subject and her world in his text, *Method in Theology*. He refers to this transformation as being a kind of conversion (*metanoia*), which as lived is existential, personal, and intimate, but is not deemed so private that it is considered solitary. Persons are, after all, part of myriad communities of discourse, in overlapping public and private spheres. Transformation as conversion has communal dimensions, and in this respect has the possibility, in passing from generation to generation, and from a cultural milieu to that of another, of becoming historical.[1] It is a prolonged process and not simply a development or series thereof; it involves a change in course as well as direction. This process, I would add, accords well with science and the notion of "evolution." The transformation as lived affects consciousness and the intentionality of consciousness. He explains that "It directs his gaze, pervades his imagination, releases the symbols that penetrate to the depths of his psyche. It enriches his understanding, guides his judgments, reinforces his decisions."[2] Understood in this way, transformation is a spiritual and ethical task.

There are four kinds of transformation, which are: (1) psychological transformation, (2) moral or ethical transformation, (3) intellectual transformation, and (4) religious transformation. Lonergan is primarily concerned with moral or ethical transformation, intellectual transformation, and religious transformation, and understands them to be an integrated part of a holistic transformative process whereby a person becomes an authentic human being—that is, genuine and therefore, real. Transformation coincides with a living religion.[3] First, psychological transformation has to do with maintaining mutuality between consciousness and the unconscious. Everyone is subject to biases that can block and distort intellectual development. Unconscious motivation is one such bias.

Second, moral transformation has to do with moving beyond the value of truth *per se* to values in general. He explains that "It sets him on a new, existential level of consciousness and establishes him as an originating value."[4] The devotion to truth is taken up into moral transformation so that there may be a deliberate response to all values. Now the pursuit of the truth is more secure, meaningful, as well as significant because it is set within this richer context. Further, one's criterion for the decisions as well as choices that are made are no longer mere satisfactions but values.[5] One is no longer driven by the satisfaction that comes from a need for control, and the desire to fortify the ego.

Third, intellectual transformation involves an ongoing commitment to the search for the reality of what is through the process of understanding.

With this kind of transformation, there is an understanding of the distinction between the immediacy and experience of the sensory world and a world that is mediated through meaning.[6] Here, truth is attained through cognitional self-transcendence, which happens by not becoming too attached to words in order that one is open to the possibility that new meaning can emerge, and by moving toward a reality that the words are pointing to—a universe filled with being.

Fourth, with religious transformation a person is grasped by what is ultimate concern.[7] The influence of Tillich's thought can be ascertained as he readily acknowledges. Religious transformation is a "falling in love" or "being-in-love" with and for the Word incarnate, and with what is the ultimate in truth, goodness, and beauty, which involves a "total and permanent self-surrender without conditions, qualifications, reservations."[8] Further, a "religiously differentiated consciousness" involves an apprehension in two different modes that are both mediated by meaning—a commonsense mode actively functioning in the world, and a mystical mode that passively withdraws interiorly.[9] The summit of transformation is being-in-love. Being-in-love is a holistic approach in that exteriority and interiority are increasingly integrated.

He devises transcendental precepts as a way to articulate what it is to be genuine—an authentic human being, and which is, therefore, a theological methodology. The transcendental precepts are: (1) Be attentive, (2) Be intelligent, (3) Be reasonable, (4) Be responsible, and (5) Be in love.[10] The first three precepts are related to intellectual transformation. The fourth precept is connected to moral or ethical transformation. Finally, the fifth precept is related to religious transformation. For Lonergan, to be in love is to be in love with the ultimate. He explains that "The transcendental notions, that is, our questions for intelligence, for reflection, and for deliberation, constitute our capacity for self-transcendence. That capacity becomes an actuality when one falls in love. . . . Just as unrestricted questioning is our capacity for self-transcendence, so being in love in an unrestricted fashion is the proper fulfillment of that capacity."[11] This kind of love leads to wisdom; it is formless and empty knowledge, hence an unknowing.[12] It coexists with scientific knowledge and serves to enrich it by adding the dimension of depth to it. Wisdom is considered the "crowning gift" of a theologian.[13] The humble mind continually seeks after what is "That deeply emotional conviction of the presence of a superior reasoning power," which is synonymous with God (theology) or the idea of God (philosophy).[14] I am now in a position to interpret and even reinterpret the transformation of reflexive consciousness.

THE REFLEXIVE TRANSFORMATION
OF CAPABLE HUMAN

I want to assert that through the ongoing integrating activity of the practice of contemplative silence, there is a reflexive transformation of capable human in understanding Ricoeur's four "I can's." Now, "I" can speak silence, "I" can practice contemplative silence, "I" can tell stories of the practice of contemplative silence, and "I" can invoke personal responsibility by practicing contemplative silence. These are four different ways of explaining and interpreting the practice of contemplative silence. This is the eighth step of the argument.

Let me proceed to a discussion of the "I can's." First, "I" can speak silence. When "I" speak silence, I am giving voice and life to silence; therefore, it is not the negation of utterance. It is a silence that is deliberate and self-conscious. It gives voice to silence, but the silence is saying nothing, on the one hand, yet is not a saying nothing, on the other hand. It is also saying not nothing. The acting and suffering capable human, just as she is capable of speaking and being able "to do things with words," is capable of speaking silence and being able to do things with silence.[15] Ricoeur launches the notion of capacity by means of the capacity "of being able to say things," so that he can confer an extension onto the idea of human action.[16] That is, by characterizing a self in terms of a capable human being, who in turn recognizes herself in her capabilities, a reflexive turn to be sure, acting is the most fitting concept to describe this approach in terms of a philosophical anthropology.

The employment of reflexivity brings together, to follow Aristotle, being as *dynamis*, or potentiality, and being as *energeia*, or act. Thus, in this study, I have throughout made a reference to the actualizable possibility for something. The notion of acting is therefore positioned in regard to its meaning deriving from the primitive polysemy—the idea of being. Beyond this, however, Ricoeur wants to reach the utterer of the utterance, the one who is speaking—the person who is not substitutable. He explains that "The self-designation of the speaking subject is produced in interlocutionary situations where the reflexivity is combined with otherness."[17] I can say here with Ricoeur, that the silence pronounced by a particular person is addressed to another person, and further, it is, on many occasions, in the form of a response from another. Self-designation through the force of the illocutionary act in the call from the other receives the attribution not only of one's proper name, but the veritable founding in terms of the speaking subject who is capable, through silence, of saying who one is. To follow Ricoeur in *Memory, History, Forgetting*, this is a silent voice, and not a mute one.[18] It is a capable voice because it is not deprived of both speech and silence. It understands how to communicate unfathomable depth and mystery through the transforming knowledge that one knows that one does not know—it is an unknowing, a conscious not-knowing in humble acquiescence to silence and language within the Word.

Second, "I" can practice contemplative silence. With regard to the "practice" of contemplative silence, it is a purposeful, deliberate action, and a ritualized action. As such, it is a concrete "thing" in the world, and not just a universal that is conceptualized and theorized. The subject who practices contemplative silence has the capacity to make the practice, which is an event in time, happen in a highly intentional way. The ascription of the practice of contemplative silence as an action to the practitioner becomes part of its meaning, insofar as there is a relation between the action of practicing contemplative silence, and the monk, nun, or agent, for example, who has the capacity to specify itself as the person who is, in fact, engaging in the action. There is a binding of what the action is with how the action is accomplished, to who has carried out the action for Ricoeur. In appropriating Kant, he says that what is significant for thought is the capacity that I possess to begin doing something all by myself. This ability to practice contemplative silence encompasses all my fragmentary actions, and confers a certain wholeness, as an integrating phenomenon, upon those actions.

The practice of contemplative silence is a ritualized action. When the monks of the Carthusian Order, for example, come together to pray the Night Office, there is a complexity of interactions that occur. Inasmuch as the monks have made vows to community life, through ongoing participation in the Night Office, and the silence that is part of the ritualized action, they have taken upon themselves and assumed initiative through which they have actualized their power to act; they are capable of acting in such a way. The deliberateness of the performances of ritualized action in the liturgical event, as well as in manual labor, transform the hearts and minds of the monks into highly energized fields of personal activity. Now, I can say that instead of speaking silence, I can enact silence through the practice. I see this in the way that the monks not only pray but carry themselves as they walk through the cloister, or when they garden, shovel the snow, or cut wood. It does not require a cloister to enact silence, that is, to practice contemplative silence. I can enact silence in the middle of the most intense of public activities, by the way in which I am present in a particular context—with thoughtfulness, mindfulness, and purposefulness. The enactment of silence can bring forth depth of being through attentive and empathic presence; it is performative insofar as I express and communicate the values I embody.

Third, "I" can tell stories of the practice of contemplative silence. In telling these stories, and reflexively talking about my narrated story of practicing contemplative silence, personal identity becomes projected as narrative identity. There is a unity of meaning that can emerge as a result of this configuring process if I follow Ricoeur here. He refers to this unifying power as "'poetry' itself."[19] Ongoing transformation transpires through this dynamic process. In the same way that the plot dictates a mutual genesis that exists between character development and a story told, so the narration of stories about the practice of contemplative silence serves as a means of transformation, insofar as I recognize new meaning or recognize myself in a new way in the stories that emerge; this is an appropriation of the narrative event, and an appropriation of the practice of contemplative silence. I must be receptive for the event to occur. What I am learning in and through this transformative process, is how to narrate myself in deliberately appropriating the silence. Ricoeur explains that "Learning to narrate oneself is also learning how to narrate oneself in other ways."[20]

Fourth, "I" can invoke personal responsibility by practicing contemplative silence. As mentioned in Chapter 6, the word, contemplative, qualifies the word, silence, by connoting the depth of meaning that is held in consciousness amid the silence. That I can carry meaning entails the capacity to hold myself accountable, in terms of responsivity, for actions to the extent of imputing them to myself. Further, I must bear whatever is the consequence of my actions, especially in the case of faults and wrongs in which another person has been harmed or made to suffer. The practice of contemplative silence is one way to invoke personal responsibility in responsively recognizing and holding those faults and wrongs in consciousness, having judged and evaluated those actions as bad (or good), and prohibited (or permitted), and too, releasing them through yet other actions of justice and mercy, and pardon and forgiveness.

In moral terms, I must hold myself accountable, especially for those vulnerable and fragile others who fall within the scope of my powers. As far as my powers extend, there is a reciprocal relatedness in my capacities in regard to the harmful effects that can occur to follow Ricoeur here. He is thinking in terms of relationships involving spatial as well as temporal proximity—that responsibility should be exercised in just measure. The practice of contemplative silence takes on spiritual and ethical import as it is one way to compassionately be with others whom I have wronged, or even to be with those whom I am unaware that I have harmed or wronged. Insofar as the practice is the means and end of spiritual transformation, I am imputing responsibility for that transformation. The word, "personal," implies a communal dimension of relationality; there are communities to which I belong, and to which I am answerable in ethical and spiritual terms. I have the capacity to specify and obligate myself to carry out this practice. Contemplative awareness can lead to spiritual and ethical activity. There is a way in which a capable human being manifests ethical and spiritual values in the manner in which I am with others. In the end, all four "I can's" can be considered activities of contemplative awareness and have to do with carrying out daily life with a higher level of awareness and purposefulness.

CONTEMPLATIVE MEDIATION IN CARMELITE TEXTS

The second way in which I interpret transformation is, in turn, by interpreting classic texts of the Carmelite tradition as performances of the transformation of reflexive consciousness, inasmuch as they constitute contemplative action. The texts that are interpreted in this part of the study are written by one figure, John of the Cross. In many respects, it can be said that his writings flow out of the practice of contemplative silence; there is an immediacy about the texts as primary sources. The desire for God, the desire for the desire for God, and being in love with God, are inherently a part of the contemplative mediation that comprises the Carmelite textual tradition. I appropriate this tradition in order to exemplify the way in which the transformation is real. These texts are capable of uttering and are capable of the transformed consciousness that I have referred to. In turning to primary texts of the tradition as expressions of the transformation, I come to an understanding of the way in which transformation has been actualized. The transformation of reflexive consciousness will therefore be interpreted. In elucidating the spiritual transformation in terms of contemplative ethical action, these texts express deep immersion in what is, which opens to uncovering the hidden beauty in life, even in tragic circumstances. Authentic life is the unitive way of seeing the unity of opposites, which through that very seeing is to transcend them. This is the ninth step of the argument.

John of the Cross

The texts of John of the Cross are performances of the transformation of reflexive consciousness. That is, the transformed consciousness exists in his texts, and hence the transformation is real. First, I want to say a few words about the corpus of his work in terms of transformation. Then I consider the poem and commentary, *The Spiritual Canticle*, that was initially mentioned in Chapter 4, followed by the *Prayer of a Soul Taken with Love*. This is a cursory reading of these texts.

There is a unity about his works considered as a whole, which is illustrative of this transformation in that he employs symbols of both light and darkness. Although John is famous for his symbol of *nada*, nothing or negation—the dark night—this is balanced by his symbol of transformation—the fire of love. They, of course, mutually imply each other. If there is a dark night, then surely the fire of love is burning; the light is brilliant—so brilliant that it is a darkness. And the flame lights the dark night. The point is that John writes about both darkness and light.

The Spiritual Canticle

Contemplative ethical action is carried out in the form of a textual commentary on the poem written for the persons to whom John provided spiritual guidance. A group of Carmelite nuns who were in Beas first read the poem, and responded in awe to the depth of profundity that it contained in its simplicity.[21] They wanted some assistance from John in probing the meaning of the symbols that he used. What evolved out of his spiritual conferences, was the writing of a commentary that cast light on the symbols and their content through an explanation and interpretation of them.

In the texts—both poem and commentary—when one begins to seek the divine, then that is the beginning of the spiritual life. Spiritual life is human life, more specifically, it is fully embodied human life; the spiritual and the sexual come together in human life. The text is a religious text insofar as it is an image of a contemplative love story, in metaphorical terms, between the human and the divine. With this religious text, the unity of meaning is between that of an image (as opposed to a thought), and the world that is signified by that image. The poem is a reworking of the Song of Songs, and gives voice to its meaning, in terms of the movement of love, or the "ways of spiritual exercise" in the life of a human being.[22]

In both the poetic text and the textual commentary, the various aspects of the movement of growth in love that comprise the spiritual life are expressed. The spiritual life is a developed relationality with the divine that is inclusive of other humans. Ethical action flows out of, and indeed is, the litmus test for the authenticity of this relationship. The poetic text itself is constructed in deeply symbolic language. The stanzas of the poem are a song whose voice sings of contemplative silence. For its duration, this symphony of love is propelled by movements of love. Moreover, the work has a tripartite structure, or, in keeping with the metaphor, three movements, based on the threefold path. The purgative way is expressed in terms of a self who seeks after the Beloved whose absence causes heartache. The Beloved also elicits stirrings of love, as the spiritual journey commences in stanzas 1–12. Whatever impedes and prevents one from growing in love of God must be rooted out at this stage. The illuminative way is depicted in terms of ongoing loving encounters between the self and the divine, which are coupled with the desire to be completely free of any hindrances that may keep the self from realizing the full flowering of mystical marriage. Spiritual betrothal occurs at this level. Stanzas 13–21 mirror this leg of the spiritual journey. The unitive way is expressed as the complete, mutual surrender of the human and the divine, and the desire for the beatific vision.[23] This is more commonly referred to as the spiritual marriage. Stanzas 22–40 reflect this third way.

It should be noted that in *The Science of the Cross*, Stein interprets the threefold way in *The Spiritual Canticle* in a deeply integrative manner in that she refers to it as "three effects."[24] She sees in the text the unity of being in that the three effects are all connected in the wholeness of a life of grace and on the mystical path taken in its entirety, although one or the other of those effects may take precedence at any given stage of the journey. She understands union to be both at the beginning and the end so that it "rules the whole" in John.[25] There is progression with the union of love as one is inwardly being drawn ever deeper.

The text beckons the practitioner of contemplative silence/interpreter into its very life, into what are the dynamics of love that transpire between the lover and Beloved, or the bride and bridegroom—between the self and God. In the third part, the unitive part of the commentary on the poem, there is a discussion of the virtues and gifts that God has bestowed on the self who has become aware of them, which include "silent music" and "sounding solitude."[26] This is an event of language and silence. The utterances that express this love are those which evoke silence. There is a stunning simplicity to the syntax that is used. Also, by alternating the syllables in a line, rapid movement is conveyed. There is a hidden vision in John's work, and in his attitude with regard to language that is congruent with modernity, according to Colin Thompson:

> But, as there, for radically different reasons: not that there is nothing, no meaning, no God in a world which can be explained in its own terms, but that human beings cannot grasp what their meaning might be until they have undertaken the harder journey within themselves, which is where the unitive path becomes revealed. Only then can the fragments of knowledge displayed so beautifully in the exterior world find their significance in the larger pattern which comes from knowledge of the self, and in that self, of a hidden God who is knowable there.[27]

In contemplative awareness, the practitioner/interpreter can hold the different contextual levels of awareness together, which is the unitive way. The interpreter's very being as immediate self-awareness is that of understanding the relation of love between the human and the divine in and through the "utterances of love" that issue forth in the poem.[28] The stanzas of the poem are all utterances, albeit metaphorical, of what is understood to be freely flowing divine love.

At the second contextual level of being with being as immediate objective awareness, the practitioner/interpreter is attentive, open, and attuned to receive "a thousand graces," as the human is one of the multitude of creatures made in the image of God and therefore endowed with beauty.[29] The interpreter can understand being with being as that which has received mystical, that is, hidden understanding of divine life that is available to anyone who would set out on the journey, or who would desire to purposefully live their own love story with the divine.

At the third reflective level of awareness, the practitioner/interpreter makes the connection between the divine and human by thinking the concept of love. The judgment that we can establish in interpreting the text is the relational reality of spiritual love—that there is a relational bond of union between the human and the divine. Moreover, the source of everything is this divine love. The textual commentary explains that "The soul says that this bed in flower is hung with purple (denoting charity), because it is only by the charity and love of the King of heaven that all the virtues, riches, and goods flourish, receive sustenance, and give enjoyment. Without such love the soul could not enjoy this bed. . . ."[30]

Further, this hidden wisdom is given "according to the mode and capacity" of the receiver.[31] The text speaks of receiving the fire of divine love through "the touch of a spark," and that "flowings" come "from the balsam of God."[32] At the reflexive level of awareness, in terms of metaphoric understanding, there is similitude between the utterance meaning (the utterances of the poetic text as objective meaning), and the utterer's meaning (what the author means and has the intention of saying as subjective meaning). That is, the poetic utterances are like the flowings from God.[33] In literal terms, the utterances are not exactly flowings from God although they can be identified as such in human experience. In textual terms, however, the interpreter can construct such a palpable world of the poetic imagination—the world of the text, in Ricoeur's terms.

For Ricoeur, meaning is not given directly; it must be achieved. The text has an overflow of meaning in that it says more than what can be perceived in the present fulfillment of meaning. With the Theoretical Mediation in its thinking activity, intermedial being mediates between "seeing," or singular representations that arise from my bodily receptivity, and "saying," which are general representations that arise from my making the conceptual determinations that are carried out in language and silence through the activity of the transcendental imagination.[34]

Whereas critical thinking combines the opposites—singular representations in terms of reference, with those universal representations in terms of meaning—religion not only unites but transcends the opposites. In terms of religious capacity as opening to a source of existence, through this power, there is a combining of saying and seeing—the meaning and the reference: "the meaning of religious discourse is itself its real reference in the world."[35]

With religious discourse, that which is said is also that which is seen. With the image, there is no reference beyond itself, to what is a perceived world, in terms of there being correspondence between what is the actual image and the perception of it. In terms of religious discourse, there is an augmentation of reality such that an image becomes more real as compared to a perceived world. What is the meaning of a religious image can instantiate its very own being. In terms of Ricoeur's theory of metaphor, "when the imagination forms an image of the new predicative congruence, the emergent meaning is not fully objectified but is also felt. The hearer or reader is thereby assimilated to the meaning precisely as she performs the predicative assimiliation."[36] Hence in addition to grasping a new congruence as that which is seen, it is felt as I carry out this work in that the thought that I have personally schematized now becomes my own individual thought through my felt participation in this process. However, at the same time, I am taken up by this activity into the light of universal reason that I share with humans as all humans have thoughts. Indeed, the meaning process draws me into participation in universal reason. And, with contemplative awareness, I am aware that this is so. Ricoeur says that feeling can be considered an intentional structure in second-order terms.[37] He explains:

> It is a process of interiorization succeeding a movement of intentional transcendence directed toward some objective state of affairs. To *feel*, in the emotional sense of the word, is to make *ours* what has been put at a distance by thought in its objectifying phase. Feelings, therefore, have a very complex kind of intentionality. They are not merely inner states but interiorized thoughts. It is as such that they accompany and complete the work of imagination as schematizing a synthetic operation: they make the schematized thought ours. Feeling, then is a case of *Selbst-Affektion*, in the sense Kant used it in the second edition of the *Critique*. This *Selbst-Affektion*, in turn, is a part of what we call poetic feeling. Its function is to abolish the distance between knower and known without canceling the cognitive structure of thought and the intentional distance which it implies. Feeling is not contrary to thought. It is thought made ours. This felt participation is a part of its complete meaning as poem.[38]

Reflexive awareness, or the truth about truth, introduces temporality, or it is reflection on the event of being in the truth. Ricoeur creates "an image of the *event* of mediation itself."[39] The event is figured as a grasping that is met by the "unveiling as 'overturning.'"[40] This figure of overturning emphasizes time as well as negativity in this event of mediation. Overturning stresses a living temporal encounter between hermeneutical inquiries and an inbreaking accentuates "the disparity and difference between inquiry and inbreaking, whether those of conceptual reflection and symbolic interpretation or those of hermeneutical mediation and divine manifestation."[41] This image of overturning itself can be interpreted in terms of a sign that has a meaning. What the sign says is that "the primordial appears only through the fallen."[42] The sign signifies that there is a "split reference: ambiguity in reference."[43] That is, manifestation occurs in two domains. The referent is a life that is refigured in openness to a divine mystery—a transfigured existence. First, in regard to the image of overturning, there is a reversal in that temporal experience is fraught with reversals. This image signifies a mediating process at work that is characterized by a discerning and the producing of new meaning as a result of the insufficiency of the literal meaning. The process at work has to do with the sentence as a whole, rather than just the word. Through the work of the productive imagination, there is a new assimilation that overturns the prior semantic collapse. This new predicative assimilation is the "act of making a similarity appear where previously only dissimilarity could be seen."[44] The interpreter sees a kinship in and through a difference. Through the metaphoric process, I am given insight as to the primordiality of my temporal existence, as a metaphor serves as a linguistic trace for a temporal schematism of my imagination.

Second, Ricoeur's image of overturning designates the actual narrative act. It is a signification of a revelational process that involves receiving, as well as being transformed, by an inbreaking of what is new being in and through a world that is projected by a religious text. This is a possibility that informs the heart of a narrative act itself. Being is intended in poetic texts in a modality of the possibility, in that they (poetic texts) refer by means of redescribing reality. An interpreter can project herself into this possible world. Religious texts, however, overturn the power that poetic texts exercise in projecting the possible. Religious texts project as well as donate an "infinite power of possibility itself, apart from any effort I might make to project a possibility on my own."[45] Religious texts carry an overflow—a superabundance.

Contemplative awareness, to recall, holds the depth of meaning of all the levels of awareness amid the silence. Contemplation for John is transformative living in the presence of God. To say I am contemplative is to say I am becoming human. There is a dynamic of growth at work. The theme of growth in love courses through the third part of the commentary. The text utters that "the soul that has reached this state of spiritual espousal knows how to do nothing else than love. . . ."[46] Although I am transformed and participating in divine love, growth in the spiritual life never ceases, and I must always be ready to engage in love as a continual exercise.[47] The text utters, too, that "[God] ever continues to communicate more love. . . ."[48] Finally, "lovers cannot be satisfied without feeling that they love as much as they are loved."[49] Thus, the practitioner/interpreter is reminded that growth is always necessary and unending.

Divine love is the source of human love, and when the human comes to recognize it as such, human spiritual love itself, inasmuch as it is in relation to divine love, is to be celebrated. This divine love is a love that is experienced in the human body. In the text, the body is a conduit for and receives divine love. The significance of the use of bodily imagery is that the idea is not to go out beyond the body, but to live more fully in the body, as the locus of human spiritual and sexual life. The stanzas of the poem, like the Song of Songs itself, are filled with sensuous references to the human body, as discussed in Chapter 4, and sexual imagery—the neck, the hand, the breast, the one hair fluttering at the neck, the eyes—all have about them, and all are the gaze of love. The gaze of love is depth—the dynamism of extraordinary depth of insight and meaning much as the symbols that are used reveal limitless content. Infinite riches await the contemplative interpreter of John's texts. Thompson aptly comments in regard to an erotic reading of John's text that "embodied in his poetry and its world of mutual self-giving, tenderness, intimacy and joy, are important insights into the nature of human love: its beauty, sensitivity and mystery, as opposed to possessiveness, abuse and self-gratification."[50]

The textual world is not one that escapes the whole of the natural world, but at the same time, it is personal, concentrating on just one small part of the world, as the textual utterances move between these two extremes.[51] Thus, there is a relationship, an integration of the part and the whole, the one and the many, the particular and the universal, which provides further textual evidence of the reality of transformation. The imagery of nature is ingredient to the poetic text. Woods, thickets, and meadows, the hill, mountains, valleys, lowlands, rivers and riverbanks, islands, waters, caverns, and love-stirring breezes, time of day—the dawn and the night both appear. There are also the forces of nature in the deadening north wind; however, this is paired up with the south wind that ushers in what breathes in the garden—the apple tree, a flowering bed with the fragrance among the flowers. There is a unity of opposites displayed in the text. And, it is all of creation that bears the mark—the divine image. But there is always an absence that remains in the presence of the image. This is, after all, a human love story. These utterances are of love sickness, of longing and search, for greater love—to become whole, to become more fully who and what I am, and to be aware that this is so.

Transformation in love in the incarnate Word is the summit of the unitive experience.[52] The contemplative seeks the divine who is hidden in the depths of the self.[53] The pursuit does not take place outside of the self.[54] The image lies within the self. What comes from God is obtained through love.[55] Nothing is known but love.[56] The inner universe of love is not a retreat from, but an enhancement of human life and the augmentation of human reality.

Contemplative awareness makes of this world a public one through sharing in the meaning of it all.

Prayer of a Soul Taken with Love

This utterance, in the form of a prayer entitled *Prayer of a Soul Taken with Love*, which is written by John, is said to have been a gloss of the exclamation of Francis of Assisi, "*Deus meus et omnia*," or "My God and all things."[57] It is a fine example of the unitive way of contemplative awareness, and another performance of the transformation of reflexive consciousness. On the unitive way, I am able to see things in a new way because I see something as other than it was previously seen to be; there is an overturning of what is seen. However, I do not discard the old meaning. I hold the old meaning, along with the new meaning. I can see things from multiple perspectives: the perspective of self as other, or empathically from the perspective of the other person, or imaginatively from the Other as divine. In other words, there is recognition of the other.

From an ethical perspective, this practice is akin to perspectival thinking, which involves intentionally choosing to understand more than one viewpoint, more than one side to an argument, more than one way of looking at things, as I recognize and acknowledge those diverse perspectives and keep in mind even different ideologically laden standpoints.[58] I want to emphasize that an individual viewpoint ideally is connected to an ethical argument as Martha Nussbaum has suggested, that is, in turn, congruent with acting for justice in the world, so that not just any individual perspective holds willy-nilly. Even if it is the case that I do not necessarily agree with those differing viewpoints or perhaps are conflicted about them, I can respect other individuals who hold them—this is to acknowledge my finitude and therefore the limits of my own position, as well as the ambiguity that exists in life. It is also to acknowledge a deep mystery about life and the mystery I am to myself; it is also to invite curiosity, wonder, and awe—even joyousness. Here, there is humility at work that can serve as an opening and introduction to a larger field of reality and meaning that one can participate in and contribute to, but never demand or command control of, as to attempt to do so is to altogether lose it.

This prayer utterance is an example of seeing creation from the perspective of the divine, as the human self who with contemplative awareness understands itself to be in the presence of God. The final lines of the prayer utterance are as follows: "Mine are the heavens and mine is the earth./Mine are the nations, the just are mine, and mine the sinners. . . ."[59] Thompson draws attention to these utterances: Contrary to what is considered the conventional use of language—through the repetition of possessive pronouns as well as adjectives that normally would suggest self-centeredness and greed—what is represented is the exact opposite of just that.[60] There is a certain impartiality and detachment from a desire to possess things for myself, such that something is remembered in freedom and appreciated for what it is in itself, rather than for what it has and can give in order to fulfill my own self-centered or wayward desires and plans.[61] He explains that "Language has been undermined, made to say the opposite of what the words appear to mean."[62] This utterance is an excellent example of the unitive way with the holding of opposites in tension, and, as such, of the transformation of reflexive consciousness—and the re-creation of language and silence within the Word.

NOTES

1. Bernard Lonergan, *Method in Theology* (Toronto: University of Toronto Press, 1971), 130–31.
2. Ibid., 131.
3. William Johnston, *"Arise, My Love . . .": Mysticism for a New Era* (Maryknoll, NY: Orbis Books, 2000), 39.
4. Ibid., 242.
5. Ibid.
6. Ibid., 238.
7. Ibid., 240; 106.
8. Ibid., 240.
9. Ibid., 273.
10. Ibid., 231.
11. Ibid., 105–6.
12. Johnston, *Mystical Theology: The Science of Love*, 84.
13. Ibid., 85.
14. Ibid., 86n22.
15. Ricoeur, CR, 94n10.
16. Ibid., 94.
17. Ibid., 96.
18. See Ricoeur, MHF, 467.
19. Ricoeur, CR, 100.
20. Ibid., 101.
21. John of the Cross, SC, 465. See Kieran Kavanaugh's introductory notes.
22. See John of the Cross, SC, theme 1. John explicitly refers to the purgative, illuminative, and unitive here.
23. Thompson, 111. Thompson comments that "The language of his poetry itself becomes a witness to the unitive experience it represents through its transcendence of the divisions literary critics assume must exist between sacred and secular, popular and learned, Eastern and Western . . . it always points to the same end and becomes a sign of the union he struggles to articulate. Whatever divisions may exist between them in the finite world, each is equal in its capacity to become signs of transcendence.

Whereas the critic asks how a poem can adopt so many styles yet retain coherence, the poet knows that at one level his words clash with each other and at another speak in complete harmony . . . the familiar can be encountered as strange, and the strange become familiar. It offers a new hearing (or reading) of its raw material, words, so that they speak with unaccustomed power and communicate across cultures and centuries. In Christian terms, this rebirth of language has a . . . sacramental quality."

24. Stein, SC, 240–41.
25. Ibid., 241.
26. John of the Cross, SC, 15; 24.6.
27. See Thompson, 279.
28. See John of the Cross, *Prologue to The Spiritual Canticle*, 2.
29. John of the Cross, SC, 5.
30. Ibid., 24.7.
31. John of the Cross, *Prologue to The Spiritual Canticle*, 2.
32. John of the Cross, SC, 25.
33. See ibid., 25.5; 25.6. See also 461, and Kavanaugh's introductory notes.
34. See Klemm, "Searching for a Heart of Gold," 100.
35. Ibid., 107.
36. Ibid., 108.
37. See Paul Ricoeur, "The Metaphorical Process as Cognition, Imagination, and Feeling," *Critical Inquiry* 5, no. 1 (Autumn 1978): 156.
38. Ibid.
39. David E. Klemm, "Ricoeur, Theology, and the Rhetoric of Overturning," *Journal of Literature & Theology* 3, vol. 3 (November 1989): 277.
40. Ibid.
41. Ibid.
42. Ibid.
43. Ricoeur, "The Metaphorical Process as Cognition, Imagination, and Feeling," 154.
44. Ibid.
45. Klemm, "Ricoeur, Theology, and the Rhetoric of Overturning," 278.
46. John of the Cross, SC, 27.8.
47. Ibid., 29.1.
48. Ibid., 33.7.
49. Ibid., 38.3.
50. Thompson, 279.
51. John of the Cross, SC, 463. See Kavanaugh's introductory notes.
52. Ibid., 1.10.
53. Ibid., 1.6.
54. Ibid., 1.8.
55. Ibid., 1.13.
56. Ibid., 1.18.
57. See Silvano Giordano, ed., *God Speaks in the Night: The Life, Times, and Teaching of St. John of the Cross*, trans. Kieran Kavanaugh (Washington, D.C.: ICS Publications, 2000), 380. See also Thompson, 278.

58. See, for example, Martha C. Nussbaum, *The New Religious Intolerance: Overcoming the Politics of Fear in an Anxious Age* (Cambridge, MA, and London, England: The Belknap Press of Harvard University Press, 2012), 25.
59. Giordano, ed., 380.
60. Thompson, 278.
61. Ibid.
62. Ibid.

Chapter 8

A Song of Hermeneutical Existence

The summoned self is the unitive way and is the key to transformation. Ricoeur explains in his essay on the summoned subject that "contemplation remains a kind of teaching because the discovery of truth is the reading within oneself of innate ideas and therefore of something always already there, but still requiring an inward discovery."[1] The actualizable possibility of the transformation of reflexive consciousness lies in the summoned self and is part of human reality. Language and symbol give possibility to transformation. The theory of discourse and silence couples with the capable self who is capable of being summoned and responding. In the fullness of time, a Word was spoken and the fallible human being was summoned into a new mode of capable human being. This mode of capable human being manifests through the practice of contemplative silence. Capable human being is summoned to ongoing response to the Word.[2] The mode of capable human being is open to continuous interpretation of the meaning of what it is to be capable human being by opening to new meaning, making meaning, unfolding meaning, discovering meaning, carrying meaning, and holding conflicting meanings (in Ricoeurian terms, the conflict of interpretations) in tension, as in nondual thinking. This mode of capable human being can be a symbol of God. A contemplative discourse of praise and celebration emerges. This is the tenth and final step of the study.

Through the ongoing transformation of reflexive consciousness, the five levels of awareness are increasingly actualized. Contemplative awareness, which carries the other four levels, can and should accompany the practice of contemplative silence, in order that the meaning of silence can be appropriated in the present moment, through hermeneutical activity. Contemplative awareness takes place in and through breathing, as well as thinking, acting, and feeling. It pulls these strands together and constitutes an integral attentiveness. My present awareness is attuned in such a way that through attentive listening through the fully embodied thinking of silence, I can extend hospitality to and welcome the word of the (textual) other in openness and vulnerability. Contemplative awareness, in carrying meanings, elicits movement in thinking, such that I can engage in the ongoing exercise of rethinking my relational realities in and for the world. The continuous movement of rethinking my relational realities which, to recall, can include my relation to God (theology) and the idea of God (philosophy), is integral to ethical action; I can open to new motivations and intentions for acting in relation to others. Through the practice of contemplative silence, capable human being, in understanding the relation between silence and language within the Word, recognizes that it has the infinite capacity to transcend itself.

There is awareness of poverty of spirit and emptiness, of utter dependence along with great desire, which correspond to the largess, the depth of contemplative human reality, and the profundity of the Word. Joy and gratitude for the grace of the silence of the Word comes in humble acceptance of finitude. Finite freedom and infinite capacity are held together in the summoned self that is the unitive way. The way in which I poetically presence my being with the other is the way of being on the way—it is a contemplative mediation. The way in which I am on the way can transform the humanness of my humanity. There is a deepening awareness of both fallibility and capability in the movement between them. They are held together in creative tension in the practice of contemplative silence; it is a fragile mediation of depth. The summoned self, in responding to the symbolic mode of capable being, mediates between accepting fallibility and opening to capability, insofar as there is openness to new meaning. In appropriating contemplative silence, one can re-create genuine human living and thus increasingly become an operative force for good in the world.[3]

My task in the remainder of this chapter is to illustrate how a further deepening and understanding of the meaning of capable human can transpire through the ongoing practice of contemplative silence. My hope is that transformation become more closely associated with movement in light of Ricoeur's concern with continuity of action. Ricoeur discusses the transformation of the summoned subject while Stein discusses transformation in terms of call and response. Initially, I shall focus on Stein's work in this regard. Second, evil is mediated in the exercise of rethinking a wrong, as a way of illustrating the importance that Ricoeur attaches to the continuation of action. Here, the practice of contemplative silence is applied to hermeneutical activity, which takes on the character of an ethical action, appearing as it does beyond the bounds of formal thinking. This exercise is integral to an understanding of the capacity for movement in mediating between fallibility and capability in hermeneutical existence. Accordingly, one can see how human expression can become more dynamic. This discussion raises, in turn, what is, I believe, a significant hermeneutical issue of how to move with increasing integrity between contexts in everyday life and in the work of textual interpretation. I pick up on this theme in the Postlude. Third, I will discuss the meaning of meaning in Stein's life and thought. In the end, I will close with a discussion of contemplative discourse within the context of the work of both Stein and Ricoeur. Further, in the spirit of Ricoeur's mediating thought, and in consideration of his work regarding movement between text and action, I will delay a conclusion and bring the study to a close with a Postlude in which I briefly ruminate on the prospects of a Third Naiveté.

First, I want to extend discussion by citing additional textual evidence using the language of the Carmelite tradition to show how the transformations have been actualized. As I consider Stein's writings, it is possible to ascertain how spiritual transformation and contemplative action are operative such that the summoned self as the unitive way, as intermedial on the way between language and silence gives way to contemplative discourse. I shall discuss the theme of call and response and the summoned subject in her work. Recall that Stein says the human is a Being-Person with an interrelation of an I, soul, spirit, and person, who has a spiritual life that flows out into the world that is disclosed to it, while at the same time keeping possession of itself.[4] One can delineate between a "*soul* being" who is oriented to the body and a "*spiritual* being" who is centered in the divine.[5] "The human I is capable" of understanding and responding to outside impressions in its exercise of personal freedom, which means that a human being is spiritual; it is a carrier of its own life as in the important sense of personally "having-oneself-in-hand."[6] This is the movement of call and response that is characteristic of the unitive way.

She explains that there is a call insofar as the intellect is attracted to something and, in turn, a person is drawn to attempt to understand what is happening.[7] There is also an attraction to reflection insofar as there is a quest for the meaning of whatever it is that has attracted a person. This movement also is an attraction to freedom as "the intellectual search for meaning" itself is representative of that free act.[8] The soul has a personal spiritual life that is integrated into a larger field of meaning. When one understands a meaning there is an attitude and behavior that accompanies the activity such that the demand must be met. There is an experience of "being-moved" deep within the being of the self so that there is "a *call* and *response*" at work; in freedom it is necessary to adopt a stance in this regard, insofar as one exercises reason in order to either negate or affirm its own standing.[9] Reason is used to refine one's position, to come to an awareness in terms of understanding in exactly what way one should conduct herself, and finally, one should exercise her personal freedom in order to pursue the necessary course of action.[10] This interiority of movement and freedom is what makes the personal I secure in itself.

When one lives a collected life, then one is situated closest to the meaning of what is happening, remains open to the demand with which it is confronted, and is positioned to assess the meaning as well as the significance of that demand. The value of living a deeply collected life is that then all the "little things" in life are more easily understood within an expanded field of awareness.[11] When one lives a collected life then one is capable of living more fully into the present moment. It should be noted that it was Stein who organized Husserl's work on internal time-consciousness. Her work unites the mind and the heart in hermeneutical activity insofar as reason in the form of self-reflexive critical and self-critical thinking is carried and held in service to the deeper life purpose of the summoned subject; it is a vocation in the sense of a calling and a summons to live more deeply. Discriminative discernment understood as an integrating hermeneutical principle is an operative force for good. To live more deeply is the vocation of the one who has been called to consequently participate through discriminative action in a larger field of awareness, of meaning and understanding. For Stein, the life of the mind and the heart work together in this developed interiority.

Stein delivers a lecture in which she discusses a vocation as a calling.[12] Vocation is connected to a formative process in that innate abilities and inherited gifts are discovered, developed, and recognized by others.[13] Examples of the transformed consciousness and the pattern of call and response appear in Stein's letters, too. She explains how acts carried out in freedom are done out of love for the divine and are the way that individual uniqueness is realized.[14] In yet another letter she discusses how she lives in gratitude and that her only desire in life is that she be a vessel of responsivity in living out her vocation.[15] This is the summoned subject.

MEDIATING ACTION IN RICOEUR'S THOUGHT

Ricoeur continually mediates polarities in his thinking, and I want to focus initially on two of them. In doing so, I hope to accentuate the overriding concern in his thought with the continuation of action. In the Epilogue to *Memory, History, Forgetting,* "Difficult Forgiveness," he discusses how I can be paralyzed in my capacity to act due to the "enigma of a fault," and yet the lifting of what seems like an incapacity is the "the enigma of forgiveness."[16] Forgiveness, while difficult, is not impossible. The possibility of forgiveness stands within the common, if elusive, horizon of memory, history, and forgetting. He formulates a polarity between avowal and hymn, that is, between fault and forgiveness. How impossible forgiveness is when someone has carried out an unpardonable act, and yet, it is the guilty who are most especially due my consideration![17] Paralysis and inertia can plague me and prevent me from taking action that would lead to healing relations. Suffering can also be an impediment to forgiveness. Suffering, in addition to physical and mental pain, involves a diminished capacity to act which I experience as a violation of my self-integrity. When suffering harbors resentment and the desire for revenge, the possibility of forgiveness is often stifled.

Spanning the polarity of fault and forgiveness are two speech acts. The first speech act is the avowal of imputability, the acknowledgment or admission of agency—the "I can" which "binds" the agent to the action.[18] The second speech act is a hymn to forgiveness which is captured in the celebrative love and joy of sapiential poetry, and which exudes, I would add, a generosity of spirit: "There is forgiveness, this voice says."[19] It is in the practice of contemplative silence that "conscience" exerts its force. Conscience is the voice of the claim of the other (relational reality) on the self at the depth of language and silence.

The second polarity is formed by placing into tension the notion of origin from *The Symbolism of Evil* and the horizon of eschatology from *Memory, History, Forgetting*. With regard to the first pole, "The symbol gives rise to thought"; it gives me something to think about. Symbol stands close to the origin of consciousness, arising, as it does, out of immediacy in life experience. This is close to the moment of originating silence and its initial interruption by *logos*. However, when I think, I bring presuppositions with me. Thinking necessarily expands from thinking about what is given to recognizing and remembering where I come from. I start with an interpretation that takes account of the original enigma contained in the symbol and that advances and shapes the meaning in the freedom of thought.[20] This act of interpretation is an original appropriation, and an event of language and, I would add, silence.[21] The poetic presencing of meaning is a "happening of truth" through what I would refer to as the "discourse-event," in which the context of meaning presents itself in a way that bestows recognizable understanding as language and silence are understood.[22] Through this process, the symbol has the power and force to disclose and unveil reality. When I interpret symbols, my self-awareness is enhanced. A philosophy that has been taught by the symbols has the work of transforming reflexive consciousness. How so? The answer is that the symbol, temporalized in metaphor, addresses the mind at the level of feeling.

The other pole is the horizon of eschatology. This pole can be related to terminating silence. Following Kant, philosophy of religion has the forward-moving agenda of setting free the original ground of goodness in human nature. "Restoration" is Kant's term for redemption from evil. The agenda of restoration should occur in the "optative mood," insofar as one expresses a wish or a choice.[23] After all, a person who is guilty is capable of so much more than her offenses or faults. The agent should be released from those very acts. To be rehabilitated, the guilty one must "be restored to his capacity for acting, and his action restored to its capacity for continuing."[24] This notion of the capacity for continuing action is drawn from Hannah Arendt's argument in *The Human Condition* regarding the dialectic of binding and unbinding under the law.[25] Unbinding the bound one requires forgiving and promising. Promising engages the capacity for acting. Forgiving permits the continuation of human action. This dialectic of binding and unbinding takes place within the ultimate horizon of an anticipated and projected restoration of goodness—a horizon of hope.

I would point out that the practice of contemplative silence can be considered as the space within which I may mediate the meaning of ultimate origin with the meaning of ultimate goal—symbols of creation are transcritically interpreted in terms of the speculative language of the coming kingdom of God, of utopia. In this space, I hold polarities open, self-consciously link them while withholding judgment, and listen to the voice of conscience. The goal is both to find the evil or negative thought I would ascribe to others in myself, and to recognize that the goodness toward which I strive is already present as the presupposition of the projection of hope.

I can manifest this mode of being and this kind of thinking in and for the world. I come to recognize myself in this movement through the practice of contemplative silence, by allowing the depth of language and silence to manifest itself in and through the activity of interpretation. I would like to consider for a moment the activity of rethinking a wrong that has been perpetrated. Suppose that in immediate response to the wrong, I suffer pain. The underlying unreflected thought is "I am in pain." I may recall that I fired back at this pain in anger, resentment, and fear. In contemplative silence I recall our (1) immediate self-awareness or the direct experience of the self as one of victim of injustice by connecting the idea of justice with the pain I face. Furthermore, I recognize my (2) immediate objective awareness or being with being as one of blaming the other, the one to whom I impute the cause of the injustice. This level is also one of unreflected immediacy. At the third level, of (3) reflective awareness I understand that I made the connection between blame and the other by thinking the concept of fault and engaging in a judgment: "She is guilty!" The relational reality I establish is one of moral fault—a rift between us.

At the fourth level, of (4) reflexive awareness, I consciously intervene in the reflective awareness by holding open blame and innocence, withholding judgment so that I may become aware of new possibilities of interpretation. I may reflect that the wrong I have suffered is itself a response to my own prior actions within a competitive cycle whose origin is unknown. I may seek the symbols of the origin of tainted relational realities in the Adamic myth, which speaks of the first sin as a broken relationship with God, the loss—through misused freedom—of primordial trust in being. I apply not only phenomenology of symbols but also a critique of hidden ideologies: Is my view skewed because of sexism, or racism, unconscious repressions, or distorted economic conditions? Once purified of systemic distortions, my practice of contemplative silence may further bring me to project my image of the day in which this relationship—and all others—will be mended and goodness restored. I might think of what action would be required to bring about the desired reconciliation—namely words of forgiveness. Finally, in (5) contemplative awareness, I am aware of the entire arc of interpretation, a complex act of selectively recalling, working through, and re-imaging the identities that reflect my relational realities. I hold together conflicting meanings and ambiguity, as I engage in nondual thinking. Nondual thinking is cessation of thinking that comes to its rest, its final end, in the unity of intuition defined as the conjunction of concept and percept, thinking and perceiving.

I confront evil and negative thought in myself. Hermeneutical activity can help me work it through in a way that enriches my humanity, and my humanity is brought into integrity. Thus, hermeneutical activity can be integrated into contemplative silence and contemplative silence can be enriched by hermeneutics. One ought to think of hermeneutical activity as ethical activity; it is not just an activity of formal thinking. Hermeneutical activity is an ethical action, and its aim is the ethical transformation of my being. Contemplative silence applied to myself and my life circumstances has ethical import.

THE MEANING OF MEANING IN THE LIFE AND THOUGHT OF STEIN

Ricoeur, in an interview with his biographer, comments that "whatever we may think about the idealistic interpretation of phenomenology of Husserl, it is to Husserl that we owe the opening of the field of the 'meaningful.'"[26] Further, he understands the transition to be the phenomenology of being as care (*Sorge*) in Heidegger's *Being and Time* in that it expands intentionality beyond idealism; hermeneutics broadens phenomenology such that phenomenology is liberated insofar as "the given is the hidden and the hidden is the given."[27] The concept of intentionality undergoes continuous development so that there is finally being-in-the-world. Husserl has been criticized for his idealism insofar as his work is in keeping within a framework of a theory of knowledge that includes the subject/object relation, although Ricoeur believes that this subject/object relationship has been overcome by the myriad ways in which human being is placed in a world, indeed, human being belongs to the world, and commits to concerned participation in the world.[28] Thus, it would be wrong to assert that this realism is opposed to idealism because realism, too, was trapped in the subject/object relationship and was, indeed, the opposite of idealism, but only in relative terms within that specified relational context for Ricoeur. The notions of textuality and the conflict of interpretations come into play here. Stein and several other of his students were critical of Husserl's philosophical idealism, but what is significant to keep in mind is that as his devoted student and protégé, she is concerned with meaning and the "meaningful" in her life and in her thought.

In her work, Stein has an abiding interest in philosophical and theological anthropology and philosophical and theological hermeneutics.[29] Not only does she ask the anthropological questions, What is the human being? and What is the being of human being? but she also asks the hermeneutical question, What is the meaning of human being? These questions necessitate the posing of a third reflexive question in order to carry out an interpretation of her work that does justice to and honors her life and thought—her Jewish roots and her Carmelite background—in addition to her intellectual pursuit of the life of the mind: What is the meaning of meaning for Stein? In order to follow these anthropological and hermeneutical questions, I shall adopt Ricoeur's approach and interpret her theology and philosophy. Stein, in her theology and in her philosophy, responds to, processes through, and carries her relational realities with integrity, mindfulness, and a profound understanding of who she is—and is not. Meaning is an integrating life principle in her spiritual and intellectual life. It is known from her autobiography and her letters that she read at least some of the works of Schleiermacher and Wilhelm Dilthey. So it is fitting to make a reflexive hermeneutical turn here to inquire what she means by the concept of the "meaningful." In other words, What is the meaning of meaning in Stein's life and thought?

Stein, in her text, *Potency and Act*, which was a forerunner to *Finite and Eternal Being*, considers the "Spiritual life as intellectual life."[30] She goes on to explain that "Living means being in motion from within. Living *spiritually* also means being aware of this motion, being illumined for oneself, being conscious of oneself and possibly of something else—*intelligere* [understanding]—, setting oneself and something else in motion from oneself."[31] Reflection, reflexivity, and the practice of contemplative silence are all at work in the relational awareness that she is referring to. She goes on to write how in God this is all one, but in humans this involves "a manifold of different acts."[32]

If one interprets Stein's life in terms of the practice of contemplative silence, I suggest as an informed possibility and a way of initiating a line of thought that the meaning of meaning in her life is to live with contemplative awareness—a spiritual awareness of depth characterized by personal self-giving in the individual soul and lived out in genuine communal life.[33] It is, moreover, individual persons in all of their primordial particularity that have been imparted with and drawn into divine life. For spiritual persons, becoming one in love involves the receiving into the self of the beloved so that the one who loves is in the image of the beloved—a generative loving union in which they completely reveal and so, disclose themselves to each other. Stein explains how in this relationship, "They bear fruit by virtue of the atmosphere which radiates from them on their environment and perhaps also by means of the works which they produce in common and through which they 'propogate' their spirit."[34] Just as Heidegger, in building on Husserl's work, is credited with developing intentionality to the point of being-in-the-world that is the temporality of finite being, it is likewise fitting to credit Stein for the further expansion of intentionality to the point of the self-transcendence of intentionality in personal self-giving. And, if I now make a theological turn and follow her, that for her is the relational awareness of eternal being—the infinite horizon of eternal being. It is being-in-the-world-in-tripersonal-relationship. "Here" in contemplative awareness, a transformation is effected in that a shift "now" occurs as the egocentric orientation gives way to a theocentric orientation.[35] It is the relational awareness of the fullness of being—what she personally experiences and names eternal being.[36]

What is at stake for Stein, beginning with her early work on empathy, is the humanness of our humanity—that qualitative depth of value wherein one realizes human life as life that is lived with and for others; I could employ Ricoeur's word, solicitude, as an analogous term here. The experience of being-affected and what it is to humbly receive from the other involves an intentional structure about feeling. According to Stein, when one empathizes in understanding the situation or perspective of the other, one is expressing care or concern, even love—in light of what she says in her later writings—for the other. *One is illumined, raised up out of superficiality into the unitive light of reason, of deepened awareness of a shared humanity—and that is what I understand to be the meaning of meaning in Stein's thought.*

CONTEMPLATIVE DISCOURSE AS THE SONG OF SONGS

Stein makes a concerted philosophical effort to account for understanding as an ongoing process and event of what it is to be a human being and what it means to be a human being who is devoted to pursuing wisdom with love, and love with wisdom; she is dedicated to living the spiritual life as an intellectual life. Stein strives to live a life of integrity as she pursues hermeneutical inquiry. And, true to the Carmelite tradition, she responsively seeks after the heart of meaning in her personal life. In her life and in her thought, she blazes a path of light as she provides one with a threefold way to follow: a path of truth, goodness, and beauty.

If I correlate contemplative awareness with truth, I am shown the way of truth in which to interpret human life. The texts of Stein can be interpreted as truthful performances of the transformation of reflexive consciousness inasmuch as they constitute at once spiritual transformation and contemplative action. I can see how the actualizable possibility of the transformation of reflexive consciousness is a part of ordinary human reality, and that inasmuch as it is an ethical and spiritual task, it warrants explanation and interpretation. The human being, in thinking, mediates between universality and particularity—between pure reflection and hermeneutical philosophy—in order to reach new understandings and unfold new meaning, and to arrive, therefore, at fresh insight about human life.[37] One pursues truth through cognitional self-transcendence, and by moving toward a reality that the words are pointing to—a universe filled with being. Truth is not purely reflexive, as each human being receives the entreaty to locate herself in a more excellent way in being, which entails a life of active involvement in the world, whatever form that may take.

If I correlate contemplative awareness with goodness, I am shown a way of goodness so that I might share in a discourse that respects human dignity—one that embraces the humanness of our humanity. How does one, in the words of the poet, Kirsten Dierking, deal with "that ache to extract meaning from vastness?"[38] When I think of how Stein met her end, I can ask, How do I go about extracting meaning from the vastness of an abyss even? If one thinks of the pursuit of goodness in human life as the ongoing moral striving to share discourse, then in the shrinking world that is ours of social media and pandemic, an enormous challenge lies in having the heart, the courage, to continually attempt to understand the situation and perspective of the other, and to act in response—not out of fearful reaction—to those understandings.[39] As I reach certain understandings of the other, I can arrive at new understandings of myself as well, and I am aware that this is so. Far from assimilating otherness, Stein's nuanced theory of empathy maintains distance in intimacy, the respectful space necessary for acknowledging that difference, personal uniqueness, and individuality are ingredients in a life of responsive freedom. And a life of responsive freedom emerges out of social and cultural life with its communal dimensions of equality, reciprocity, and responsivity.[40] Then it becomes an actualizable possibility to lift each other up—to "carry" each other—without resentment, rejection, or blame, and respond in new and larger fields of meaning and reality, rather than to marginalize, demonize, ostracize, isolate, alienate, segregate, execute, torture, terrorize, rape, and victimize one another. Stein astutely writes that "People are neither brutes nor angels, because they are both in one. Their bodily sentient being differs from the sentient being of brutes, and their spirituality differs from that of angels."[41]

If I correlate contemplative awareness with beauty, I am shown a way of beauty—that is, an aesthetically pleasing way to appropriate the meaning of silence in the here and now through the hermeneutical endeavor. In appreciating the silence that envelops and punctuates discourse and communication, and in appropriating the meaning of silence, human being as finite, embodied freedom, recognizes in understanding the relation between silence and language within the Word, that it has an infinite capacity to transcend itself through meaning-making activity. And, in understanding the relation between fallibility and capability, hermeneutical existence as such can be seen to be a form of spiritual and ethical growth, as the aesthetic joy of living a beautiful life more and more takes hold. "We meet this splendor," Stein says, "in the world of sense in the radiance of physical light . . . in the loveliness of physical forms and bodies."[42] This splendor is also met in the spiritual beauty of the human soul insofar as its manner and actions are in accord with an intellectual clarity characteristic of reason.[43] What distinguishes the created spirit is having experientially become aware of the accord "with all other existents in that it, too, is permeated by the law and order of all that which is."[44] Contemplative discourse can create space to understand a shared humanity—and I am aware that this is so. Then, contemplative discourse becomes the song of songs. It is the sheer blissful joy in knowing, loving, serving; it is the joyous and "free self-giving of this gift of life."[45]

CONTEMPLATIVE DISCOURSE: A SONG OF HERMENEUTICAL EXISTENCE

In the spirit of Ricoeur who is always probing the mystery of existence, that is, of what it is to be human and the meaning of being human, I shall relate an enigma of hermeneutical existence: In the epilogue to the epilogue of *Memory, History, Forgetting*, Ricoeur says that "recognition is . . . the small miracle of memory . . . in the silent evocation of a being who is absent or gone forever, the cry escapes: 'That is her! That is him!'"[46] A moment of recognition. One can think, "Who can *say*, who can *see* . . . who I am?"[47] A moment of truth. I can respond with my Yes to life, my Yes to acting and to suffering in the acceptance of all that is which means that I am capable human being—'I can' be with, 'I can' live through, and 'I can' transcend paradox and contradiction as I understand my manifestation of lived experience in a new way. In changing my relationship to language by recognizing silence I change my relationship to myself; in changing my relationship to myself I change my relationship to language and silence, and integrally so.

A hermeneutics of contemplative silence manifests a deeper level of awareness as a poetics of presencing a shared human solidarity, "In which being there together is enough," in the words of Wallace Stevens.[48] I can come to recognize myself in a new light as I understand more and more continually so, the responsive words: *"There is forgiveness,"*[49] or *"you are better than your actions."*[50] I can remember the uniqueness to the way in which the voice proclaims the words of forgiveness, which come from above.[51] Ricoeur explains, "It is a silent voice but not a mute one. Silent, because there is no clamor of what rages; not mute, because not deprived of speech. An appropriate discourse is in fact dedicated to it, the hymn. A discourse of praise and celebration."[52]

A hymn to humanity is sung and can be sung and sung again: I can continually refer truth claims back to my existence as I strive to live my life with integrity, and in greater depth. Given the Ricoeurian "I can" and my capability, I can, indeed, continue to make, unfold, discover, and carry meaning, and interpret my lived experience—in harmony with the lovely poetic words of *the* song of songs: "Arise, my love, . . . the time of singing has come, . . . let me hear your voice, ..."[53]

SUMMARY OF THE STUDY AND A DELAYED CONCLUSION

The significance of this study is that I have shone a philosophical eye on the practice of contemplative silence. I have done so using the thought of Paul Ricoeur and the hermeneutical tradition, and primary texts of the Christian theological, spiritual/mystical tradition, especially the work of Edith Stein as well as John of the Cross, and the Carmelite tradition. I provided an explanation of how the practice is possible. The context was theoretically determined in terms of fallibility and capability. The context was religiously determined in terms of the purgative, the illuminative, and the unitive ways, as well as the *via negativa*. In so doing, I established a hermeneutical and a phenomenological context, in addition to a historical and religious/theological context, for the practice of contemplative silence.

Toward these goals, in Chapter 1, I explained Ricoeur's philosophical anthropology, and his reflection on fallible human being. In Chapter 2, I explained his methodological change from reflection to hermeneutics, and his work on a hermeneutics of symbol. I then shifted focus in Chapter 3 to capable human and the role of silence in the creation of meaning. I identified the elements that warrant this shift, including in addition to Ricoeur's transition to hermeneutics, his interpretation theory, which included a discussion of expression and discourse, and the relation of silence to discourse using the work of Dauenhauer, and finally the hermeneutical self of Ricoeur with personal, narrative, moral, and aesthetic identities. I grafted the practice of contemplative silence onto Dauenhauer's third irreducible moment of silence. I constructed capable human who understands the relation of silence to discourse. Chapter 4 was a description of the practice of contemplative silence as a historical phenomenon, using textual testimony and avowal to the practice in telling what the practice is. The Carmelite spiritual tradition was privileged in Chapter 5 in order to associate Stein with this school of spirituality which she practiced, as well as to ground her thought in the work of John of the Cross.

With Chapter 6, I turned to the practice of contemplative silence and explained it as the means and end of spiritual transformation. I accomplished this task by engaging in an analysis of the meaning of the practice of contemplative silence. I also provided an ontic example of the practice, in the Carthusian school of spirituality, which is representative of the practice as a religious phenomenon. The practice is undertaken in a reflexive space of consciousness that involves a dialectic between silence and language within the Word. In order to understand the transformation, next, I mined the philosophical tradition in order to provide knowledge of the five levels of awareness ingredient in the phenomenon itself as potentialities—immediate self-awareness, immediate objective awareness, reflective awareness, reflexive awareness, and contemplative awareness. Contemplative awareness and the transformation of reflexive consciousness culminate in the idea of the summoned subject with contemplative awareness. Given the consideration of the practice of contemplative silence itself, and the five contextual levels of awareness, all the elements were in place so that one could understand the meaning of capable human.

Chapters 7 and 8 addressed the meaning of the practice—the meaning is the transformation. The transformation was interpreted in a threefold way. In Chapter 7, first, I reinterpreted Ricoeur's four "I can's," in terms of the practice of contemplative silence as a transformative spiritual and ethical activity. Second, select texts of John of the Cross, representative of the Carmelite tradition, were interpreted to illustrate that the transformations are real. The texts were shown to be capable of uttering, and capable of the transformed consciousness. Then in Chapter 8, I explained the notion of the summoned subject in Ricoeur and the theme of call and response in Stein. I also extended my engagement with the Carmelite textual tradition in taking up Stein's texts once again and posed a reflexive question, What is the meaning of meaning for Stein? in order to carry out an interpretation of her work that recognizes her life and her thought—her Jewish roots as part of a vibrant tradition, as well as the Carmelite tradition—in addition to her life of scholarly inquiry. Whereas in Chapter 7, transformation involved metaphor and "overturning," in Chapter 8, transformation was discussed in terms of movement and continuity of movement, something that Ricoeur emphasizes in his thought.

I present by way of this summary, the summoned self as being the unitive way and the key to the transformation. Fallible human was summoned into a new mode of capable being, which manifests through the practice of contemplative silence. Capable human being is what it means to live hermeneutical existence, which is, in turn, a form of spiritual and ethical maturity. One way to think about the nature of the practice of contemplative silence is as an ongoing mediating activity of understanding the relation between fallibility and capability in lived hermeneutical existence. Lived hermeneutical existence lies at the heart of contemplative human reality. Contemplative human reality is the heart of meaning. In the spirit of Ricoeur's mediating thought, I will delay a conclusion and proceed to the Postlude in which I briefly ruminate on the prospects of a Third Naiveté.

NOTES

1. See Paul Ricoeur, "The Summoned Subject in the School of the Narratives of the Prophetic Vocation," *Figuring the Sacred: Religion, Narrative, and Imagination*, trans. David Pellauer, ed. Mark I. Wallace (Minneapolis: Augsburg Fortress Press, 1995), 270.

2. See David E. Klemm, "The Word as Grace: The Religious Bearing of Paul Ricoeur's Philosophy," *Faith and Philosophy*, vol. 10, no. 4 (October 1993): 503; 517. Klemm clarifies the religious import of Ricoeur's philosophy: "Ricoeur describes how the word as word (language as such) functions as grace such that philosophical thinking, which is necessarily referred to words and symbols as the medium of its own thinking of being, is itself always already a religious thinking."

3. See John Wall, *Moral Creativity: Paul Ricoeur and the Poetics of Possibility* (New York: Oxford University Press, 2005), 155; 179. Given the unity of contemplation and action, I want to direct attention to Wall's work. He considers moral life and thought to be radically creative. He draws from Ricoeur's work on hope that is directed to the future and his "affirmation of the human capability for goodness made by faith." Importantly, he addresses evil in a poetic sense in that "it is a failure to create the world itself anew, a failure to render productive through meaningful life in common the two-way tensionality of passivity and agency together." This tensionality is rendered productive, I maintain, in contemplative awareness.

4. Stein, FEB, 364; 374.
5. Ibid., 461.
6. Ibid., 370.
7. Ibid., 438.
8. Ibid., 439.
9. Ibid.
10. Ibid.

11. Ibid., 440.
12. Stein, Woman, 59.
13. Ibid., 60.
14. Stein to Sr. Agnella Stadtmüller, OP, October 29, 1939, Letter 306, in SPL, 313.
15. Stein to Mother Petra Brüning, OSU, April 16, 1939, Letter 300, in SPL, 309.
16. Ricoeur, MHF, 456–57.
17. Ibid., 458.
18. Ibid., 457–58.
19. Ibid., 458.
20. Ricoeur, SE, 348–50.
21. See Martin Heidegger, "The Nature of Language," *On the Way to Language*, trans. Peter D. Hertz (New York: Harper and Row Publishers, Inc., 1971), 59. Heidegger explains that "In experiences which we undergo with language, language itself brings itself to language."
22. See Heidegger, "The Origin of the Work of Art," 69; 44.
23. Ricoeur, MHF, 493. See also OA, 218, in which he explains that "Human (free) choice appears to carry with it an original wound that affects its capacity for determining itself for or against the law; the enigma of the origin of evil is reflected in the enigma that affects the actual exercise of freedom. The fact that this penchant is always already present in every opportunity to choose but that it is at the same time a maxim of (free) choice is no less inscrutable than the origin of evil."
24. Ricoeur, MHF, 493.
25. Ibid., 486; 493. See also Ricoeur, "Ethics and Human Capability: A Response," 290. Ricoeur, in quoting Hannah Arendt, says that "'the continuation of action' may be the ultimate concern of ethical action." See Hannah Arendt, *The Human Condition*, 2nd ed., intro. Margaret Canovan (Chicago and New York: The University of Chicago Press, 1998), 230–47.
26. Reagan, 104.
27. Ibid.
28. Ibid.
29. Stein, Life, 397; 502n184. She notes the importance of the work of Max Scheler and Wilhelm Dilthey in this regard. While she also notes in a letter to Roman Ingarden that she has four volumes of the original edition of Schleiermacher's sermons, it would be of interest to know if she had access to his *Hermeneutics and Criticism* and his lecture notes on the theme of dialectic at the University of Berlin. See Stein to Roman Ingarden, October 10, 1918, Letter 53, in Letters to Roman Ingarden, 141; 142n5. See also Wilhelm Dilthey, *Introduction to the Human Sciences*, vol. 1, Selected Works, ed. and intro. Rudolph A. Makkreel (Princeton, NJ: Princeton University Press, 1989).
30. Edith Stein, *Potency and Act: Studies Toward a Philosophy of Being*, vol. 11, The Collected Works of Edith Stein, trans. Walter Redmond, ed. L. Gelber and Romaeus Leuven, intro. Hans Rainer Sepp (Washington, D.C.: ICS Publications, 2009), 129.
31. Ibid.
32. Ibid.

33. Ibid., 466; 458.

34. Ibid., 466.

35. See "Husserl and Aquinas: A Comparison," 32. In her discussion of Husserl and Aquinas, she delineates between transcendental phenomenology and Catholic philosophy and explains that "the latter has a *theocentric* and the former an *egocentric* orientation."

36. Stein, FEB, 466.

37. Ibid., 318. Stein explains that "Only when it knows can the intellect have an 'authentic understanding' of what *knowledge* and *truth* really are."

38. Kirsten Dierking, "Sailing on Lake Superior," *Northern Oracle* (Minneapolis, MN: Spout Press, 2007), 12.

39. Stein, FEB, 318.

40. See Edith Stein, *An Investigation Concerning the State*, vol. 10, The Collected Works of Edith Stein, ed. and trans. Marianne Sawacki (Washington, D.C.: ICS Publications, 2006), 171. Stein makes an important distinction between "ethical duty" and "ethical quality." While ethical duty is connected to one's individual freedom and the choice one has to do what is necessary in a given situation, with ethical quality, one is always dependent on others as the inclination to adopt values and the way one gains them is not entirely up to the individual—one is dependent on others in this regard. Nevertheless, one must still exercise one's freedom to listen and to seek them out even if they are unattainable at the time; there is a dynamic of interdependence at work.

41. Ibid., 371.

42. Ibid., 323.

43. Ibid. Stein quotes here Thomas Aquinas.

44. Ibid., 320.

45. Ibid., 371.

46. Ricoeur, MHF, 495.

47. Ricoeur, FM, Chapter 2.

48. Wallace Stevens, "Final Soliloquy of the Interior Paramour," *The Collected Poems of Wallace Stevens* (New York: Vintage Books, 1990), 524.

49. Ricoeur, MHF, 466.

50. Ibid., 493.

51. Ibid., 467.

52. Ibid.

53. Song of Solomon 2:10–14 (NRSV). See also Paul Ricoeur, *Critique and Conviction: Conversations with François Azouvi and Marc de Launay*, trans. Kathleen Blamey (New York: Columbia University Press, 1998), 184–86. Ricoeur remarks that "between the aesthetic and the religious . . . there is a zone of overlap," continuing, "one of the richest examples of . . . overlap of the religious and the aesthetic is, undoubtedly, the Canticle of Canticles." This poetry contains the verticality of the divine and human relationship, and yet, at the same time, love brings with it reciprocity "that can imply crossing the threshold between the ethical and the mystical.

Where ethics maintains the vertical dimension, mysticism attempts to introduce reciprocity; the lover and loved occupy equal, reciprocal roles. Reciprocity is introduced into verticality by means of the language of love and thanks to the metaphorical resources of the erotic." He also refers to "its capacity to introduce tenderness in the ethical relation."

Postlude

Toward a Third Naiveté

Stein pursued truth in her life and in her thought. She carried a faith tradition forward while she was true to herself in continuing to probe what it is to be human and the meaning of being human as the philosopher and theologian that she was. She also remained meaningfully engaged with the faith tradition of her roots. A crucial question that emerges from her work is, How can one facilitate movement between different contexts, theological, philosophical, and otherwise in terms of critical hermeneutical philosophy, and at the same time, remain true to the relational realities of one's lived existence in this present moment of history and historical consciousness? That is, as a moral agent, I have the capability to respond to the signs of the times in a world fraught with systemic injustice, inequality, and violence.

Chauvet, in *Symbol and Sacrament*, suggests the need for a "third" naiveté, which remains a naiveté, he reminds the reader, because symbolic action involves the entire subject, and not just the brain.[1] He also says that prophetic criticism places one in the realm of ethics, of action. One can ask, What action shall I respond with? I would advocate for self-critical, self-reflexive action with a difference, as an initial response. Let me explain. A third naiveté goes beyond issuing a judgment in terms of intellectual transformation. Also, it is not simply a return to a naïve understanding in critically justifiable terms. With contemplative awareness, I am attentively responsive to discourse—language and silence, and I am in the process of—on the way to—learning how to be with my words and my silence and that of others in and through my action. A "third naiveté" not only breathes, sees, and hears, but responds to language as well as the silence that resides in the spaces of my moving relations of meaning in my being in the world. This is precisely what is unthought in the work of Ricoeur. It involves holding my relational realities in and through text and action. Thus, text and action (Ricoeur) and contemplation and action (Stein) have silence and the relation of silence to discourse as an integrating principle in terms of living relational realities. Moreover, there is the possibility to arrive at deeper coherence of meaning in this dynamic movement. Whereas the second naiveté does not explicitly include the relation of silence to discourse, a third naiveté includes the relation of silence to discourse and explicitly acknowledges the role of silence in the creation of meaning. Contemplation in and through my action enables, ennobles, and empowers me to mindfully move from context to context with growing integrity, while space is created in terms of my relational realities. A deeper appropriation is possible in living out of an expanded nondual awareness, even as critical thinking and self-critical thinking connected to ethics and a spirituality, is held amid it all. I therefore can move continually, inclusively, and integrally beyond issuing a judgment to contemplative awareness in carrying out the process of discriminative discernment. Capable human—human capability—increasingly can become an operative force for good in the world. This is, in part, what it is to do justice in and through relational realities.

Second, recall that Yannaras discusses how in the Areopagitical writings whereas natural knowledge corresponds with the self-sufficiency of human fallenness and presupposes individual verification, and therefore, individual doubt and divisiveness, with the apophatic knowledge of God, comes the experience of personal relationship, which does not divide, but brings nature and knowledge into harmonious relationship.[2] Further, knowledge serves as merely the starting point—a dynamic one to be sure—for realization and "awareness," I would add, of the empirical relationship with reality. Yannaras explains that the human capacity to approach reality through apprehension requires the coordination of many different factors such that in the realization (and awareness) of this relationship of knowing, the otherness of respective approaches and the freedom of approach is preserved.

For Stein, this has to do with the development of interiority. She likens this growth to mystical theology insofar as a person is being transformed in a new way of knowledge, Christian mysticism, although it be in the negative. In following Pseudo-Dionysius, as well as Thomas Aquinas (who, in turn, follows Aristotle), she explains how positive and negative theologies upon completing an ascent "come together at the summit of 'mystical theology' where God himself unveils his mysteries but at the same time imparts a feeling of their impenetrability."[3] Negative theology serves as a corrective and a complement for positive theology, she says, "And something will appear in both theologies that turns any knowledge of God into the experience of God: the personal encounter with him."[4] I have arrived at what is the heart of personal life for Stein.

The transformation of reflexive consciousness and cognitive self-transcendence hinge on both the way in which I am on the way with my empirical relational realities—that is, the dispossession of myself, the renouncing of myself, self-giving, and self-reflexive critique in terms of critical hermeneutical philosophy. Here I am in the realm of "self-reflexively providing a critical reflection or deconstruction of . . . [my own] narrative of agency," to employ the words of Susan Abraham in her work on postcolonial hermeneutics.[5] She explains the importance of Catholic decolonial theology being attentive to contextual concerns—"economic, political, cultural, and multi-religious"—but that in light of global Catholic theology its limits must also be taken into consideration.[6] Further, one of the merits she sees in contemporary postcolonial hermeneutics is the different regional variation that is expressed globally.[7] She discusses the work of Anthony J. Godzieba and Lieven Boeve, and the latter's call for Catholic theology to become a "radical hermeneutical theology"; however, what can be regarded as spirituality is dependent upon particular languages in addition to the grammars of the particular context.[8] Decolonization is discourse carried out from particular contexts, deconstructive in and of itself; this involves historicized spirituality such that self-securing truth claims are deconstructed in recontextualizing theology.[9]

I take this to mean that one must proceed modestly, but the important point is that one must proceed; one gives, and in and through the process, one receives. I see the possibility for this process to be an important spiritual practice, a discipline, for those who take seriously the necessity to make sense of and appropriate the Catholic intellectual tradition—that is, to genuinely, critically, and self-critically engage it and make meaning of it—and not a form of relativism for, as Yannaras explains, "the Church's theology is a witness to its experience" beginning with the witness of the apostles to a historical person.[10] What is the changeable element is language, specifically the language of relation as an expression of love that continually is modified and renewed such that new expression of these relational realities is never exhausted.[11] I would add silence here so as to include discourse in its entirety.

Stein, too, explains how the meaning in language understood as a process evolves: "that words no longer have their original meaning must be attributed to the historical process of semantic change in its various forms . . . when we use an individual proper name to designate a particular thing, this name is *poor* in content and meaning compared to the richness of its intentional object. . . ."[12] Further, doctrine develops, that is, it "evolves"[13] to follow John Henry Newman in that there is, indeed, growth, even as this unfolding and flowering is realized in the middle of continuity and permanence.[14] One can think of continual growth in the spiritual life of the *ecclesia* as the beautiful and magnificent flowering of awareness in the garden of eternal relational reality. As for the Church—the *ecclesia*—it "is the realization of this divine gift . . . the mode of the Trinity, the mode of freedom from every existential necessity, made a reality from created human existences—it is existence as relation. . . ."[15] Given the relational reality of the triadic, tripersonal God and the human being as ecclesial, "will or freedom is not an individual property, something exercised or achieved, but a fact and realization of relation self-transcendence—it is love as *mode of existence*," explains Yannaras.[16] Love is performative and ecstatically joyous; it is the unending divine symphony—the song of songs. If one is listening well, it is celestial music heard now in and through the pulsating heart of a shared humanity and experienced as relational awareness.

If one looks at proceeding on the way as traveling lightly with utter humility, and the necessity of proceeding as engaging in critical and self-critical hermeneutical philosophy, I believe this locates one within the context of this study, in the realm of discourse and silence, and the five contextual levels of awareness that culminate in contemplative awareness. The various dimensions of contemplative silence and its reflection in discourse as well as action and form of life are different ways to think through transformative human experience.

McGinn uses the term, "mystical consciousness," as a worthwhile way to think about the modes of special encounter with God that Christian mystics have spoken of, "primarily because consciousness emphasizes the *entire process* of human intentionality and self-presence, rather than just an originating pure feeling, sensation, or experience easily separable from subsequent acts of thinking, loving, and deciding."[17] He goes on to explain in his rationale that someone who investigates mystical consciousness tries to analyze the texts and life witness of these mystical teachers "for what they reveal about all the forms of thinking and loving in which the human subject achieves self-transcendence and transformation through an encounter with God, the ultimate Source and final Goal."[18] And, mystical consciousness makes the further claim that beyond the consciousness of objects, as well as the consciousness or self-presence as an agent in the acts as an I, or reflexively in the self-appropriation of the act of intending, there is a "consciousness-*beyond*" or "meta-consciousness," McGinn explains in quoting Merton.[19] This "meta-consciousness" can be thought of as the "co-presence of God in our inner acts . . . not as an object, but as a goal that is both transcendent and yet immanent."[20] There is an infinite horizon that includes all of knowing and loving, which "somehow becomes really 'here' in a new form of awareness. . . ."[21]

Stein wrote philosophical treatises on that goal and, as she did so, was reflexively aware—of who she was and who she was not as a human being, as can be seen and understood in her texts. At the same time, she wrote about the ongoing transformative process of living out her relational realities with integrity, while also recognizing the spiritual beauty that was unfolding in the depths of her personal being, a mystery at the heart of her existence that could only be lived out by being attentive to others—by generously sharing her life with others. Stein knew it was in the giving that she would receive. She lived out of the heart of reality; she understood the heart of meaning.

NOTES

1. Chauvet, *Symbol and Sacrament*, 265.
2. Yannaras, *On the Absence and Unknowability of God: Heidegger and the Areopagite*, 90–91.
3. Stein, "Ways to Know God: The 'Symbolic Theology' of Dionysius the Areopagite and Its Objective Presuppositions," 89.
4. Ibid., 116.
5. Susan Abraham, "Postcolonial Hermeneutics and a Catholic (Post)Modernity," *Beyond Dogmatism and Innocence: Hermeneutics, Critique, and Catholic Theology*, eds. Anthony J. Godzieba and Bradford E. Hinze (Collegeville, MN: Liturgical Press, 2017), 226.
6. Ibid.
7. Ibid.
8. Ibid.
9. Ibid., 226–27. Abraham draws from the work of Lieven Boeve here.
10. Christos Yannaras and Norman Russell, *Metaphysics as a Personal Adventure: Christos Yannaras in Conversation with Norman Russell* (Yonkers, NY: St. Vladimir's Seminary Press, 2017), 72–73. Yannaras explains that "the Church's gospel, the witness of ecclesial experience, does not have elements dependent on their historical 'context' in a specific culture, so that when the culture changes, it is inevitably required that the significance of ecclesial experience should also change. . . . The Church only sets down its experience that if the mode of existence changes—if humanity wishes to exist and struggles to do so only in order to love and because it loves, if it fights to free itself from the ego—then its life becomes a celebration, a foretaste of the freedom that Christ granted to human nature."
11. Ibid., 73.
12. Stein, FEB, 79–80.
13. My thanks to Keith J. Egan for sharing an important insight concerning the use of "evolution" in his scholarship on the Carmelite charism in relation to Newman's *An Essay on the Development of Christian Doctrine*, so as to reflect the fruitful contemporary friendship between science and theology. I would add that the significance of this relationship cannot be overstated in the light of religious fundamentalism and the dangerous and harmful influence of anti-science bias on contemporary life.
14. See John Henry Newman, *An Essay on the Development of Christian Doctrine*, fwd. Ian Ker (Notre Dame, IN: University of Notre Dame Press, 1989).
15. Yannaras and Russell, 72.
16. Ibid.
17. Bernard McGinn, "Mystical Consciousness: A Modest Proposal," *Spiritus* 8, no. 1 (Spring 2008): 46. My thanks to Keith J. Egan for bringing this article to my attention.

18. Ibid., 46–47.
19. Ibid., 47.
20. Ibid.
21. Ibid.

Bibliography

Abraham, Susan. "Postcolonial Hermeneutics and a Catholic (Post)Modernity." In *Beyond Dogmatism and Innocence: Hermeneutics, Critique, and Catholic Theology*, edited by Anthony J. Godzieba and Bradford E. Hinze, 203–27. Collegeville, MN: The Liturgical Press, 2017.

Ackerman, Jane. *Elijah: Prophet of Carmel*. Washington, D.C.: ICS Publications, 2003.

Arendt, Hannah. *The Human Condition*. 2nd ed. Introduction by Margaret Canovan. Chicago and London: The University of Chicago Press, 1998.

Aristotle. *Nicomachean Ethics*. 2nd ed. Translated and Introduction by Terence Irwin. Indianapolis and Cambridge: Hackett Publishing Company, Inc., 1999.

Beiser, Frederick C. *German Idealism: The Struggle Against Subjectivism, 1781–1801*. Cambridge, MA and London: Harvard University Press, 2002.

Benedict. *The Rule of St. Benedict in English*. Edited by Timothy Fry. Collegeville, MN: The Liturgical Press, 1982.

Bernard of Clairvaux. *On the Song of Songs I*. Cistercian Fathers Series 4. Translated by Kilian Walsh. Introduction by M. Corneille Halflants. Kalamazoo, MI: Cistercian Publications, Inc., 1971.

Bernard of Clairvaux. *On the Song of Songs III*. Cistercian Fathers Series 31. Translated by Kilian Walsh and Irene M. Edmonds. Introduction by Emero Stiegman. Kalamazoo, MI: Cistercian Publications, Inc., 1979.

Bernard of Clairvaux. *On the Song of Songs IV*. Cistercian Fathers Series 40. Translated by Irene Edmonds. Introduction by Jean Leclercq. Kalamazoo, MI: Cistercian Publications, Inc., 1980.

Bible. New Revised Standard Version. Nashville, TN: Thomas Nelson, Inc., 1989.

Blundell, Boyd. *Paul Ricoeur Between Theology and Philosophy*. Bloomington: Indiana University Press, 2010.

Bonaventure. *The Soul's Journey into God, The Tree of Life, The Life of St. Francis. The Classics of Western Spirituality*. Translated and Introduction by Ewert Cousins. Preface by Ignatius Brady. Mahwah, NJ: Paulist Press, 1978.

Borden Sharkey, Sarah. *Thine Own Self: Individuality in Edith Stein's Later Writings.* Washington, D.C.: The Catholic University of America Press, 2010.

Burrows, Mark S. "'Raiding the Inarticulate': Mysticism, Poetics, and the Unlanguageable." In *Minding the Spirit: The Study of Christian Spirituality*, edited by Elizabeth A. Dreyer and Mark S. Burrows, 341–62. Baltimore and London: The Johns Hopkins University Press, 2005.

Cassian, John. *The Conferences.* Ancient Christian Writers 57. Translated and Annotated by Boniface Ramsey. New York and Mahwah, NJ: Paulist Press, 1997.

Cassian, John. *The Institutes.* Ancient Christian Writers 58. Translated and Annotated by Boniface Ramsey. New York and Mahwah, NJ: The Newman Press, 2000.

Changeux, Jean-Pierre and Paul Ricoeur. *What Makes Us Think?: A Neuroscientist and a Philosopher Argue about Ethics, Human Nature, and the Brain.* Translated by M. B. DeBevoise. Princeton, NJ, and Oxford: Princeton University Press, 2000.

Chauvet, Louis-Marie. *Symbol and Sacrament: A Sacramental Reinterpretation of Christian Experience.* Translated by Patrick Madigan and Madeleine Beaumont. Collegeville, MN: The Liturgical Press, 1995.

Chauvet, Louis-Marie. *The Sacraments: The Word of God at the Mercy of the Body.* Translated by Madeleine Beaumont. Collegeville, MN: The Liturgical Press, 2001.

Clauteaux, Elbatrina. "When Anthropologist Encounters Theologian: The Eagle and the Tortoise." In *Sacraments: Revelation of the Humanity of God: Engaging the Fundamental Theology of Louis-Marie Chauvet*, edited by Philippe Bordeyne and Bruce T. Morrill, 155–70. Collegeville, MN: The Liturgical Press, 2008.

Crowe, Benjamin. *Heidegger's Religious Origins: Destruction and Authenticity.* Bloomington and Indianapolis: Indiana University Press, 2006.

Cunningham, Lawrence S., ed. *Thomas Merton: Spiritual Master: The Essential Writings.* Foreword by Patrick Hart. Preface by Anne E. Carr. New York and Mahwah, NJ: Paulist Press, 1992.

Dauenhauer, Bernard P. *Silence: The Phenomenon and Its Ontological Significance.* Bloomington: Indiana University Press, 1980.

Descartes, René. *Discourse on Method and Meditations on First Philosophy.* Lexington, KY: BN Publishing, 2007.

Dierking, Kristen. *Northern Oracle.* Minneapolis, MN: Spout Press, 2007.

Dilthey, Wilhelm. *Introduction to the Human Sciences.* Vol. 1 of *Selected Works.* Edited and Introduction by Rudolf A. Makkreel. Princeton, NJ: Princeton University Press, 1989.

Downey, Michael, ed. *The New Dictionary of Catholic Spirituality.* Collegeville, MN: The Liturgical Press, 1993.

Driscoll, Jeremy. "*Apatheia* and Purity of Heart in Evagrius Ponticus." In *Purity of Heart in Early Ascetic and Monastic Literature*, edited by Harriet A. Luckman and Linda Kulzer, 141–60. Collegeville, MN: The Liturgical Press, 1999.

Egan, Keith J. "Carmel: A School of Prayer." In *Carmelite Prayer: A Tradition for the 21st Century*, edited by Keith J. Egan, 7–23. Mahwah, NJ: Paulist Press, 2003.

Egan, Keith J. "The Solitude of Carmelite Prayer." In *Carmelite Prayer: A Tradition for the 21st Century*, edited by Keith J. Egan, 38–62. Mahwah, NJ: Paulist Press, 2003.

Bibliography

Franke, William, ed. *On What Cannot Be Said: Apophatic Discourses in Philosophy, Religion, Literature, and the Arts.* Vol. 1 of *Classic Formulations.* Notre Dame, IN: University of Notre Dame Press, 2007.

Gadamer, Hans-Georg. *Philosophical Hermeneutics.* Translated and edited by David E. Linge. Berkeley, Los Angeles, London: University of California Press, 1977.

Gadamer, Hans-Georg. *Truth and Method.* 2nd rev. ed. Translated by Joel Weinsheimer and Donald G. Marshall. New York: Continuum, 2000.

Giordano, Silvano, ed. *God Speaks in the Night: The Life, Times, and Teaching of St. John of the Cross.* Translated by Kieran Kavanaugh. Washington, D.C.: ICS Publications, 2000.

Gregory of Nyssa. *The Life of Moses. The Classics of Western Spirituality.* Translated, Introduction, and Notes by Abraham J. Malherbe and Everett Ferguson. New York, Ramsey, Toronto: Paulist Press, 1978.

Hegel, Georg W. F. *The Phenomenology of Spirit (The Phenomenology of Mind).* Translated by J. B. Baillie. LaVergne, TN: Digireads.com, 2009.

Heidegger, Martin. *Being and Time, A Translation of Sein und Zeit.* Translated by Joan Stambaugh. Albany: SUNY Press, 1996.

Heidegger, Martin. "Building Dwelling Thinking." In *Poetry, Language, Thought*, translated and introduction by Albert Hofstadter, 141–59. New York: Harper and Row, Publishers, Inc., 1971.

Heidegger, Martin. *Contributions to Philosophy (From Enowning).* Translated by Parvis Emad and Kenneth Maly. Bloomington and Indianapolis: Indiana University Press, 1999.

Heidegger, Martin. *Discourse on Thinking.* Translated by John M. Anderson and E. Hans Freund. Introduction by John M. Anderson. New York: Harper and Row, Publishers, Inc., 1966.

Heidegger, Martin. "Language." In *Poetry, Language, Thought*, translated and introduction by Albert Hofstadter, 185–208. New York: Harper and Row, Publishers, Inc., 1971.

Heidegger, Martin. *On the Way to Language.* Translated by Peter D. Hertz. New York: Harper and Row, Publishers, Inc., 1971.

Heidegger, Martin. "The Origin of the Work of Art." In *Poetry, Language, Thought*, translated and introduction by Albert Hofstadter, 15–86. New York: Harper and Row, Publishers, Inc., 1971.

Heidegger, Martin. "Postscript to 'What Is Metaphysics?'" In *Pathmarks*, edited and translated by William McNeill, 231–38. Cambridge and New York: Cambridge University Press, 1998.

Heidegger, Martin. "The Question Concerning Technology." In *The Question Concerning Technology and Other Essays*, translated and introduction by William Lovitt, 3–35. New York: Harper and Row, Publishers, Inc., 1977.

Heidegger, Martin. "What Is Metaphysics?" In *Pathmarks*, edited by William McNeill and translated by David Farrell Krell, 82–96. Cambridge and New York: Cambridge University Press, 1998.

Howells, Edward. *John of the Cross and Teresa of Avila: Mystical Knowing and Selfhood.* New York: The Crossword Publishing Company, 2002.

Husserl, Edmund. *The Essential Husserl: Basic Writings in Transcendental Phenomenology*. Edited by Donn Welton. Bloomington and Indianapolis: Indiana University Press, 1999.

Into Great Silence. Directed by Philip Gröning. Berlin, Germany: Zeitgeist Video, 2005. DVD.

Jasper, David. *The Sacred Desert: Religion, Literature, Art, and Culture*. Malden, MA and Oxford: Blackwell Publishing, 2004.

John of the Cross. *The Collected Works of St. John of the Cross*. Translated by Kieran Kavanaugh and Otilio Rodriguez. Revisions and Introductions by Kieran Kavanaugh. Washington, D.C.: ICS Publications, 1991.

Johnston, William. *"Arise My Love . . .": Mysticism for a New Era*. Maryknoll, NY: Orbis Books, 2000.

Johnston, William, ed. *The Cloud of Unknowing and The Book of Privy Counseling*. New York: Doubleday, 1973.

Johnston, William, ed. *Encyclopedia of Monasticism*, vol. 2. Chicago and London: Fitzroy Dearborn, 2000.

Johnston, William. *Mystical Theology: The Science of Love*. Maryknoll, NY: Orbis Books, 1995.

Kant, Immanuel. *Critique of Pure Reason*. Translated and Edited by Paul Guyer and Allen W. Wood. Cambridge and New York: Cambridge University Press, 1998.

Kant, Immanuel. *Religion within the Boundaries of Mere Reason*. Translated and Edited by Allen Wood and George di Giovanni. Introduction by Robert Merrihew Adams. Cambridge and New York: Cambridge University Press, 1998.

Kavanaugh, Kieran. "Contemplation and the Stream of Consciousness." In *Carmelite Prayer: A Tradition for the 21st Century*, edited by Keith J. Egan, 101–18. New York and Mahwah, NJ: Paulist Press, 2003.

Kearney, Richard. "Capable Man, Capable God." In *A Passion for the Possible: Thinking with Paul Ricoeur*, edited by Brian Treanor and Henry Isaac Venema, 49–61. New York: Fordham University Press, 2010.

Klemm, David E. *The Hermeneutical Theory of Paul Ricoeur: A Constructive Analysis*. Lewisburg, PA: Bucknell University Press, 1983.

Klemm, David E. "Levinas' Phenomenology of the Other and Language as the Other of Phenomenology." *Man and World* 22 (1989): 403–26.

Klemm, David E. "Philosophy and Kerygma: Ricoeur as Reader of the Bible." In *Reading Ricoeur*, edited by David M. Kaplan, 47–69. Albany: SUNY Press, 2008.

Klemm, David E. "Ricoeur, Theology, and the Rhetoric of Overturning." *Journal of Literature & Theology* 3, no. 3 (November 1989): 267–84.

Klemm, David E. "Schleiermacher's Hermeneutic: the Sacred and the Profane." In *The Sacred and the Profane: Contemporary Demands on Hermeneutics*, edited by Jeffrey F. Keuss, 61–75. Burlington, VT: Ashgate Publishing Company, 2003.

Klemm, David E. "Searching for a Heart of Gold: A Ricoeurian Meditation on Moral Striving and the Power of Religious Discourse." In *Paul Ricoeur and Contemporary Moral Thought*, edited by John Wall, William Schweiker, and W. David Hall, 97–111. New York: Routledge, 2002.

Klemm, David E. "The Word as Grace: The Religious Bearing of Paul Ricoeur's Philosophy." *Faith and Philosophy* 10, no. 4 (October 1993): 503–20.

Lebech, Mette. *The Philosophy of Edith Stein: From Phenomenology to Metaphysics*. Bern: Peter Lang, 2015.

Levinas, Emmanuel. *Totality and Infinity: An Essay on Exteriority*. Translated by Alphonso Lingis. Pittsburgh: Duquesne University Press, 1969.

Lonergan, Bernard. *Method in Theology*. Toronto: University of Toronto Press, 1971.

MacIntyre, Alasdair. *After Virtue: A Study in Moral Theory*. 2nd ed. Notre Dame, IN: University of Notre Dame Press, 1984.

McGinn, Bernard, ed. *The Essential Writings of Christian Mysticism*. New York: Random House Publishing, Inc., 2006.

McGinn, Bernard. *The Foundations of Mysticism: Origins to the Fifth Century*. Vol. 1 of *The Presence of God: A History of Western Christian Mysticism*. New York: The Crossroad Publishing Company, 1991.

McGinn, Bernard. *The Growth of Mysticism: Gregory the Great through the 12th Century*. Vol. 2 of *The Presence of God: A History of Western Christian Mysticism*. New York: The Crossroad Publishing Company, 1994.

McGinn, Bernard. "Mystical Consciousness: A Modest Proposal." *Spiritus: A Journal of Christian Spirituality* 8, no. 1 (Spring 2008): 44–63.

McIntosh, Mark A. *Mystical Theology: The Integrity of Spirituality and Theology*. Malden, MA, and Oxford: Blackwell Publishers, Inc., 1998.

Merrill, Christopher. *Things of the Hidden God: Journey to the Holy Mountain*. New York: Random House, 2005.

Merton, Thomas. *The Climate of Monastic Prayer*. Foreword by Douglas V. Steere. Spencer, MA: Cistercian Publications, 1969.

Merton, Thomas. *Contemplation in a World of Action*. Foreword by Robert Coles. Notre Dame, IN: University of Notre Dame Press, 1998.

Merton, Thomas. *Contemplative Prayer*. Introduction by Thich Nhat Hanh. New York and London: Doubleday, 1996.

Merton, Thomas. *New Seeds of Contemplation*. New York: New Directions Books, 1961.

Morrill, Bruce T. "Building on Chauvet's Work: An Overview." In *Sacraments: Revelation of the Humanity of God: Engaging the Fundamental Theology of Louis-Marie Chauvet*, edited by Philippe Bordeyne and Bruce T. Morrill, xv–xxiv. Collegeville, MN: The Liturgical Press, 2008.

Morrill, Bruce T. "Time, Absence, and Otherness: Divine-Human Paradoxes Bonding Liturgy and Ethics." In *Sacraments: Revelation of the Humanity of God: Engaging the Fundamental Theology of Louis-Marie Chauvet*, edited by Philippe Bordeyne and Bruce T. Morrill, 137–52. Collegeville, MN: The Liturgical Press, 2008.

Newman, John Henry. *An Essay on the Development of Christian Doctrine*. Foreword by Ian Ker. Notre Dame, IN: University of Notre Dame Press, 1989.

Nussbaum, Martha C. *The New Religious Intolerance: Overcoming the Politics of Fear in an Anxious Age*. Cambridge, MA, and London, England: The Belknap Press of Harvard University Press, 2012.

Origen. *An Exhortation to Martyrdom, Prayer and Selected Works*. The Classics of Western Spirituality. Translated and Introduction by Rowan A. Greer. Preface by Hans Urs Von Balthasar. Mahwah, NJ: Paulist Press, 1979.

Peters, John Durham. *Speaking into the Air: A History of the Idea of Communication*. Chicago and London: The University of Chicago Press, 1999.

Picard, Max. *The World of Silence*. Preface by Gabriel Marcel. Wichita, KS: Eighth Day Press, 2002.

Plato. "Charmides." In *The Collected Dialogues including the Letters*, edited by Edith Hamilton and Huntington Cairns, 99–122. Princeton, NJ: Princeton University Press, 1989.

Prétot, Patrick. "The Sacraments as 'Celebrations of the Church': Liturgy's Impact on Sacramental Theology." In *Sacraments: Revelation of the Humanity of God: Engaging the Fundamental Theology of Louis-Marie Chauvet*, edited by Philippe Bordeyne and Bruce T. Morrill, 25–41. Collegeville, MN: The Liturgical Press, 2008.

Pseudo-Dionysius. *The Complete Works*. The Classics of Western Spirituality. Translated by Colm Luibheid with Paul Rorem. Preface by Rene Roques. Introduction by Jaroslav Pelikan, Jean Leclercq, and Karlfried Froehlich. New York and Mahwah, NJ: Paulist Press, 1987.

Reagan, Charles E. *Paul Ricoeur: His Life and His Work*. Chicago and London: The University of Chicago Press, 1996.

Ricoeur, Paul. *The Conflict of Interpretations: Essays in Hermeneutics, I*. Edited by Don Ihde. Evanston, IL: Northwestern University Press, 1974.

Ricoeur, Paul. *The Course of Recognition*. Translated by David Pellauer. Cambridge, MA, and London: Harvard University Press, 2005.

Ricoeur, Paul. *Critique and Conviction: Conversations with François Azouvi and Marc de Launay*. Translated by Kathleen Blamey. New York: Columbia University Press, 1998.

Ricoeur, Paul. "Ethics and Human Capability: A Response." In *Paul Ricoeur and Contemporary Moral Thought*, edited by John Wall, William Schweiker, and W. David Hall, 279–90. New York and London: Routledge, 2002.

Ricoeur, Paul. *Evil: A Challenge to Philosophy and Theology*. Translated by John Bowden. Introduction by Graham Ward. London and New York: Continuum, 2007.

Ricoeur, Paul. *Fallible Man*. Revised translation by Charles A. Kelbley. Introduction by Walter J. Lowe. New York: Fordham University Press, 1986.

Ricoeur, Paul. *Figuring the Sacred: Religion, Narrative, and Imagination*. Translated by David Pellauer. Edited by Mark I. Wallace. Minneapolis: Augsburg Fortress Press, 1995.

Ricoeur, Paul. *Freedom and Nature: The Voluntary and the Involuntary*. Translated and Introduction by Erazim V. Kohák. Evanston, IL: Northwestern University Press, 1966.

Ricoeur, Paul. *Freud and Philosophy: An Essay on Interpretation*. Translated by Denis Savage. New Haven, CT, and London: Yale University Press, 1970.

Ricoeur, Paul. *From Text to Action: Essays in Hermeneutics, II*. Translated by Kathleen Blamey and John B. Thompson. Evanston, IL: Northwestern University Press, 1991.

Ricoeur, Paul. "The Hermeneutical Function of Distanciation." *Philosophy Today* 17 (1973): 129–69.

Ricoeur, Paul. "Intellectual Autobiography." In *The Philosophy of Paul Ricoeur*. The Library of Living Philosophers 22, edited by Lewis Edwin Hahn and translated by Kathleen Blamey, 3–53. Peru, IL: Open Court Trade and Academic Books, 1995.

Ricoeur, Paul. *Interpretation Theory: Discourse and the Surplus of Meaning*. Fort Worth: Texas Christian University Press, 1976.

Ricoeur, Paul. *Memory, History, Forgetting*. Translated by Kathleen Blamey and David Pellauer. Chicago and London: The University of Chicago Press, 2004.

Ricoeur, Paul. "The Metaphorical Process as Cognition, Imagination, and Feeling." *Critical Inquiry* 5, no. 1 (Autumn 1978): 143–59.

Ricoeur, Paul. *Oneself as Another*. Translated by Kathleen Blamey. Chicago and London: The University of Chicago Press, 1992.

Ricoeur, Paul. "The Power of the Possible." In *Debates in Continental Philosophy: Conversations with Contemporary Thinkers*, edited by Richard Kearney, 42–46. New York: Fordham University Press, 2004.

Ricoeur, Paul. "Religious Belief: The Difficult Path of the Religious." In *A Passion for the Possible: Thinking with Paul Ricoeur*, edited by Brian Treanor and Henry Isaac Venema, 27–40. New York: Fordham University Press, 2010.

Ricoeur, Paul. *The Rule of Metaphor*. Translated by Robert Czerny with Kathleen McLaughlin and John Costello. London and New York: Routledge, 1977.

Ricoeur, Paul. *The Symbolism of Evil*. Translated by Emerson Buchanan. Boston: Beacon Press, 1967.

Ricoeur, Paul. "Toward a Hermeneutic of the Idea of Revelation." *Harvard Theological Review* 70, nos. 1–2 (January-April 1977): 1–37.

Scharlemann, Robert P. "Being 'As Not': Overturning the Ontological." In *Inscriptions and Reflections: Essays in Philosophical Theology*, 54–65. Charlottesville, VA: University Press of Virginia, 1989.

Scharlemann, Robert P. *The Being of God: Theology and the Experience of Truth*. New York: The Seabury Press, 1981.

Scharlemann, Robert P. "The Being of God When God Is Not Being God: Deconstructing the History of Theism." In *Inscriptions and Reflections: Essays in Philosophical Theology*, 30–53. Charlottesville, VA: University Press of Virginia, 1989.

Scharlemann, Robert P. "The Question of Philosophical Theology." In *Being and Truth: Essays in Honour of John Macquarrie*, edited by Alistair Kee and Eugene T. Long, 3–17. London: SCM Press Ltd., 1986.

Scharlemann, Robert P. "The Textuality of Texts." In *Meanings in Texts and Action: Questioning Paul Ricoeur*, edited by David E. Klemm and William Schweiker, 13–25. Charlottesville and London: University Press of Virginia, 1993.

Schleiermacher, Friedrich. *Dialectic or, The Art of Doing Philosophy. A Study Edition of the 1811 Notes*. Translated, Introduction, and Notes by Terrence N. Tice. Atlanta, GA: Scholars Press, 1996.

Schleiermacher, Friedrich. *Hermeneutics and Criticism*. Translated and Edited by Andrew Bowie. Cambridge and New York: Cambridge University Press, 1998.

Shannon, William H., and Christine M. Bochen and Patrick F. O'Connell. *The Thomas Merton Encyclopedia*. Maryknoll, NY: Orbis Books, 2002.

Sheldrake, Philip. *The New Westminster Dictionary of Christian Spirituality*. Louisville, KY: Westminster John Knox Press, 2005.

Stein, Edith. *Essays on Woman*. 2nd rev. ed. Vol. 2 of *The Collected Works of Edith Stein*. Translated by Freda Mary Oben. Washington, D.C.: ICS Publications, 1996.

Stein, Edith. *Finite and Eternal Being: An Attempt at an Ascent to the Meaning of Being*. Vol. 9 of *The Collected Works of Edith Stein*. Translated by Kurt F. Reinhardt. Washington, D.C.: ICS Publications, 2002.

Stein, Edith. *The Hidden Life: Essays, Meditations, Spiritual Texts*. Vol. 4 of *The Collected Works of Edith Stein*. Translated by Waltraut Stein. Edited by L. Gelber and Michael Linssen. Washington, D.C.: ICS Publications, 1992.

Stein, Edith. *An Investigation Concerning the State*. Vol. 10 of *The Collected Works of Edith Stein*. Edited and Translated by Marianne Sawacki. Washington, D.C.: ICS Publications, 2006.

Stein, Edith. *Knowledge and Faith*. Vol. 8 of *The Collected Works of Edith Stein*. Translated by Walter Redmond. Washington, D.C.: ICS Publications, 2000.

Stein, Edith. *Life in a Jewish Family: An Autobiography, 1891–1916*. Vol. 1 of *The Collected Works of Edith Stein*. Translated by Josephine Koeppel. Edited by L. Gelber and Romaeus Leuven. Washington, D.C.: ICS Publications, 2016. First published in 1986.

Stein, Edith. *On the Problem of Empathy*. 3rd rev. ed. Vol. 3 of *The Collected Works of Edith Stein*. Translated by Waltraut Stein. Washington, D.C.: ICS Publications, 1989.

Stein, Edith. *Philosophy of Psychology and the Humanities*. Vol. 7 of *The Collected Works of Edith Stein*. Translated by Mary Catherine Baseheart and Marianne Sawacki. Edited by Marianne Sawacki. Washington, D.C.: ICS Publications, 2000.

Stein, Edith. *Potency and Act: Studies Toward a Philosophy of Being*. Vol. 11 of *The Collected Works of Edith Stein*. Translated by Walter Redmond. Edited by L. Gelber and Romaeus Leuven. Introduction by Hans Rainer Sepp. Washington, D.C.: ICS Publications, 2009.

Stein, Edith. *The Science of the Cross*. Vol. 6 of *The Collected Works of Edith Stein*. Translated by Josephine Koeppel. Washington, D.C.: ICS Publications, 2002.

Stein, Edith. *Self-Portrait in Letters: 1916–1942*. Vol. 5 of *The Collected Works of Edith Stein*. Translated by Josephine Koeppel. Edited by L. Gelber and Romaeus Leuven. Washington, D.C.: ICS Publications, 1993.

Stein, Edith. *Self-Portrait in Letters: Letters to Roman Ingarden*. Vol. 12 of *The Collected Works of Edith Stein*. Translated by Hugh Candler Hunt. Introduction by Hanna-Barbara Gerl-Falkovitz. Editing and Comments by Maria Amata Neyer.

Notes prepared in collaboration with Eberhard Avé-Lallemant. Washington, D.C.: ICS Publications, 2014.

Stevens, Wallace. *The Collected Poems of Wallace Stevens*. New York: Vintage Books, 1990.

Stewart, Columba. "Introduction." In *Purity of Heart in Early Ascetic and Monastic Literature*, edited by Harriet A. Luckman and Linda Kulzer, 1–16. Collegeville, MN: The Liturgical Press, 1999.

Teresa of Avila. *The Book of Her Foundations, Minor Works.* Vol. 3 of *The Collected Works of St. Teresa of Avila.* Translated by Kieran Kavanaugh and Otilio Rodriguez. Washington, D.C.: ICS Publications, 1985.

Teresa of Avila. *The Book of Her Life, Spiritual Testimonies, Soliloquies.* Vol. 1 of *The Collected Works of St. Teresa of Avila.* 2nd rev. ed. Translated by Kieran Kavanaugh and Otilio Rodriguez. Washington, D.C.: ICS Publications, 1987.

Teresa of Avila. *The Way of Perfection, Meditations on the Song of Songs, The Interior Castle.* Vol. 2 of *The Collected Works of St. Teresa of Avila.* Translated by Kieran Kavanaugh and Otilio Rodriguez. Washington, D.C.: ICS Publications, 1980.

Thérèse of Lisieux. *Story of a Soul: The Autobiography of Saint Thérèse of Lisieux.* 3rd ed. Translated by John Clarke. Washington, D.C.: ICS Publications, 1996.

Thompson, Colin. *St. John of the Cross: Songs in the Night.* Washington, D.C.: The Catholic University of America Press, 2003.

Tillich, Paul. *The Courage to Be.* Introduction by Peter J. Gomes. New Haven, CT, and London: Yale University Press, 2000.

Treanor, Brian, and Henry Isaac Venema. "Introduction: How Much More Than the Possible?" In *A Passion for the Possible: Thinking with Paul Ricoeur*, edited by Brian Treanor and Henry Isaac Venema, 1–21. New York: Fordham University Press, 2010.

Turner, Denys. *The Darkness of God: Negativity in Christian Mysticism.* Cambridge and New York: Cambridge University Press, 1998.

Wall, John. *Moral Creativity: Paul Ricoeur and the Poetics of Possibility.* New York: Oxford University Press, 2005.

Wallace, Mark I. *The Second Naiveté: Barth, Ricoeur, and the New Yale Theology.* Macon, GA: Mercer University Press, 1995.

Weil, Simone. *Waiting for God.* Translated by Emma Craufurd. Introduction by Leslie Fiedler. New York: HarperCollins, 2001.

Welch, John. *The Carmelite Way: An Ancient Path for Today's Pilgrim.* Mahwah, NJ: Paulist Press, 1996.

Williams, Robert R. *Recognition: Fichte and Hegel on the Other.* Albany: SUNY Press, 1992.

Yannaras, Christos. *On the Absence and Unknowability of God: Heidegger and the Areopagite.* Edited and Introduction by Andrew Louth. Translated by Haralambos Ventis. London and New York: T&T Clark International Ltd., 2005.

Yannaras, Christos, and Norman Russell. *Metaphysics as a Personal Adventure: Christos Yannaras in Conversation with Norman Russell.* Yonkers, NY: St. Vladimir's Seminary Press, 2017.

Index

a priori conceptions, 8, 21n25, 79, 128
Abraham, Susan, 187
aesthetic identity, 57–58, 152–55
affective mediation, 12–18
alienation from self, 17, 26, 27, 35, 37
Anselm of Canterbury, 109n29, 135, 146n119
apophasis:
    Denys' dialectics of apophaticism, 92n56;
    John of the Cross on, 71, 83;
    the negative way, as more than, 72, 91n49;
    personal relationship with God, acquiesce to, 186;
    Pseudo-Dionysius on, 77–78;
    as unknowing, 70, 92n57
Aquinas, Thomas, 122, 182n35, 182n43, 186
Arendt, Hannah, 172, 181n25
Aristotle, 10, 14, 19, 56, 70, 115, 152, 186
Augustine of Hippo, 71, 81, 87, 122, 146n119
awareness, five levels of, *xvii–xviii, xxiii*, 113, 120, 142, 167, 179, 188

Barth, Karl, *xi*
Basil the Great, 76, 119

Being and Time (Heidegger), 46, 120, 121, 173
Beiser, Frederick C., 21n22
Bergson, Henri, *xi*
Bernard of Clairvaux, 79–80, 93n76
bios, 18, 24, 25, 116, 117
Blundell, Boyd, 44, 67n128
Boeve, Lieven, 187
Bonaventure, 80–82
Borden Sharkey, Sarah, *xxvn1*
Brück, Maria, 101
Brüning, Petra, 181n15
Burrows, Mark S., *xxvn2*

the capable human:
    contemplative silence, manifesting through, 149, 167, 168;
    essential elements of, 36, 40, 46, 53;
    ethical maturity in, 180;
    good in the world, contributing to, 186;
    recognition of, 60, 177;
    reflexive transformation in, 152–55;
    silence in relation to discourse, as understanding, 46, 47, 53, 179
Carmelite tradition, 70, 155:
    Carmelite spirituality, 97–100, 179;
    John of the Cross and, 82–84, 149, 156;

Stein and, 85–87, 100–3, 169, 174, 175;
Teresa of Avila as a leading figure of, 72–74, 82;
Thérèse of Lisieux and, 84–85
Cassian, John, 85, 90–91n42
cataphasis, 70–72, 74, 77, 78
Chauvet, Louis-Marie, 126, 140–42, 185
Clement of Alexandria, 75
Cloud of Unknowing text, 72
Conrad-Martius, Hedwig, 101, 109n31
contemplative silence, 58, 108, 125, 149, 152, 179:
in apophatic/cataphatic framework, 70–72, 74, 83;
capable being, manifesting *via* practice of, 167–68, 180;
in classic Greek education, 75;
conscience, exerting its force within, 171;
contemplative awareness as accompanying, 142, 167, 188;
Dauenhauer, in phenomenology of, 36, 51, 179;
ethical import of, 173;
God, depth level of understanding *via,* 136;
in *Into Great Silence* film, 118, 120;
Gregory of Nyssa on, 76–77;
hermeneutical context for, 20, 113, 178;
idle forgetting, providing the opportunity for, 62;
John of the Cross, as inspiring writings of, 155;
as a mediating space, 172;
Merton as practicing, 87, 88;
moments of recognition provided by, 58;
ontic example of practice, 117–20;
personal responsibility, evoking through, 154;
as a ritualized action, 153;
solitude and simplicity in the method of, 69;

Spiritual Canticle and, 156, 157;
Stein, practice of, 86, 107, 174;
Thérèse of Lisieux on, 84–85;
third moment, as within, 114, 115, 117
Course of Recognition (Ricoeur), 54n93
critique, 39, 67n128, 173;
as "2" in 1-2-3 structure, 51;
"desert of criticism" as the reflexive endpoint of critique, 38;
ideological critique, 46;
intellectual critique, Stein on the necessity of, 131;
Kantian critique, Heidegger shifting from, 120;
of onto-theology, 122, 137;
self-reflexive critique, 186–87
Critique and Conviction (Ricoeur), 182n53
Critique of Pure Reason (Kant), 21n25, 66n113, 159
Cunningham, Lawrence S., 95–96n132

Dalbiez, Roland, *xi*
Dauenhauer, Bernard P., 36, 47, 48–53, 65n61, 178–79
Dierking, Kirsten, 176
Dilthey, Wilhelm, 174, 181n29
Dionysius the Areopagite, 71–72, 77–79, 84, 139, 186
distanciation, 36, 37, 44
The Divine Names (Dionysius the Areopagite), 78
Dülberg, Hedwig, 111n77

Eckhart, Meister, 72, 126
Egan, Keith J., 90n27, 91n43, 94n97, 94n107, 189n13, 189n17
Emerson, Ralph Waldo, 64n30
Epictetus, *xii*
Ernst, Maria, 111n81
"Ethics and Human Capability" (Ricoeur), 181n25
Evagrius Ponticus, 90nn41–42
evil, 18, 37, 168, 180n3:

actualized self-awareness, as the
source of, 35;
confronting of evil within
oneself, 172, 173;
fallibility, as linked with, 25–26,
27–28, 51;
human being and experience of,
2, 11, 36;
origin of, 12, 181n23;
restoration as redemption from
evil, 171;
symbols of, 30–32
existential negation, 28

the fallible human, 6, 20, 32,
167, 178, 180
Fallible Man (Ricoeur), *xx, xxvi*n3,
*xxvi*n8, 3, 19
feeling, 17, 26, 29, 160–61, 186:
of abandonment, 85;
in the affective perspective, 4;
Bernard on, 80, 93n75;
contemplative awareness, as
part of, 167;
eros as a fundamental feeling, 14;
essential *vs.* spiritual feelings, 5;
in *Fallible Man,* 3;
Gefühl as the feeling of absolute
dependence, 135;
happiness and, 10–11, 18;
illusory feeling of empty words, 107;
intentional structure of, 75, 159, 175;
knowing, rising together with, 25;
moral feeling of respect, 24;
poesis, role in, *xxv*n2;
recognition of, 9–10, 28, 56,
57, 120, 129;
Ricoeur on the dimension of,
13–14, 15;
symbol, addressing the mind at the
level of, 171;
the texture of feeling, 12;
in theory of empathy, 125
Fichte, Johann Gottlieb, 15, 21n22, 26

Finite and Eternal Being (Stein),
xiii, 106, 174
forgiveness, 61, 62, 154, 170–
71, 173, 178
Francis of Assisi, 162
freedom, 9, 20n1, 24, 27, 63n3, 106:
apatheia along the path of, 76;
apophaticism, linking to, 79;
approach, freedom of, 78–79, 186;
in Carmelite spirituality, 99;
divine freedom as differing from
human freedom, 2;
embodied freedom, 1, 177;
ethical duty, as linked to, 182n40
evil and, *xxi,* 11–12, 28, 29, 30;
in existence-as-relation, 187;
finite freedom in the
unitive way, 168;
free choice, Ricoeur on, 181n23
freedom of judgment and
the verb, 19;
freedom of thought, 171;
human nature, freedom granted
to, 189n10;
individual uniqueness as realized
through, 170;
mediating being and finite
freedom, 4;
misused freedom, 173;
the other, affirming the freedom of,
16, 61, 62;
relation self-transcendence, as
realization of, 188;
remembrance in freedom, 163;
responsive freedom, 176;
of the spiritual life, 107–8;
surety, as linked with, 169
Frege, Gottlob, 64n35

Gadamer, Hans-Georg, *xi,* 36
Gregory of Nyssa, 72, 76–77
Gregory of Palamas, 71–72
Gröning, Philip, 118

Hamilton, Edith, 63n3

Hegel, Georg W. F., 15–16, 66n120
Heidegger, Martin, *x, xi*, 79,
   80, 122, 175:
  aletheia, 125, 132;
  Befindlichkeit, 125;
  Being and Time, 46–47,
    120, 121, 173;
  "Building Dwelling
    Thinking," 145n102;
  *Contributions to Philosophy (From
    Enowning),* 146n120;
  "Conversation on a Country Path
    About Thinking," 126n64;
  Dasein concept, 121, 123, 124;
  enowning, understanding through,
    136, 146n120;
  Gelassenheit and letting go, 125–26;
  "Memorial Address," 144n60;
  mitsein, xxiii, 124;
  the nothing, addressing the question
    of, 122–23;
  "Origin of the Work of Art," 131n99,
    132n104, 171n22;
  "Postscript to 'What Is
    Metaphysics?,'" 143n39;
  "What Is Metaphysics?," 122n35
hermeneutics, 26, 36, 44, 62, 70:
  appropriation, hermeneutical
    process of, 35;
  of contemplative silence, 19, 108,
    113, 167–68, 173, 178;
  continual interpretation as
    part of, 134;
  existence, hermeneutics of, 177, 180;
  On First Principles as an exercise in
    hermeneutics, 75;
  the hermeneutical self, 53–54,
    134, 141, 178;
  inquiry process in, 129,
    159, 174, 175;
  integrity and ethical activity as part
    of, 169, 173;
  "is not" awareness as
    crucial, 120, 122;
  mediation concept within, 168;
  philosophical hermeneutics, 27, 32,
    37, 46, 176, 185, 188;
  postcolonial hermeneutics, 187;
  reflection, role of, 27, 28;
  as reflexive interpretation, 132, 133;
  Song of Songs, examining, 75–76;
  Stein, hermeneutical activity of,
    129, 140, 170;
  symbol, hermeneutics of, 29–32
Hermeneutics of Symbols: I
  (Ricoeur), 33n29
Hermeneutics of Symbols: II
  (Ricoeur), 33n41
hope:
  eschatological hope, 5;
  the future, directing hope
    toward, 180n3;
  horizon of hope, 172;
  for re-creation of language, *xxi;*
  as spiritual feeling, 5
The Human Condition (Arendt), 172
Husserl, Edmund, *x,* 122, 175:
  appresentation of the other,
    64n30, 129;
  egocentric orientation, 182n35;
  as an idealist, 173–74;
  internal time-consciousness,
    65n61, 170;
  Logical Investigations, 19, 86

idem-identity, *xxii,* 54
the illocutionary act, 42–43, 152
the illuminative way, 75, 76, 156–57,
  163n22, 178
imago Dei, 103
Ingarden, Roman, 101, 109n29, 181n29
The Interior Castle (Teresa of
  Avila), 73, 82
the interlocutionary act, 42, 45,
  48–49, 152
Into Great Silence (film), 118–20
ipse-identity, *xxii,* 54

James, William, 64n30
Jasper, David, 95n113

Index

John of the Cross, 85, 99, 100, 105:
as an apophatic theologian, 71, 72, 83;
Ascent of Mount Carmel, 83, 104;
as a Carmelite, 82, 83, 102, 149, 155;
contemplation as transforming and humanizing for, 160;
Dark Night, 83, 94n98;
night in mystical worldview of, 86–87;
night of the senses, 104;
night of the spirit, 104;
Prayer of a Soul Taken with Love, 162;
Spiritual Canticle, 83–84, 156–57

Kant, Immanuel, 8, 38, 59, 80, 153:
Critique of Pure Reason, 21n25, 66n113, 159;
on intuition, 7, 59;
Religion within the Boundaries of Mere Reason, xxi, 11;
on restoration as the redemption from evil, 171
Kaufmann, Fritz, 101, 109n30
Kavanaugh, Kieran, 83
Kearney, Richard, *xxvi*n3, 20n1
Klemm, David E., *xxvi*n18, 20n18, 32n1, 63n16, 146n119, 180n2
Kopf, Callista, *xiv*n10, 109n25, 110n36

Lebech, Mette, 143n27
Levinas, Emmanuel, 61–62
Life of Moses (Gregory of Nyssa), 76–77
linguality *(Sprachlichkeit)*, xii, 23, 36
Lipps, Theodor, 86
Logical Investigations (Husserl), 19, 86
logos, 14, 18, 24, 25, 57, 116, 117, 118, 130, 142, 171
Lonergan, Bernard, 150–51

MacIntyre, Alasdair, 115–16
Martha and Mary (biblical figures), 73, 80

McGinn, Bernard, 75, 76, 78, 90n32, 93n75, 188
McIntosh, Mark A., 78
meaning and mode of being, 131–33
Memory, History, Forgetting (Ricoeur), 61, 152, 170, 171, 177
Merrill, Christopher, 88n1
Merton, Thomas, 87–88, 95–96n132, 115, 188
metanoia (conversion), 150
the metaphorical process, 138–39, 140, 160
metaphysics, 126
Method in Theology (Lonergan), 150
misery, 2, 5, 13, 23, 24
mood:
continual transformation of, 57;
mitsein as a mood dimension, 124;
mood of anxiety in the face of nothing, 123;
the optative mood, 171;
in Stein's theory of empathy, 125;
subjective consciousness, as linked to, 120
moral identity, 55–57, 152–55
Morrill, Bruce T., 147nn144–45
The Mystical Theology (Dionysius the Areopagite), 78
myth, 31, 35:
Adamic myth, 31–32, 172–73;
critique, disintegration of myth in, 38;
foundational myth of the Carmelite Order, 98;
mythological language, 28, 30, 37

narrative identity, 55, 153–54
New Seeds of Contemplation (Merton), 87
Newman, John Henry, 187, 189n13
Nicomachean Ethics (Aristotle), 115
nouns, study of:
John of the Cross, use of nouns, 84;
noun-verb conjunction, *xx*, 19–20, 40, 41, 44;

pronouns, 41, 44, 162–63;
see also verbs, study of
Nussbaum, Martha C., 162

On First Principles (Origen), 75
On the Problem of Empathy
(Stein), x, xi
Oneself as Another (Ricoeur), *xxii*, 27, 29, 54, 181n23
Origen of Alexandria, 70, 74–76, 79

Parmenides text, hypotheses of, 78
perception, 19, 59, 121, 129, 159;
  abandonment of perceptions in the negative way, 71;
  comprehension as differing from, 123;
  felt sense perception of aesthetic striving, 25, 57–58;
  objective commonness and, 140;
  passivity, as characterized by, 81;
  perspectival perception, 6–7;
  primordial experience of the inner perception, 122;
  in the second contextual level of awareness, *xxiii;*
  silence as established in, 50;
  three elements of reciprocity and, 56–57
perlocutionary effect, 42
personal identity, *xxii*, 26, 53–54, 152–55
Peters, John Durham, 64n30
Philo of Alexandria, 70
Picard, Max, 114
Plato, 63n3, 70, 80, 91n44
Plotinus, 70, 75, 91n44
Potency and Act (Stein), 174
practical mediation, 9–12
Prayer of a Soul Taken with Love (John of the Cross), 162
Pseudo-Dionysius. *See* Dionysius the Areopagite
the purgative way, 75, 76, 156, 178
purity of heart, 76, 90–91nn41–42

Reagan, Charles E., *xiii*n2, 181n26
referent, 128, 139, 144n79:
  in the dialectic of sense and reference, 43;
  divine mystery, openness to, 160;
  in *Fallible Man,* 19;
  God, double referent of, 137–38;
  naming and creation of, 140;
  referential activity of language, 38–39
Religion within the Boundaries of Mere Reason (Kant), *xxi,* 11
respect, 11–12, 57, 79, 162:
  distance in intimacy, as showing, 176;
  moral feeling of, 24;
  in mutual recognition, 16, 60;
  in philosophical anthropology of Ricoeur, 9;
  self-respect, 56
Ribot, Felip, 98
Ricoeur, Paul, 124, 129, 136, 158, 169:
  Aristotle, building on, 10, 14;
  the capable human, 57, 60, 152–55, 167, 180;
  communication as an enigma, 42;
  conflict of interpretations, 46, 51, 167, 174;
  continuity of action, ethics of, 168, 180n3, 181n25;
  Course of Recognition, 54n93;
  critique, 38–39, 67n128;
  discourse, theory of, 40, 41–42, 43–46, 48, 52;
  ethical intention, 56;
  "Ethics and Human Capability," 54n92, 54n94;
  evil, contemplations on, 2, 11–12, 25–32, 171, 181n23;
  existential difference, *xxi;*
  Fallible Man, xx, xxvin3, xxvin8, 3, 19;
  false consciousness as pretense, 38;
  feeling, theory of, 17, 24;
  the first naiveté, 37–38;

Freud and Philosophy, 26n8;
heart, on the fundamental
 openness of, 15;
hermeneutical arc, 45–46;
hermeneutics of symbol, 28, 29–32;
Hermeneutics of Symbols: I, 33n29;
Hermeneutics of Symbols: II, 33n41;
hermeneutics of the self, 141;
"I can's" of transformation, 60, 149,
 152–55, 178;
Interpretation Theory, xxii
langue and *parole,* distinguishing
 between, 40;
mediating action, 170–73;
Memory, History, Forgetting, 61,
 152, 170, 171, 177;
Oneself as Another, xxii, xxvi, 27, 29,
 54, 181n23;
original affirmation, *xxi,* 5, 28
overturning concept, 30–31, 138,
 139, 159–60;
the paradox of feeling, 13;
philosophical anthropology, 5, 9, 12;
"The Power of the
 Possible," 56n107;
recognition, structure of,
 58–62, 67n122;
Rule of Metaphor, 138–39;
the second naiveté, 37, 39–40, 51,
 134, 139, 186;
semantic autonomy of the
 text, *xx,* 44;
solicitude, defining, 56–58, 175;
the summoned subject, 167, 168,
 169, 170, 179;
synthesizing, guiding the
 activity of, 8;
text and action, silence contained
 within, 185;
on textuality, 23, 36, 44,
 46, 133, 174;
theory of metaphor, 159;
understanding, on the evolution
 of, 121–22;

worth, feeling of as the summit of
 self-consciousness, 17
Rule of St. Benedict (Benedict of
 Nursia), 79

Saccas, Ammonius, 75
sacrament, 99, 140–42, 164n23, 185
Saussure, Ferdinand de, 63n19
Scharlemann, Robert P., 128,
 137–40, 144n79
Scheler, Max, 86, 181n29
schematism, 8–9, 14–15, 17,
 30–31, 159–60
Schleiermacher, Friedrich, 134–35, 136,
 146nn119–20, 174, 181n29
Science of the Cross (Stein), 86,
 103, 104, 157
the second naiveté, 37, 39–40, 51,
 134, 139, 186
semiotics, 40, 41, 46
sense:
 dark night of senses, 104;
 in dialectic of sense and
  reference, 43;
 as hylectic data, 64n30;
 as meaning of experience, 42;
 as represented content, 19;
 sense impressions, *xxiii;*
 sense objects, 117;
 in the sign, 127
sentence, 121, 130, 160:
 dialogue, in the event of, 42;
 outside referent, as directed to, 43;
 as a primary unit of meaning,
  18–19, 116;
 propositional content of, 41;
 science of the sentence, 40;
 Stein on universal validity in the
  sentence, 129;
 utterance meaning in the textual
  sentence, *xx,* 44;
 verification of truth/falsehood in, 59
sign, concept of, 26, 29, 116,
 118, 128, 133:
 duality, first sign of, 17;

208 *Index*

expression as a sign, 19;
finitude as a sign, 2;
God as a sign, 137, 140;
happiness, perceiving the sign of, 10;
in the hermeneutical arc, 45;
the hermeneutical self,
   recognizing, 133;
hidden meaning in sign, 121;
infinitude as a sign, 2–3;
other signs, referring to, 43;
overturning, sign in the
   image of, 160;
in reflective awareness, 127;
the science of signs, 40;
signs of the times,
   responding to, 185;
symbol, distinguishing from, 30;
transcendence, sign of, 163–64n23;
utterance, systematically related
   signs of, 47;
will united to God, sign of, 73
silence:
   originating silence, 50, 51, 52–53,
     114, 116, 171;
   pervasive silence, 50, 51, 114, 117;
   terminating silence, 50, 51, 52–53,
     114, 117, 171;
   see also contemplative silence
Song of Songs, 70, 108, 178:
   affective experience and, 81;
   bodily references in, 161;
   bridal mysticism of, 82, 83–84;
   as contemplative discourse, 175–77;
   as an epithalamium, 76;
   Origen, deeper degree in analysis
     of, 75, 79;
   Spiritual Canticle as a reworking
     of, 83, 156
Spiritual Canticle (John of the Cross),
   83–84, 156–57
Stadtmüller, Agnella, 181n14
Stein, Edith, 124, 129, 131, 177, 187:
   on artistic expression as
     religious, 132–33;
   being, characterizing as "not," 123;

Being-Person, on the human
   as, 122, 169;
call and response in writings of,
   168, 169, 170;
Carmelite background, 70,
   85–87, 100–3;
contemplation and action, on their
   seamlessness, 107–8;
contemplative silence, as a
   practitioner of, *xvii*, 174;
empathy, theory of, 125, 176;
*Essays on Woman, xii*n10;
Finite and Eternal Being,
   xiii, 106, 174;
finite being, 122, 131, 175;
finite mind, 125, 130;
indwelling, describing as
   threefold, 105–6;
integrity, on sharing your life
   with, 188–89;
intentionality, on developing the
   concept of, 175;
interiority, on the
   development of, 186;
An Investigation Concerning the
   State, 182n40;
Jewish roots, *xii,* 179, 185;
metaphor use in the process of
   understanding, 139–40;
Potency and Act, 174;
On the Problem of Empathy, x, xi;
Science of the Cross, 86,
   103, 104, 157;
Self-Portrait in Letters: 1916-
   1942, *xiv*n10;
Self-Portrait in Letters: Letters to
   Roman Ingarden, 109n29;
semantics and, 130, 187
Stevens, Wallace, 178
Story of a Soul (Thérèse of Lisieux), 84
the summoned subject, 167, 168,
   169, 170, 179
symbol, 32, 131:
   in Adamic myth, 172;

of God, in the illuminating
process, 62;
hermeneutics of symbol, 178;
night as a symbol, 86–87;
in philosophical thinking, 180n2;
second meaning, as providing, 30;
the second naiveté, symbolic
expressions of, 39;
Symbol and Sacrament, 185;
symbolic mode of capable
being, 168;
The Symbolism of Evil, 171
Symbol and Sacrament (Chauvet), 185
Symbolism of Evil (Ricoeur), 171

Teresa of Avila, 72–74, 82–83,
99, 102, 105
textuality *(Schriftlichkeit),* xii, 23, 36,
44, 46, 133, 174
Thannisch, Ottilia, 143n42
theoretical mediation, 5–9, 158
Thérèse of Lisieux, 84–85,
94n108, 94n110
the third naiveté, 169, 180, 185–89
Thompson, Colin, 94n98, 157, 161,
162, 163–64n23
Tillich, Paul, 123, 151
transformation, 161, 173, 179–
80, 185, 188:
of the capable human, 152–55;
in the Carmelite tradition,
xx, 168, 169;
five levels of awareness, role in,
xxiii–xxiv, 113, 120;
as a gift of contemplative life, 106;
language, transformation
appearing in, 40;
in the night of the spirit, 104–5;
as an ongoing process, 58, 139;
practice as the means and end
of, 116, 117;
of the psychic into the noetic, 42–43;
recognition, role in, *xxii,* 62;

of reflexive consciousness, *xvii, xx,
xxiv, xxv,* 32, 58, 69, 149–50, 151,
155, 162, 163, 167, 176, 179, 186;
to a theocentric orientation, 175;
in the unitive way, 76, 84
*Treatise of St. Basil on the Holy
Spirit* text, 119
truth:
cognitional self-transcendence,
coming through, 151, 176;
as correspondence, 125;
as divine, 81, 105, 140;
event and disclosure of, 131–32;
of faith, 104;
first truth, 26;
happening of truth as the discourse-
event, 171;
inner truth, out of inner
necessity, 55, 126;
judgment, truth in issuing, 128;
as lived claim, *xxv;* 43, 176, 178, 187
revealed truth, 139;
spiritual truth, 131;
subjective truth, 126;
as a temporal event, *xxiii,* 159
as a transcendental, 25, 151, 176;
verification of, 59
Turner, Denys, 91n49, 92nn56–57

the unitive way, 70, 155, 162, 168, 178:
call and response as
characteristic of, 169;
contemplation and action as,
72–74, 76;
opposites in tension, holding, 163;
as the spiritual marriage, 157;
as the summoned self, 167, 180

Van Gogh, Vincent, 131–32
verbs, study of, *xxv–xxvi*n3, 121, 139:
adverbs, 44, 84;
noun-verb conjunction, *xx,* 19–20,
40, 41, 44;
the power to judge, as
revealing, 22n66;

verbs as ascribing what is, 41

Wall, John, 180n3
Weil, Simone, 127
World of Silence (Picard), 114
Wyschogrod, Edith, 147n144

Yannaras, Christos, 78–79, 89n2, 186, 187, 188, 189n10

About the Author

Michele Kueter Petersen received her M.A. in Theology from the University of Notre Dame, B.A. in History and Political Science, M.A. in History and Ph.D. in Religious Studies from the University of Iowa. She has taught in the Department of Philosophy at Clarke University, the Department of Religion at Cornell College, and the Department of Philosophy and Religious Studies at Mount Mercy University. Her work is in the area of Philosophy of Religion. Her research interests include the religious philosophy of Paul Ricoeur, Edith Stein, and John Henry Newman, the Carmelite textual tradition, Catholic-Jewish dialogue, and ethical responses to religious diversity and religious pluralism. She has published essays on Ricoeur, Stein, and Newman. She lives in Iowa City, Iowa.

Printed in Great Britain
by Amazon